Little Farm
HOMEGROWN

By Susan Colleen Browne

MEMOIRS OF COUNTRY LIFE

Little Farm in the Foothills:
A Boomer Couple's Search for the Slow Life

Little Farm Homegrown: A Memoir of Food-Growing, Midlife,
and Self-Reliance on a Small Homestead

VILLAGE OF BALLYDARA SERIES

MORGAN CAREY ADVENTURE SERIES

Little Farm

HOMEGROWN

A Memoir of Food-Growing, Midlife, and Self-Reliance
on a Small Homestead

Little Farm in the Foothills, Book 2

SUSAN COLLEEN BROWNE

With John F. Browne

Whitethorn Press

*To Sasha, Collin, Carrie and Meghann
and all our grandchildren*

Welcome to the Little Farm

It was the Great Septic Blowout that did it.

That is, the event that inspired this "Little Farm" sequel. As a novelist, I always figured my original *Little Farm in the Foothills* memoir would be my first, last and only true-life book—a story about starting a small homestead in the Pacific Northwest, and how my husband and I pursued our dream of moving to the country for a simpler life. But when our septic tank very spectacularly belched a river of sewage into our shop, I had an epiphany. Actually, after three days of mucking out the mess and sanitizing everything in sight, *and* taking another full day to recover from the trauma, *then* I had my epiphany.

Being a former city girl—moving out to the Cascade Mountains' Foothills as a germophobe cupcake gardener—I'd learned so much about organic food-growing and coping with our new, more self-reliant life in the country. Why not write a second book, to help other backyard farmers and food gardeners avoid the same expensive and time-consuming boo-boos that John and I made?

Some of you may know me as my other persona—Susan Colleen Browne, spinner of Irish tales in my Village of Ballydara series. But when I'm not at my computer dreaming up Irish stories, I'm dressed in dirty Carhartts and an ancient red Pooh Bear sweatshirt, immersed in running our little corner of food-raising heaven, Berryridge Farm.

Our place is ten acres of logged-off land tucked in the lower elevations of the Cascade range. John and I started out with a cleared one-half acre plot, a modest manufactured home, a well and pumphouse, an uninsulated pole building that serves as a combination shop/barn, and enough space for a small orchard and garden. Initially, our cleared area seemed like plenty for an immense garden, compared to what we had in the city. With the untamed spaces surrounding us, our acreage was a veritable wooded wonderland, tucked within a larger 73-acre clear-cut tract. A jungle of young birch and alder trees sheltered hemlock, cedar, and Douglas fir saplings, interspersed with more natives like big leaf and vine maples, bitter cherry, mountain ash and Indian plum trees. Layers of logging slash tangled with wild blackberry bushes of all sorts—Himalayan, evergreen, black-cap and trailing. Among the trees grew a thicket of thimbleberry, sword fern and brackenfern, Oregon grape and native bleeding heart.

Ringed by mature firs, the tract was teeming with black-tailed deer, rabbits, and songbirds: robins, towhees, grosbeaks, goldfinches, chickadees and sparrows, and in the warmer months, hummingbirds with their distinctive chatter and dogfights filled the air. Raptors like bald eagles and red-tailed hawks sailed high above the trees, and in summer, nighthawks, a species of swallow, swooped at dusk. As the only residents along the mile-long lane through the clear-cut, John and I felt our property had a real "Home on the Range" kind of vibe.

But as I indicated above, mistakes, as they say, were made. Our biggest error happened right at the start: our half-acre wasn't nearly enough for all that we wanted to do, and grow here. (Why, oh why, didn't we have our contractor clear two acres? Five? Or even more?) Once John and I settled into our new life, we didn't want to mechanically bulldoze any more of our lovely little woods, compacting the soil and displacing, or even killing, so many wild creatures.

Instead, we decided to clear more garden space by hand. Over the years, with a pickax, saw, shovel, pruning loppers and elbow grease, the two of us have hacked out not only more vegetable garden areas, but spaces for two more orchards, plus four woodsheds, two storage sheds, a carport and good-sized chicken coop and run that John designed and built by himself. Still, John and I (a couple of Boomers who didn't know about hard work until we moved here) realized over the years that we could have avoided many of our failures. Too, so much of what we've done could have been accomplished more easily, with far less gnashing of teeth. If all that energy-wasting wasn't bad enough, we spent a *lot* of money on projects that didn't pan out.

The Gardening School of Hard Knocks is actually a super-effective way to get an education, but I'd like to save you from learning everything the hard way. While *Little Farm Homegrown* will not be a comprehensive guide to country life and food-growing, my intention is to show the next phase of how a midlife couple has made a dream of living in the country come true. The book also relates family events that tested our ability to keep our homestead going, especially as we've grown older. Since John and I are hearty eaters with a passion for local, organic food, this book would not be complete without sharing how we've produced enough fruits and vegetables to sustain two adults for easily half a year, with extra for our family and friends!

If you follow my Little Farm in the Foothills blog, you may find some familiar passages, but I've expanded many of these events to show their effect on Berryridge Farm's big picture. As John did for the first Little Farm book, he'll contribute his perspective here and there. Whether you're someone who dreams of a place in the country, or you're ready to start a backyard farm, it's my hope that you'll find plenty of inspiration in this book to pursue your vision...*and* help you begin your new life.

If the first Little Farm book was about *looking* for the slow life, this second memoir is the story of *finding* it—coping with the challenges and discovering the joys of living closer to the land. By the way, I'll provide the full skinny on the septic tank back-up later in the book. Warning: you may learn far more than you'll ever want to know about on-site septic systems!

PART I

Boomers on Board

'Tis the gift to be simple, 'tis the gift to be free...

—From "Simple Gifts" by Joseph Brackett

1 🐾 Cruisin'

We had it All Figured Out.
Berryridge Farm was in its summer glory, and our first, tumultuous year in the Foothills was a distant memory. With that wake-up call behind us, I'd recently published *Little Farm in the Foothills*, about the same time that John and I were embracing a more ambitious, self-sufficient outlook. We learned we could survive without the power company—for short periods of time, at least—and after our first taste of farm-fresh eggs, we envisioned getting a flock of laying hens. Through all the ups and downs, we'd somehow created a simpler, hands-on lifestyle in a place our city friends regarded as the Middle of Nowhere.

Yet self-reliance doesn't have to mean living like hermits.

The first couple of years in the Foothills, I'd loved the peace and silence of our place—just me, John and the wildlife. Among the young trees and brush surrounding us, it was so quiet that when a raven flew overhead, you could hear the swish of its wings.

John and I, the sole residents of the seven-parcel clear-cut, had truly found our spot of paradise. With practice, I'd taught myself not to be a scaredy-cat, walking along our deserted mile-long lane while pretending that we didn't have bears and cougars lurking in the woods only a few feet away. Our solitude wasn't going to be permanent, though: the other six properties were gradually being purchased. We felt lucky when a lovely woman bought the parcel closest to ours and started building her home. Still, who knew what kind of folks might buy the five remaining lots.

We were especially nervous about who might end up on the second one adjoining ours. The original developer dug three wells for six parcels, and stipulated that each well would be shared with the two closest lots. (The seventh lot—the farthest from ours—

didn't have a well.) This arrangement meant that our well would be co-owned by an as-yet unknown property owner.

John and I didn't have a problem with sharing—not exactly. Garrett, our Oracle of Infrastructure, had built us a large, sturdy pumphouse with a 119-gallon water tank, plenty for two households (in theory). The well co-owners would only have to figure out how to split the small electric bill for the well. Still, I couldn't stop fretting: what if some big family buys the property, and uses an insane amount of water? (Leaving none for us!) Or what if there are unforeseen hassles with bill paying? And the most pressing worry, what if the buyers turned out to be...well, difficult?

Up the main road, among the lovely woodlands and small farms around us, was a field right next to the roadway, one of those hoarder properties. About half a mile away as the crow flies, the place was littered with junked mechanical equipment, broken appliances and abandoned utility trucks, all in varying states of rust and disrepair. I'd seen a few flatbed and cargo trucks appear in different spots in the driveway, so some of the vehicles were clearly functional. The rest of the stuff, however, was a blot on an otherwise picturesque landscape of a blueberry farm and a stand of firs, tucked up against a wooded foothill.

As the months passed, new trash appeared on the property: a bunch of busted-up camper-trailers, mountains of empty wooden pallets, and dozens, if not hundreds, of fifty-gallon metal drums slowly accumulated next to one of the dead trucks.

Each day, passing the place on my bike, I'd gaze at the mess with dismay, wondering what could be in the drums. Illegal drugs? Hazardous waste? Wasn't there a law prohibiting that kind of material on private property? My bigger worry was if some of those drums were leaking, and whatever was inside was percolating down to the aquifer that supplies water to our entire area. On the upside, I never detected any nasty odors that might hint at dangerous chemicals. In fact, what was maybe the most unusual aspect of the place was the faint aroma of donuts you got passing by.

Still, all that garbage was beyond unsightly. And this disaster of a property, so close to ours, made me fear the worst: what if a junkyard-keeper moves next to us?

Growing older has its undeniable drawbacks—if it's not the new wrinkles on your face, it's yet *another* ache in your joints. But there's one thing about the years passing that never fails to surprise and delight me—it's realizing how small the world actually is. You might run into a classmate halfway across the world, discover someone in your writer's group once lived in your hometown, or learn that back in the day, two of your new neighbors once shared the same zip code. Coincidence, or fate? In any event, when John and I heard the empty parcel next to us had been sold, we never anticipated the buyer would be a friend!

Our new neighbor, Jake, was a younger colleague of John's from the police department where he'd spent his thirty-year career. Jake was a likeable guy with a strong independent streak. Preferring to run his own show, he and his partner, Barb, also a police officer from John's department, decided they weren't up for well-sharing. They had a new well dug, built their own pumphouse, and Jake even installed an above-ground manual water pump in case of power outages.

And no schlepped-together structures for Jake—he built his entire water system by hand, as well as a shop with a large apartment upstairs, and a beautiful gazebo, each project meticulously designed and executed. Having friends become your neighbors was pretty ideal—and even better was that Jake and Barb buying the place meant we had two more law enforcement officers in the immediate area. I definitely felt a little safer from intruders—whether bear, cougar or the two-legged kind.

Although our site guy Garrett had skimped on clearing land for our garden, he'd been lavish about infrastructure. Besides our roomy pumphouse, he'd installed a septic system that was twice the size required by county regulations. Garrett had also included another septic outflow pipe in our shop, so we could eventually add a third toilet. Despite this skookum septic array, he assured us that the upkeep of the OSS (on-site septic) would be minimal.

On Garrett's last day of work at our place, John and I stood nearby as our Oracle dispensed his final words of wisdom. "Once a year, take off your septic tank cover, pull up the filter, and give it a rinse with a hose," he told us.

"Sounds easy enough," said John. "We can do it, no problem."

We? I looked at John without saying anything. *Yeah, good luck with that, getting me to hose down a sewage-coated filter.*

"And get your tank pumped every four years," Garrett added.

"Four years," I repeated. "I'll remember that."

Although John and I had barely started our new, slower life, I had already discovered how fast time goes by—yet I had no idea how quickly four years could pass. And guess what—the annual filter-rinsing somehow got pushed to the bottom of the priority list. Besides, John always said he knew lots of people who went for years and years without pumping their tank.

And hey—we had that oversized system, a veritable septic of champions. What could go wrong?

Once Jake and Barb started developing their place, the 73-acre neighborhood began a rapid transformation as three additional lots were purchased. Two more families now lived here full-time, in their custom-built houses. I tried not to be envious—our manufactured home in all its plastic glory served our needs—but one house had three stories with vaulted ceiling, a real stone fireplace and geothermal heat, and the other had the elegant silhouette of an Asian temple.

However, both families were so nice, how could I hold their gorgeous homes against them? And I admit, the previously vast-feeling 70-plus acres felt more secure. There was still plenty of wildlife around, but the new neighbors' dogs kept wild critters like bears and coyotes at a comfortable distance.

I'd never been much of an animal person—babies were my thing. Starting at age seven, when I wasn't at school I was babysitting my younger brother, and when my baby sister came along six years later, I became a quasi-parent to her as well. At twenty-two, I became a mother for real, and by my mid-forties, I was a grandmother. So kids, not pets, have always been on my radar.

Yet these neighbor dogs turned out to be great fun. Fiona, a super-friendly golden retriever, gave me (a bicyclist who's been chased—and even bitten—by more aggressive dogs than I care to count) new faith in canine companions. Another neighbor's dog, a blue heeler named Nellie, became John's pal. He'd be clearing brush in the woods, and over she'd come with a stick in her mouth. He'd throw the stick, Nellie would fetch it, and of course, being a breed who likes having a job, she wanted to do it All Day Long.

Clearly, John was fond of this dog, and every once in a while he and I would talk about getting one of our own. But once we decided to acquire a flock of hens, we concluded a dog wasn't in the cards. I already felt time-challenged with my writing career and looking after Berryridge Farm, so how would I fit in all the new responsibilities of a pet? Then there was making sure we could spend enough quality time with a dog. With six grandchildren, including a newborn and three toddlers, we often left our place to make short visits or to help with childcare.

Time wasn't standing still for other family members either. John's sister Becky was undergoing cancer treatments, and his mom Wanda, as sharp as she was, needed more support as she grew more frail. At any rate, bringing a dog around new babies and sick folks, or leaving it home alone, simply didn't seem feasible.

Besides, I was sure a dog would be more work than chickens.

2 🕿 Self-Reliant Foodies

I really was living my dream.

Little Farm in the Foothills had been well-received, and with the last years of sod-busting, John and I had created the life we'd envisioned—even if our place didn't resemble your typical homestead. From what I'd observed, most folks with a small acreage who are seriously raising food will till up a large square, then plant in rows. When we first put pickax to soil, however, we took a more unconventional approach.

John had long wanted to craft a Japanese-style garden. He'd visited Japan as a young man, and was struck by the beauty of their outdoor designs, the simplicity and balance of stone accents and carefully selected plantings. Not that our place in any way resembled the Japanese garden of his dreams, you understand. First of all, most of our space was devoted to fruit and vegetables. And in our eagerness to start producing crops as soon as possible, we dug each garden bed one at a time, filling it with plant starts right away. We'd leave room for a path around the bed, then start another planting area. On the pathways between the beds, inspired by the gardens he remembered so vividly, John covered the ground with gravel. He finished the paths with another Japanese touch—a border made from the soccer-ball sized rocks we'd unearthed from our digging.

The gravel paths did lend our place a certain elegance, I suppose, even if the whole effect seemed pretty haphazard. Even eccentric. Given the photos in my favorite homesteading magazines, it would have been more practical to cover the foot-traffic areas with a thick, weed-suppressing layer of straw or wood chips.

Our quirky layout aside, John and I were determined to protect our crops from whatever Mother Nature's minions had in store. Our cleared ground was surrounded by a Russian nesting-doll arrangement of a six and a half foot fence, and inside that, our garden beds were encircled by poultry wire, with bird netting protecting the berry crops at harvest time. Here and there, little wire "huts" John had fashioned from more poultry fencing provided an extra layer of protection for individual plants—whatever it took to guard our food from the unrelenting thievery of deer, rabbits, and robins.

And our hard work was paying off. From the rich, virgin soil I'd talked about in the first Little Farm book bloomed bushy potato plants, carrot tops a foot high, and pea vines taller than John's six feet climbed up a steer-wire trellis. The asparagus crowns John and I planted had developed into vigorous ferns, and we were eagerly waiting for the following spring, when we could pick as many spears as we liked.

A transforming moment came to John and me when we discovered *Animal, Vegetable, Miracle*, a terrific homesteading memoir by Barbara Kingsolver. In the book, she relates her family's experience of eating locally for a year. In an especially memorable passage, her daughter, hungry for fresh breakfast fruit after a long winter, plaintively asks her mother for something local they could eat, and Kingsolver suggests rhubarb.

Well, how about that: rhubarb, a spring delicacy you could harvest weeks before the rest of your garden starts producing, could be good for more than dessert—and John and I had two vigorous crowns right here in our yard.

The truth is, I'd never really given much thought to where my food came from. For years, I'd had a glass of orange juice for breakfast every day, assuming the fruit came from Florida or California. Then one spring day, idly perusing the label on my favorite juice brand, I discovered where the concentrate hailed from.

"Brazil!" I exclaimed to John.

He poured a cup of coffee. "What?"

"This juice is from Brazil!" I said indignantly. "Do you believe that?"

"Aw, what can you do," he said sympathetically, then finished his meal, but I was really steamed. Staring out the kitchen window, I didn't really see the garden we'd created so we could feed ourselves. Instead, I imagined tanks of O.J. traveling from South America in huge container ships, then trucked from some far-off port to a processing plant. At that moment, buying such long-distance food simply didn't feel *right*. That glass of breakfast juice turned out to be my last.

Quickly swapping orange juice for stewed rhubarb turned into a beta-test of our *Animal, Vegetable, Miracle*-inspired mindset. Soon after our first rhubarb harvest, our strawberries were ready—and our crop was *insane*. We feasted on bowlfuls for breakfast, strawberry shortcake for dessert, and still had twenty quarts to freeze for the following winter.

The fruit trees in our orchard were putting on height and girth, providing John and me with more insurance for our home-grown food supply.

That is not to say we didn't encounter the occasional setback. Um...setbacks.

Early in the game, full of newbie homesteader zeal, we bought a young fig tree from our neighborhood Foothills nursery, twelve miles away. I didn't care for figs, but I agreed with John, why not try something *really* new? We tucked the sapling into a cozy bed on the south side of the shop, surrounded with boulders to retain heat—the warmest spot in the yard. Our $30.00 experiment died with the first hard frost.

Still, what were we thinking? Despite the nursery's proximity to our house, winter temperatures there could be five degrees warmer, and during the winter, the staff often covers their tender plants. Conclusion: even though the nursery could grow a California transplant doesn't mean we could.

In this experimental phase, John and I also planted not one, but two kiwi plants, a male and a female. Why kiwis? I dunno. We heard they were chock-full of vitamin C, yet neither of us really *ate* kiwis. They had a frustrating growing habit too: both kiwis would appear to completely die in the winter, then when spring arrived, virtually *explode*, swiftly producing twenty-foot long canes. Yet with all that growth, we never got any flowers from those darn kiwis, much less fruit.

Despite our failure with the fig tree, and the head-scratching kiwi idea, we decided we'd produce apricots—fruit that would be easy to dry and store. And since apricot trees grew just fine at our Foothills nursery, why not? (We are slow learners.) After buying two, John built a lovely little arbor with an Asian touch next to the trees, to support them through the worst of the winter winds.

Wind wasn't the problem. Blight was. Around the time I was putting the finishing touches on my book, John was standing under his apricot arbor, pruning out blackened, foot-long new growth. And speaking of things you don't want turning black, I hadn't quite recovered from my most recent, quite spectacular homesteading failure.

The previous fall, I'd harvested our first real garden successes: a bumper crop of potatoes, onions and huge Blue Hubbard squashes. Kneeling in the muddy potato patch one rainy November day, I'd harvested my spuds from the wet, chilly soil, my fingers going numb. But the yield of all three crops was worth the discomfort: at least sixty pounds of potatoes, enough onions to last us all winter, and over a dozen winter squash. I surveyed my vegetables with great satisfaction as I settled the whole caboodle in our unheated, uninsulated shop—thinking of the steaming baked potatoes in my future, the rich, sweetness of onions in my pasta sauce. And most of all, the delicious squash pies I would make, since the taste and texture of Hubbards was so very superior to canned pumpkin!

Six weeks later, the Foothills were smacked by a late December Northeaster, and the temperature plummeted to the single-digits. I didn't remember my stored crops until it was too late. The next day, I found every last vegetable had frozen hard as baseballs. *How could I have been so stupid!* I railed at myself. I thought I could save the crops, until the weather warmed up. That's when I discovered I was the proud owner of onions turned to mush, ruined squashes, and a half-dozen grocery bags full of blackened, squishy potatoes. I almost cried.

Yet I'd been full of country living naiveté before my potato debacle. That same season, I decided to try Brussel sprouts—I was a big fan, but the ones in the store looked kind of yucky. Although John and I had never raised anything in the cruciferous family (broccoli, cabbage, kale, or Brussel sprouts, among others), now that we had garden space to burn, I was ready! Freshly weeding a plot, I set in a half-dozen nursery starts, and the plants grew like crazy.

I'd heard of cabbage moths—the main pests of cruciferous vegetables—but I thought they only bothered bigger growers. Or that the moths were more of a *town* pest, where there were lots of other gardens to feast on. They wouldn't find our tiny veggie patch, tucked away in the woods.

I was stunningly wrong. The moths found our garden patch just fine, obviously laying their eggs. By the time the sprouts were ready to pick, every last plant was riddled with fat, green worms. The chewed-up foliage was unsightly enough, but the worm poo, scads of it, was *everywhere*. It was the most disgusting sight I'd seen in any garden of mine—and the few un-poo'd on, edible sprouts I'd rescued were hardly worth the trouble.

Much more costly were the misjudgments John and I made establishing our orchard. Cutting down dime-a-dozen birch and alder saplings for garden space was satisfying, but digging fruit trees out of the ground—the fig being the first of many—due to our own ignorance or over-confidence was painful. Not to mention a big, fat waste of time and money.

Still, as all you gardeners know, hope springs eternal. AKA, there's always next season. So the following summer, John and I anticipated Berryridge Farm being bigger, better, and moving forward.

But unbeknownst to us, trouble was afoot. Or should I say, underfoot.

My Favorite Martian

"The Martian," starring Matt Damon, has become one of my all-time favorite movies, says John.

As a science-fiction movie buff, whether old-time classics or modern blockbusters, I don't say "favorite" lightly. The challenge of humans going into space, especially in the "Star Trek" or "Star Wars" films really captivates me. But in "The Martian," the astronaut main character, Watney, portrays a modern-day Robinson Crusoe—one of the stories I loved at a kid. He's a man marooned alone in a hostile place, Man vs The Elements. And Watney, through creativity and improvisation, survives against long odds.

I see a few parallels with life here on Berryridge Farm—even if our daily routine isn't quite a fight to the finish against such an unforgiving environment. Like in the Crusoe storyline, Sue and I have had to improvise to overcome challenges and setbacks. Often, like Watney, I've found my way around problems using older technology and hands-on, jerry-rigged solutions, along with some rough carpentry skills I picked up from my dad. And at our place, hand tools are just as important as power tools.

If you've seen the movie, you probably remember Watney's biggest brainwave: potato growing. That's another reason the movie personally resonates with me. Potatoes were the first-ever garden vegetable I grew as a kid. I was about eleven years old when I saw my mother get out a bunch of spuds to peel. When I asked her what those funny knobs were on the potatoes, Mom explained about the "eyes" and how they grew into plants. That day, she gave me a couple of potatoes to cut up and plant, and for the next months, I watched in wonder as the foliage grew. Later that summer, I ended up harvesting only about a dozen taters, but still, it felt like a big accomplishment. These days, with modern, climate-controlled potato storage, you don't see many eyes on grocery-store taters, so the process wouldn't work now as well as it did back then.

With our man Watney having to be self-reliant to survive, the author of "The Martian" chose the best vegetable for his story: potatoes are filling, with lots of calories, and a "renewable" crop. If you've got some potato "seed," you can grow spuds indefinitely. The first time I watched the movie, when Watney spies his vacuum-packed potatoes, I knew exactly what he was going to do. For sure, the "humanure" element adds some comic reality to his mission!

Every time I view the "The Martian," I'll get a bit choked up— especially when the first potato leaves emerge from the soil, and Watney talks to those little sprouts, the only other living thing in his life. I've been known to talk to plants myself—that is, after I'm done chatting with Berryridge Farm's deer, bunnies, birds and bees, as well as the ladybugs who keep showing up all over our kitchen.

Sue always scoffs at astronaut Watney's whole potato-growing project, that it's not really accurate. "The guy would need several months for his potatoes to grow eyes," she'll say. "Besides, it's such a longshot, for vacuum-packed potatoes to even sprout at all!"

"That's all true," I'll admit. "But I'm not going to argue with a great story."

3 ☞ Six Inches Under

One summer day, after I'd been away from the garden for several author events, I decided to pick some new potatoes. I'd planted organic seed for the first time and couldn't wait to find out how they'd taste. My thirty-hill potato patch, our biggest so far, was in the site we'd cleared the year before, next to the woods—which unfortunately meant the weeds were that much closer. And while I'd been busy with my book, the weeds had taken over—pretty much every square inch of my potato plot was dense with unwanted greenery.

Still, when I was ready to harvest my spuds, the robust, bushy tops pointed to a successful crop. I knelt in the patch, parted the weeds and eased my handfork into the bed. I carefully wielded my fork to loosen the soil, and scooped up…two teensy tubers.

I sat back on my heels and stared at the tiny spuds, puzzled. Compared to our earlier production, this seemed very modest. I'd recently met a woman at a book event, an experienced gardener, and in the middle of my rhapsodizing about our productive soil, she shook her head. "Just wait," she said darkly.

"Oh?" I asked politely. I'd never seen garden plants grow as prodigiously as they did at our place.

"The soil will get worn out very fast," she said.

Feeling deflated, I decided she didn't know what she was talking about. For all I knew, she could have been growing her veggies in the same site for decades, and her soil had given up the ghost a long time ago. At Berryridge Farm, I'd been rotating my crops from the get-go. And every time John and I dug in a fresh spot, I'd seen an abundance of mycorrhizae. One of the best predictors of productive soil, mycorrhizae are little white threads of soil fungus that thrive in undisturbed or carefully tended earth.

Now, in my potato bed, I moved to the next hill, then the one after that, and discovered more of the same. Where were my impressive, fist-sized spuds of yore? Had this woman been right after all, and our lovely woodland dirt was losing nutrients already? Or had I let the weeds draw all the nutrition away from my food crops?

Just as doubt was settling in, I pushed my fingers into the soil again, and detected a nice big specimen. Okay, Berryridge Farm still had *it*! Elated, I pried out a big potato—but a good third of it was...*gone*. Bitten clean away.

I couldn't believe my eyes. Had my spuds been attacked by some kind of virulent pest? After seeing what cabbage worms could do above ground, I wondered if there was some evil potato bug doing the same damage below—although the chances of any insect eating such a large quantity of flesh seemed really remote.

So there I was, with a ruined crop and no clue how it could have happened. As summer drifted into fall, I was stressed and time-crunched with author tasks. So I didn't give my tater mystery the attention it deserved.

4 ☞ A Gift to Remember

John had been making sketches all winter, and by the spring thaw, he'd come up with a final design for a new structure. We were ready to begin the next phase of our little homestead. Farm animals!

For months, John and I had been deep-diving into backyard farming books. We were especially inspired by the aforementioned *Animal Vegetable Miracle* by Barbara Kingsolver and *Farm City* by Novella Carpenter. Both memoirs extensively covered small-scale poultry-raising—Kingsolver and her family homesteading in a lovely hollow in the Appalachian mountains of Virginia, while Carpenter shared the comic ups-and-downs of her turkey and chicken operation in the middle of Oakland, California. So...why not bring hens to Berryridge Farm?

John and I couldn't wait for this new facet of self-sufficiency—after all, we were big egg eaters, John especially. Breakfast was never a grab-'n-go kind of meal for my husband's family—the first meal of the day, in their minds, required eggs, bacon, and all the sides. John's son Collin could sometimes stray from the Browne tradition, though. As a young teen, in a cookbook produced by the extended family, he offered this entry:

Breakfast
Go to store. Purchase favorite cereal. Pour required amount into a large bowl. Add milk to desired floatation level. Sprinkle with white or brown sugar as desired. Eat.

Despite Collin's recipe, John, like me, wasn't a big fan of cold cereal, especially the national brands made up of grains and sweeteners from who knows where. Plus, I figured keeping laying hens on your place was about as local as you could get. Having one less item to buy at the grocery store was the frosting on the cake.

Six chickens sounded about right—so few would be very little trouble, I was sure. Country life had tamed the worst of my germ fears, so I felt primed to deal with a bit of animal manure. And on the off-chance a zombie apocalypse (or any other kind of breakdown of modern life as we know it) came along, John, our family, and I could hole up on Berryridge Farm and still survive! At any rate, given our hugely disappointing potato crop, with on-site egg producers, we would have some good quality protein to sustain us.

Luckily, we'd saved our income tax return to pay for our chicken project. We quickly nixed the cutesy premade chicken houses just coming into fashion. Besides, no catalogue-ordered coop kit would do. John's hand-built chicken coop was even sturdier than his woodsheds—it reminded me of one of those 50s-era Chevy trucks that aren't exactly pretty, but lasts forever.

Building the Coop

I'd completed several woodsheds with three sides, but the henhouse would be my first fully-enclosed structure. Sized at 8' x 8', it would be the largest building you can construct in our county without needing a permit. Half the building would be for the chickens' living area, and we could store garden equipment and chicken supplies in the other half. After all, a homestead can never have enough storage.

I used siding panels for the walls, which is a kind of pressboard coated with primer on one side. I cut out three good-sized windows and covered them with poultry fencing for safety, and made one-piece shutters for each one with more siding material, hinged at the top. For the partition between the coop and the storage area, I kept the upper third open, and covered that with poultry wire as well. I figured with openings on all four sides, the hens would have plenty of ventilation. Since Sue and I decided we weren't going to do this project on the cheap, I installed a steel roof, with a "1 in 12" pitch. The final touch was distributing a layer of crushed rock along the interior walls, for better drainage of the dirt floor.

Next, I started on what Sue and I called the "safety zone," a 10-foot square caged run next to the coop, enclosing all four sides and top with poultry wire and steer fencing. Adjacent to the run, I created another "chicken exercise yard" that I didn't cover, with a doorway leading to our newest orchard space. This way, our future chickens would have room to explore outside their compound. To give the whole area a finished look, I lined the fence with more crushed rock.

When Sue saw my completed project, she grinned ear-to-ear. "It looks amazing," she said. "So neat and tidy." You've probably have guessed by now Sue is pretty big on neat and tidy.

Last, I constructed a roost, three dowels on a frame in a stair-step arrangement, which took up most of the coop's space. I cut a man-sized door leading into the safety zone, again using a piece of siding hinged on one side, then carved out another small opening for the hens about a foot and a half off the ground. For their ramp, I propped up a scrap of siding.

Sue had studied up on all kinds of chicken husbandry, and showed me photos of nesting structures. "This one looks doable," she said, pointing to one design: nest boxes on the outside of the coop. She'd grown more comfortable around animals the last few years, but I could tell she was relieved she wouldn't have to go inside the coop to collect eggs. I created an oblong box big enough for three nests and attached it to the north side of the coop, about four feet off the ground, then added a little hinged top. A hen would have all the privacy she needed to lay, and we would have easy access to her eggs. Now all we needed were some actual *chickens*.

After John completed what I thought was quite a genius chicken compound, I could see he was far more into our chicken project than I'd ever hoped. Thinking I would surprise him, on the down-low I'd been making some phone calls. I got the name of a gal who supervised the youth livestock program at the county fair and inquired about buying chickens, and she gave me the number of a local chicken farmer. When I called the farmer, she said she wasn't selling any hens, but she had a friend with a flock in the Foothills south of us, and gave me her email.

Connecting with Shannon over the phone, I discovered she was Scottish, and was every bit as nice as she seemed in her emails. She and her family lived on a homestead about twenty-five miles away, and she said she'd have some pullets ready by early summer. I told her we were hoping for six chickens, and asked how much she wanted for them.

"What do you think of fifteen dollars each?" she said.

I'd learned pullets are young hens that are just starting to lay, and that their eggs can be more nutritious than mature hens'. For sure, $15.00 per bird was a steal! "Sounds great," I told her. "When will they be ready?"

"Not until July," she said regretfully. "I know that's a long time to wait—why don't you come out and see them?"

After settling on a date, I thanked her and hung up, almost rubbing my hands in anticipation. John's birthday was approaching, and *finally*, I would give him something he'd remember.

My loved ones' birthdays are sort of a problem. When it comes to gifts, I have a definite block. Sometimes I wonder if I use up all my creativity on my writing, and never have any left over for my personal life. You see, I never know what to give people, and I always think whatever gift I come up with will disappoint the recipient. To make matters worse, I hate shopping. Wait—I loathe it. I'd rather clean toilets than go to the mall, and I find online shopping overwhelming.

I'm a far cry from John's sister Becky, gift-giver extraordinaire. Her presents were never ostentatious, or overly expensive, but always somehow just *right*. Even exactly what you needed. Her wedding gift to John and me was a clever little salsa pitcher, with a glass topper that looked like a hot pepper. It was Pinterest-ready long before the platform was a gleam in a techie's eye. One Christmas she gave us an oversized platter, sturdy enough for the giant turkeys we always roasted.

Becky had a whimsical streak that matched mine too. One of her most memorable gifts was a book of fairy illustrations with accompanying personality profiles of the fairies (loved it!). Along with the book was a ceramic Fairy King, a handsome guy with whiskers that formed a cup. You could hang the King of the Fairies on the wall and keep your keys in his beard.

John had definitely inherited his family's great-gifts gene. His first present to me was a big teddy bear dressed in a purple flannel shirt that matched the one he was wearing. Many years later, after we moved to the Foothills he gave me the electric chainsaw I'd hinted about, one of his best presents ever. Now, with my chicken gift in mind for him, I could finally give *him* something special that would require no shopping whatsoever.

5 🐓 Buck-buck-buck buh-GAW!

The afternoon of John's birthday, on a sunny June day, I asked him ever-so-casually, "How about a nice country drive before we go to dinner?"

My easygoing husband said yes right away. He knew something was up, but was nice enough not to spoil any surprise I might have for him. We climbed into his '97 Ford Ranger and headed to the river valley south of us. Following Shannon's directions, we turned off the highway, traversed a low-lying road that was still covered with water from the spring rains, and meandered down another road tucked up against a wooded hill. After another mile or two, I saw a mailbox with the house number Shannon had given me.

We bounced into her driveway and looked around. Her place seemed like a much *realer* homestead than ours, with a picturesque, if higgledy-piggledy look. A short distance from the driveway was a one-story wood cabin, but Shannon's homestead was dominated by a large chicken run. Bare of vegetation, the pen was filled with strawberry-blond chickens of every size. A coop four times the size John had built stood in the center, the whole area covered with black commercial fishing net. Clearly, this area of the Foothills was home to the same chicken-eating raptors we had in our neighborhood. Outside the run, near the hillside, was a plot of thigh-high grass.

On the near side of the chicken pen, a few sheep grazed in a small fenced area, and a rise surrounded with a split-rail fence held four or five goats, one standing atop a pile of dirt. As John and I climbed out of the truck, a big hound, a smaller mixed-breed and a terrier ran over to us, all three barking vociferously.

Shannon stepped out of the house to greet us, shushing the dogs. A pretty, thirtysomething woman with short brown hair, Shannon had two young boys at her side, who were about four and six years old. After we introduced ourselves, she showed us around, her youngest son trailing us. She waved toward the far-from-secure fence around the goats, making the usual joke—that since there's never been a fence invented that will hold goats, why try? Glad I'd worn my oldest pair of gardening boots, we entered the chicken run to get a closer look at her operation.

Fifty or so clucking chickens busily pecked the ground. I watched nervously as some pecked each other, and I tried to keep my distance as others flapped their wings or skittered around. "All of them are Sexlinks," Shannon explained.

Despite the bizarre name, it was a breed known for good egg production. The birds were certainly attractive, their feathers a hundred shades of red-blond. We peeked inside the coop, and Shannon showed us her nest boxes. I did wonder why the nests were at the ground level—easier to build, maybe?—but didn't say anything.

She took us over to a barbed wire pen a short walk from the chicken run, where two porkies wallowed in the mud. Stepping inside, Shannon scratched them between the ears, wearing a fond smile. "Pigs are a lot of fun—really intelligent."

John drew closer. "I see you've got a solar panel here."

The panel was about the size of a magazine. "Yes," Shannon replied, "it's to power the fence, to keep the pigs in."

Very smart, I thought, not having to run an electric line down the middle of your homestead—although these two peaceable-looking critters didn't look like they were eager to escape.

On the way back to the house, her little boy approached us. "Look what I found, Mommy." He held a dead chicken in his arms.

"Go get rid of that!" Shannon scolded and waved toward a brushy area on the other side of the house. "And wash your hands!" she called as he ran off. "Sorry about that," she said to us, looking nonplussed but not terribly worried. "I'll take a look at the hen later," she added, then the phone rang inside the house. "Can you give me a minute?"

"Sure," John and I said at the same time. With our hostess away, I glanced back at the run. All of the birds appeared vigorous and healthy, despite their kind of dog-eat-dog existence. The dead bird had showed no sign of injury. And since Shannon had been so highly recommended by the chicken farmer, it seemed really unlikely that she'd sell us sick birds. Maybe, I thought, chickens were like a lot of other animals. Sometimes you ended up with a few runts or weaklings that just couldn't make it.

With Shannon still in the house, I checked out her vegetable patch, close to the road. Covered with bird netting draped on poles, the garden was like the homestead itself, messy but productive. Off to one side was a much smaller, wire-enclosed pen, holding a couple of dozen all-white chickens. From my research, I knew they were meat birds, but now, I could see how different they were from layers. Huddled in a mass in the far corner, the chickens trembled like a vibrating feather pillow. The red-blond hens seemed like scrappy critters, but this bunch seemed like they'd have trouble surviving an itty-bitty rainstorm.

By the time Shannon emerged, I had fetched our checkbook from the truck so we could pay her in advance. Thanking us, she said, "The chickens should start to lay in another month—let's touch base then."

We shook on the deal, and John and I climbed back into the Ranger. Despite desperately wanting to wash my hands, I was so excited about our future chickens I *almost* forgot my germiphobiness.

On the way home John pulled up at our locally-owned farmer supply store. We had chicken equipment to buy! And I quickly decided I could actually enjoy shopping after all, if I got to shop at a store for farmers.

After stepping carefully around Shannon's chicken pen, dotted with bird droppings, I had one big priority: muck boots for both of us—our first real farmer's footgear. Next, into our oversized shopping cart went a galvanized metal chicken feeder and a waterer, along with a bag of grit for the hens' digestion and oyster shell flakes to make strong eggshells. After we drove around to the back of the store to pick up a fifty-pound sack of feed pellets and a bale of straw for bedding, our grand total came to $234. It was the last of our tax return, but what did we care? We were ready for our chicken adventure!

6 🐓 C-Day!

Five weeks later on a sunny Saturday in July, John and I headed south again. In the bed of the Ranger sat three durable, nearly pristine boxes we'd saved from our move years before. When we pulled up at Shannon's place for the second time, she was ready for us.

The chickens, however, were not. The pullets she'd chosen for us were stubbornly resistant to being apprehended. A couple of them ran into the tall grass. "Hiding spots from the hawks," Shannon told us, as her older boy ran after the birds. John and I brought our boxes over to the run, then watched the two skilled chicken-chasers.

Rounding up the escapees took about twenty minutes, but finally, Shannon and her son had captured six chickens. As they protested vociferously, Shannon, with John's help, got two birds in each of our boxes. Taping the boxes, John left several inches open between the cardboard slats for air. He and I loaded the boxes into the truck bed, and said our farewells to Shannon and her son.

When we arrived back at Berryridge Farm, the shut-in-their boxes birds were definitely freaked out, and continued to squawk and peck as John released them into their new run. I cringed to see the previously clean boxes soiled with manure. I mean, the drive had only been forty-five minutes! Couldn't they hold it that long?

Ruined cardboard, I reminded myself, seemed a small price to pay for farm-fresh, homegrown eggs. Our new hens didn't know it yet, but they were going to be treated to a great life. Even if we didn't have one of those cute little coops you see in magazines, the chickens would reside in what I liked to think was a veritable luxury chicken resort.

Did I say a dog would be more work than chickens?

I soon discovered keeping a small flock of hens was a *far* bigger deal than I thought it would be. Despite my inexperience with animals, I clicked with our birds right away—although I did feel a little beleaguered when they pecked at my hands and legs when I stepped into the pen. John, being of sterner stuff, didn't mind it, and would often sit on a stump in our newest orchard where we let the chickens scratch all day, and take a bird up on his knee.

Of course we gave our "girls" names. John called the biggest, most assertive hen Chloe O'Brien, after the character on one of his favorite shows, "24." (The human Chloe O'B. could kick butt too.) The lightest-blond one was Marilyn (as in Monroe), and two we couldn't tell apart were Daisy and Maisy. Girl #5 was a dark honey color with one small white dot on her thigh, so she became Dottie. Then we seemed to run out of inspiration, and never did come up with a name for the last one.

One element to keeping hens I hadn't anticipated was the extra noise they brought to our place. You see, silence was my *jam*. The quieter the better. You couldn't consider the birdsong filling the air of Berryridge Farm *noise*—like the wind in the trees, the wild birds created the symphony of the woods.

The hens? Not so much. The steady clucking, the *buck-buck-buck-buh-GAH*, the startling *Squawk!* when a bird got pecked by her sister, and the constant squeaking of the feeder broke into my peace. Yet all the sounds soon became part of the background music of our place. The biggest surprise, though, was discovering what good company the hens were. Watching the chickens' funny little waddle-stride was entertaining, and when you entered the pen, they'd come running like they adored the ground you walked on, jockeying for who could get the closest to the door before you opened it. Of course, I knew it was because their "human" was bringing them food, but still.

All the girls would follow you around loyally, making you feel even more wanted and needed—though the way they got underfoot was not only awkward, but often hazardous! And just as our chicken lady Shannon had predicted, the girls started laying soon after we got them home, large brown beauties, with yolks a rich yellow-orange. All in all, I felt like we, and Berryridge Farm, had made a quantum leap in the homesteading biz.

7 ✍ Birds of a Feather

L ike I said before, our six birds were *work*. Fresh feed every day, and water every couple of days. The waterer needed cleaning and sanitizing at least once a week, and more often in hot weather. On rainy days, I didn't always feel like putting on my work pants and muck boots to go into their pen, but there the hens were—letting you know, quite vocally, that they didn't like being neglected.

We soon found out they didn't like getting wet either. So John and I draped a tarp over the steer wire roof of the safety zone.

The hens were messy. Although I learned scratching is a healthy chicken behavior, we soon discovered how compulsively chickens tear up the ground. During our flock's first night they'd obliterated the neat row of gravel inside the coop, so rocks were scattered all over the dirt floor. Within a couple of days, ditto for the gravel John had laid so carefully around their pen.

Most eye-opening of all: chickens weren't a cheap date.

We'd bought only the one sack of pellets. When it was nearly empty, I read the label, then examined the feed more closely. The manufacturer indicated that the product was mostly processed corn and soy with some vitamins, yet the pellets didn't seem to contain any recognizable food particles. I decided then and there that if you're going organic with your homestead, you might as well go all the way.

Be prepared to open your wallet, though. The pellets had been $12.50 for fifty pounds. I checked around and found local, organic feed from a new, boutique feed business. The layer mix was chockfull of raw, unprocessed grains, split peas, and what I guessed to be a protein/vitamin meal. The cost was, *gulp*, $28.00 for twenty-five pounds. (But soy-free!) A same-size sack of organic chicken scratch (more raw grains) was $21.00. Sure, we could have probably found something less expensive, but we were committed to local products.

The real challenge with chickens wasn't the cost of their feed, or tending them daily. It was cleaning the coop.

The job fell to me by default: between John and me, I was the one small enough to squeeze inside the coop. So despite my dread of germs, every other day, rain or shine, I'd don my coop clothes. Besides my stained Carhartts, I wore a sweatshirt over my tee-shirt with the hood securely pulled up, with another long-sleeved fleece on top of it. I put a broad-brimmed hat on top of my hood, then elbow-high rubber gloves. I wore this get-up even on the hottest days, you understand. Although my pathogen-avoidance had improved, I never claimed to be cured, did I?

Carefully maneuvering around the roost, peering in every corner, I found there was guano not only *on* the roost, but splashed on every wall. (I never did figure out how the chickens managed that. And they weren't telling. Obviously what happens in the coop stays in the coop.) For poo-scooping, I appropriated a garden tool from our collection, a curved trowel with a varnished wooden handle—it was a gift from John's daughter Sasha, purchased at Williams Sonoma. I just hoped she never found out what we used it for.

Despite the window openings, the coop was dim inside. I'd pick up the most obvious piles of manure off the dirt floor to dump into a pail, then squint at the gravel the hens had scattered all over the place, trying to figure out what was a rock and what was poo. "There's got to be a better way," I said to John one night, and showed him another roost design. He liked it, but the coop was pretty much a done deal. See, for any new manure-catching system, he'd have to disassemble the roost, but he couldn't fit inside the coop to do it!

We also discovered our biggest design error—the nesting boxes—and why Shannon's boxes had been at ground level. A laying hen likes to be the top dog, and a flock has a definite pecking order—it's not a play on words, but a real fact. The highest perch on the roost is the most desirable spot, taken by the leaders of the flock, while the less assertive birds are forced to roost on the lower rungs. Turns out, the top of our roost held four birds, maybe five if they cozied up. So any bird slow to turn in at dusk would be stuck on the second rung.

It was usually Dottie, the most sociable of our flock. She'd hang around with John and me well into the evening, often until it was nearly dark, when we went inside. We soon discovered that she'd figured out a way to score a top spot after all—having a lovely repose exactly where she wasn't supposed to: in one of the nesting boxes.

After learning that nesting boxes need to be lower than the roost, we also found out that as much as chickens poo'd all over the place, they did most of it while they slept! Naturally, if Dottie or any other girl had been sleeping in a box, any egg laid would be right in the mess the guilty parties had deposited in the night. In the middle of all our late summer chores, tearing up the coop to build nest boxes lower to the ground was a job John and I couldn't find time for.

We checked our chicken-raising books and found out a way around the problem: a nest guard. John created a little moveable fence with a rope attached to it, so you could raise and lower the guard as needed from outside the coop.

It wasn't convenient; you'd have to make sure the guard was secured before the chickens retired for the evening. Then, so they'd have access to the nests by early morning, you'd have to go back outside to lower the guard after they were asleep. But John's design seemed to do the trick—unless a bird roused in the night and snuck back into a nest. And after John found a scrap of siding to slide under the top roost to catch some of the nightly manure, the coop was much easier to clean. I decided to dial down my cleaning to twice a week, which made life easier too.

As the fall rains began, John installed a gutter along the coop's overhanging roof, so we wouldn't get drenched collecting eggs on rainy days. Ever mindful of the girls' comfort in cold weather, he figured they should have some outside shelter. Within days, inside their safety zone, he'd constructed a small roost with a pitched roof. Then, when it rained they could keep their feet dry.

As I admired his outdoor roost, John commented, "Well, if we didn't feel like homesteaders before, we sure do now that we have animals."

A few months into our chicken-keeping, despite our mistakes, John and I felt we had this chicken thing down pat. Meanwhile, the rest of Berryridge Farm seemed to be going down the tubes.

8 ✐ Helpless

As a retired police officer, John has a locker full of weapons. The locker isn't an arsenal or anything—simply a secured location for the shotguns, handguns and Bowie knives my husband keeps strictly for emergencies. While his small collection of black-powder historical-style firearms isn't terribly practical, he possesses the guns for what they represent: respect for history, and for the land. John is no hunter either—the closest he ever got to obtaining game was when he was a young dad. During a brief survivalist phase, he bought a couple of meat rabbits and butchered, skinned, and cooked them.

I hadn't been around guns since I was little. Although as a youth, my dad often hunted with his father, Dad took us kids on exactly one pheasant-hunting expedition during my childhood (we stayed in the car). Other than that one occasion, Dad kept my grandfather's old shotgun in a felt case, tucked deep in the bowels of our family basement. As a kid, out of curiosity I once dug the gun out of the closet to look at it; otherwise, Dad's shotgun was out of sight, out of mind.

Although my husband is well prepared for any eventuality, as Dad did with his old shotgun, John's firearms stay in his locker. On our Foothills' walks, John carries a five-foot maple bough as a walking stick, and tucks a Bowie knife in his belt. It's only the days when one of the neighbors reports a cougar or bear sighting that he brings his .380 handgun. And since we have lots of wild critters around I wouldn't want to meet face-to-face, he's ready to protect us, and our place. But the summer we brought the chickens into our lives, there was a predator at work, the wiliest of all.

One we were powerless to combat.

At our place, rabbits are a 24/7 pest. If you're familiar with the *Tale of Peter Rabbit*, you know exactly what Peter Cottontail eats, starting with Farmer MacGregor's carrot tops. He's certainly eaten ours when he's snuck past the chicken wire. Given the number of bunnies roaming our area, John and I are well acquainted with their eating habits. They eat every tender annual flower you ever dare to put in the ground—and that's only the beginning. They eat your beet greens, spinach, kale and asparagus. When it comes to berries, they love strawberry foliage and during the winter, they've made mincemeat of cranberry plants and blueberry shrubs. They bite off the tops of cultivated caneberry shoots too. But because we're not up for having John take potshots at bunnies all the livelong day, we've enclosed pretty much everything we grow in poultry wire.

Rabbits don't eat rhubarb (someone gave them the heads up that the leaves are poisonous maybe?), squash, or potato leaves, but that's pretty much all they leave alone. One thing was sure, anything else above ground was at risk.

But below?

Garden Devouring Machines

Protecting your garden from bunny predation is a given. Besides surrounding all your beds with poultry fencing, you've got to secure any gaps, no matter how small. If you don't, sure as shootin' a rabbit will find its way inside.

If they do sidle into your fenced garden beds, be prepared for mass destruction. But although they're fast, if you're strategic, you can catch them. One spring morning, Sue was standing at the glass sliding doors. She suddenly said, "John, there's a rabbit in the south strawberry bed!" I went to the door and sure enough a small bunny had managed to nose its way under the chicken wire fencing around the bed. But once inside it couldn't find an exit.

I grabbed a sweatshirt, put on my shoes and went out to remove the intruder. Several minutes of chasing the animal didn't help, but once I'd figured out how to maneuver closer to it, I was able to get the bunny cornered and fling my sweatshirt over him. I gathered up the shirt with the bunny inside it and gently tossed both over the two-foot high fence. The bunny worked its way out the sweatshirt and ran out of the garden. Now, all I had to worry about was where he'd gotten inside in the first place.

The organic seeds John and I tucked lovingly into the soil before we got the chickens had produced swathes of healthy seedlings, nestled safe from rabbits in their fenced beds. Then suddenly, *pouf,* like magic, they were gone. Beets and broccoli, pea and bean plants completely disappeared, leaving only a small hole in the ground. Like, now you see 'em, now you don't. Since the rabbits weren't eating them, what was?

When our first summer root crops were ready to harvest, the mystery deepened. In the potato patch, I found the same situation as last summer: far fewer potatoes per hill, mostly tiny ones. Almost all the larger potatoes had big chunks missing. One evening, John and I started picking our carrot rows. I pulled up a big carrot, then stared at the bizarre vegetable shell in my hand. "John, what is this?"

He gazed at it too, looking perplexed. "I have no idea."

John is a far more experienced gardener than I am; still, he'd never seen anything like this particular specimen. You'd pull on a perfectly-formed carrot top, but the carrot itself would be hollowed out, leaving only an outside skin. And the damage was extreme: about three of every five carrots were ravaged. We visited our local nursery to make inquiries, then went online. What we discovered wasn't only dismaying. It was chilling.

The culprit? Voles.

"Voles?" people would say when John and I mentioned our garden problem. "You mean moles?"

"No, voles," we'd answer patiently. Most people have never heard of them, but voles are a common rodent. They're about the size of moles, and live underground in a vast network of tunnels, often using the same passages made by mice or moles. Folks with lawns might declare moles as the biggest pain, given the unsightly piles of soil they leave all over the place, but give them credit: moles are carnivores that eat bugs and other soil organisms. If only voles ate the same!

But no—these critters are *vegetarians*. The crafty little buggers are voracious eaters of just about everything in your garden, above and below ground: your carrots, beets, peas, kale, spinach, broccoli, and yes, your potatoes. They don't eat onions, but they'll nibble on onion roots, stunting the plant so the bulbs don't develop properly.

Other roots weren't immune either. As John and I began to investigate our yard more closely, we found destruction everywhere. Empty spots in the asparagus beds showed vole holes—and those missing crowns were gone for good. Vole holes were rife in the strawberry beds. We'd often find a half-eaten berry sitting in a hole. The evil little creature had clearly parked himself right under the plants, merrily eating a berry while completely out of harm's way.

There were holes beneath the blueberry shrubs too, with scraps of root material strewn above ground. Beneath the apple trees, the ground was spongy. Yep, more vole holes. The nursery folks had told us mice would wreak havoc in your orchard, eating the tender, soil-level bark of young fruit trees. John and I found that voles did *far* more damage with their unrelenting root-eating: several fruit trees weren't putting on much height, and their trunks were so scrawny they didn't look like they could support the tree.

Well. This was all-out *war*. Voles were ruining Berryridge Farm.

Problem: You couldn't catch 'em—we tried. John set mouse traps and rat traps, but voles were too smart for that. You couldn't shoot 'em—the smallest and wiliest of predators, they were the least seen. We went high-tech: we read about these solar-powered spikes you stick into the ground and emit a high-pitched buzz that supposedly voles can't abide. John went to the hardware store and found them, at $19.95 apiece. Despite the cost, we bought six and set them around the yard.

Within a day or two, I found more vole holes, right next to the spikes! And it was *me* who couldn't stand the electronic buzz. Outside for hours each day, I could hear the noise from every corner of the yard, and it drove me *nuts*. With six spikes giving off a tone every thirty seconds, the sweet, pure silence of our place was shattered. I finally pulled all the spikes up and stuck them in the shop. And that was $120 plus tax we'd never see again.

One other element to our vole problem had no solution. Here we were, growing tender-footed crops for humans in the middle of the woods, with hardy, native weeds, shrubs and trees growing like crazy no matter how much vole-noshing went on. And except for some neighbors one-third of a mile away, a farm family who had a garden (surrounded by a machine-maintained lawn and pasture), we were the only food growers for miles around. Without any mechanical noise and vibrations that might disturb them, every vole in this part of the Foothills had likely moved into our yard. What in the world were we going to do?

The thing was, John and I had learned to focus on the vegetables that grew reliably in our climate. In the Foothills, those were root crops. You couldn't count on enough hot summer days to confidently raise warm-weather produce, but even with cool and rainy weather, potatoes, carrots, parsnips and the like would thrive.

So what if we gave up on root vegetables? The previous year, we'd had a bumper crop of squash and tomatoes, but this year both were a total bust. Conclusion: if we didn't do root veggies, our dreams of self-sufficiency would go up in smoke.

Okay, we could always focus on fruit. We had oodles of orchard trees. Yet our strawberry yields—berries that had somehow survived the voles—had gone downhill too. I knew that after three years or so, strawberry plants generally develop a virus that makes the crowns weak, and the berries tiny. Clearly it was time to replace our strawberries, but I wondered if I should bother—the plants would meet the same fate as the rest of our crops.

Despite all these snags, as summer drifted into fall, I had to let go of my garden concerns. John and I had a whole new worry—one that far eclipsed a few hungry rodents.

9 ☞ The Times, They Are A Changin'

John's not one to fret. In fact, faced with any challenging situation, whether it's bad weather, power outages, or a family problem, he accepts it calmly and says, "It is what it is." But he *was* anxious about his mom.

Wanda Mae McDonald Browne was of hardy Midwestern stock, the granddaughter of Irish immigrants who raced for a homestead in the Oklahoma Land Rush of the 1890s. Strong and independent, she was like a Cadbury Crème egg, firm on the outside, but soft and sweet on the inside. From her, John got his questing mind, artistic sensibilities, and cooking skills, not to mention her homebody gene. But like Berryridge Farm, she was losing ground.

Wanda still lived in the split-level house where John had grown up, in a tree-filled suburb near Seattle. For nearly twenty years, John's sister Becky had lived with their mom. But Becky's cancer had metastasized, necessitating ongoing chemotherapy, which added to John's anxieties. Wanda no longer drove, so errands were up to John's sister. One day she had a one-car accident that left her badly shaken, though not injured.

Becky was not only swiftly losing mobility, but having frequent falls, unable to get back on her feet without assistance. Wanda was calling 911 on a regular basis. Still, well into her eighties, John's mom was in no condition to be a caregiver for her daughter. The family made a difficult decision: Becky would go into semi-assisted living in a small city on the eastern side of the state, near John's older brother Sid and lots of medical facilities.

Becky was heartbroken to be leaving her mother. "We're a team," she said many times, but neither of them could go on much longer, given the stress of her illness and the strain on Wanda.

Becky's move was just in time. Six years into widowhood, Wanda was going deaf, turning the radio on full blast to catch the Art Bell Show every night. She still read extensively, but with chronic back pain, she spent most of her days sitting at the kitchen table. Now housebound, not even going outdoors to get the mail, she was living in that big house, alone. With two flights of stairs.

Her home, over a half-century old, was also showing its age. Never remodeled, or having had more than basic repairs, the structure's wood siding was failing, and the neighborhood woodpeckers were going to town on wood-burrowing bugs. John's brother Sid, who had professional carpentry skills, patched the siding holes with a sheet of metal. Which unfortunately didn't stop the woodpeckers—they'd peck on the metal, creating an unholy din.

Wanda's deck, slick with moss, was rotting, and there was more rot in the downstairs bathroom. John and Sid, who also lived a three-hour drive away, would try and talk to her about repairs, but there were a couple of stumbling blocks. First of all, Wanda tended to be a bit of a procrastinator, living that time-honored motto, "Never do today what you can put off until tomorrow." The second, bigger delay was that Wanda, although financially comfortable, was too frugal to hire a contractor. She wanted her sons to repair the house, or not at all.

Her grandson, John's nephew, looked in on her regularly and brought her groceries, but he lived thirty miles away. So John came up with a plan. "Wouldn't it be great if my mom would come up here to live?" he'd dream aloud. "She always said how much she loved *The Egg and I*—maybe she'd be game to live in the country. She could buy a little park home and we'd put it on the property."

For sure, the classic memoir by Betty MacDonald, about greenhorns and their wacky adventures in the boondocks had to be more fun to read than to live. Still, John's proposal sounded doable: with a doctor's note, county zoning regs would allow a second small home on the property. Wanda could leave that crumbling house—and at the same time, keep her independence. Plus John could check on her every day. With that in mind, he persuaded her to make her first visit to Berryridge Farm.

One Saturday in November John drove down to the family home to pick Wanda up. Once they'd arrived here, he was ready to show her around, but she was hardly able to take more than a few tottering steps around the garden.

She stayed one night, and by morning, couldn't hide her eagerness to return home. Still, over breakfast, John asked her hopefully, "How do you like our place?"

She didn't smile. "It's so...dark."

So that was that. Wanda would stay in her fifty year-old house. Her own mother had lived to be nearly one hundred, so my sweet mother-in-law could be living alone for a very long time.

Change had come to my side of the family too.

My younger daughter's marriage was slowly disintegrating, and all I could do was offer Meghann support from afar. Carrie, my older girl, was offered a promotion that meant a temporary assignment to the Detroit area. She jumped at the opportunity—she, my son-in-law Kevin and granddaughter Megs would be away eighteen months. Carrie was close to her dad's extended family, who all lived around central Michigan, only a couple hours' drive from Carrie's new home. She and Kevin found a condo in a tony Detroit suburb on a lake, perfect for my son-in-law's boating hobby. I put on a good face, but inside, I was grieving. A year and a half seemed like forever, Michigan a world away.

Two months into their move, Carrie sent me a photo of our granddaughter, whom everyone called "little Megs," dressed in her Halloween costume: a deliciously macabre corpse bride, with a make-up scar on her cheek, like in the Tim Burton film. I gazed at Megs' beloved face. At nine, my granddaughter was growing up far too fast. Missing her until I ached, a spark went off in my mind: a children's story, something I'd never written before. I'd been working on my first Irish novel, but I set it aside to write a Halloween/Day of the Dead paranormal tale of a young girl (who strangely enough, closely resembled our granddaughter) who dresses up as a dead bride—only to bring on a curse in which the costume won't come off!

A few weeks later, *Morgan Carey and The Curse of the Corpse Bride* was finished, and John designed a cover for it. We got a few books printed and sent one to Little Megs and her mom. Megs promptly brought her book to school for show-and-tell, and it turned out to be a big hit—surely the highest honor for a grandma. Megs' and Carrie's pleasure in my story made the distance between us seem not so great after all. Still, I wondered: if Carrie turned her temporary job into a permanent one, what would happen to my relationship with my daughter and her family?

10 🐾 Chicken Weatherproofing

With winter came a fresh chicken learning curve.

The hens seemed to do all right during cold snaps, but when another January Northeaster dropped the temperature below twenty, John and I felt downright guilty that they had to live in an unheated space. He rigged up a rudimentary heater he'd seen his dad design: a 60-watt incandescent bulb set inside a coffee can, with holes punched in the can to let excess heat escape. He connected his makeshift heater to a 200-foot industrial-strength extension cord and plugged it into one of the shop's outlets. And what do you know, that bit of heat seemed to liven up the flock.

Not that a little warmth had any effect on the piles of manure in the coop. When the winter temperatures dropped into the 20s or below, that fancy Williams-Sonoma trowel really came in handy: for cleaning, instead of scraping manure off the coop board, you'd have to chisel it.

We also discovered that if our girls didn't like getting wet, they especially hated snow. All six of them would not so much as step foot—or claw—into it. Although they did have a roof of sorts over their caged safety zone, provided by the tarp, that limited dry space wasn't enough. When it snowed they'd congregate beneath the plastic sheet, which meant the chicken-poo patties were much more concentrated.

Nor was the tarp an ideal cover. Since it wasn't perfectly taut, when it rained—which is almost daily during our winters—you'd have to go into the run and push up on the tarp where puddles had formed, necessitating yet another change into chicken-cleaning getup. Rain or snow would readily accumulate in any sagging areas, which soon led to leaky spots. And this mix of mud and manure, so unpleasant to walk in, was not a healthy environment for hens. Our newest orchard space, then, really came in handy.

Encouraged by the robust growth of the fruit trees we'd planted our first year here, an Akane, Elstar and Florina apple and two European pears, a Red Bartlett and Comice, John and I created a larger orchard with more apple trees: a Jonagold, Red Gravenstein, Tsugaru, Williams Pride, and our *real* pride and joy, a Honeycrisp. To that we added a couple of heirlooms: a Karmijn de Sonnaville, and Ashmeads Kernal, plus a Centennial crabapple. Plums joined the apples, a Saxton, a Japanese plum, and two prune plums. Next to the chicken compound, near the apricot trees, we established a third orchard area, with two Asian pear trees, and more apples, a Queen's Cox and Early Macintosh. Besides having all the apples we'd ever want for pie, cider, and best of all, fresh eating, we had space for the hens to roam.

With springtime, our six hens were happily settling back into scratching up every shred of vegetation in their pen, not to mention everything in the orchard next to it. In the bare spots, they gave themselves dust baths: hens will scratch up a hole big enough to settle into, then flap their wings and sort of squeegee down into the dirt. Apparently this helps eliminate pests and parasites on their skin and among their feathers.

To create more areas for dust baths, John built a narrow, fenced-in "tunnel" adjacent to our woodshed complex, so the hens would have ample safe and dry spots. The girls also liked to hang out beneath a young, yet robust fir tree that stood at the edge of the orchard—another safe, dry place for dust-bathing.

Luckily, with all this soil-scrabbling, the birds didn't bother our two apricot trees. Besides, maybe a little chicken manure would invigorate the trees' growth enough to stay ahead of the blight. While the hens were able to fly very short distances, they never breached the four-foot fence separating the orchard from our main garden.

The chickens went gaga over dandelions and wild spinach—although after a few weeks of scratching, they'd devoured every shred of green left in the orchard area. So after weeding the vegetable beds, John and I would bring them handfuls of greens. The girls loved bugs and worms of every kind too, so beware the poor beetle who ventured into their lair! Between their feed and scratch grains we fed them, they were eating almost constantly. With all this nice organic fuel, they were producing a bounty of eggs, at least four or five a day. Sometimes six, which was *waaaay* more than we could eat. John and I shared dozens with my brother Ty, the Wood Guy, and with Burl, my stepdad, who was big on farm eggs. We usually had six or seven dozen in the fridge, so it was a boon to get our first regular egg customer, a friend of John's who happily paid $3.00 a dozen. We were like, real farmers!

Then came the day I returned from errands in town, and found John outside…in his underwear.

11 🐾 First Casualty

Earlier that day, I'd looked out the kitchen window to see a red-tailed hawk. It swooped over the chicken compound and settled on one of the fence posts overlooking the hens' run. I jammed my feet into some boots and bolted outside, waving my arms. "Go on! Get away!" The hawk lazily took off, as if not the least bit intimidated by my yelling. Meanwhile, our six hens had taken shelter beneath the young Douglas fir in the orchard, and there they stayed, quaking in terror.

I returned to the house to get ready to leave for town, but before long, the hawk was back, alighting on the post again. Same drill: I ran into the yard, shouting, but this time, the imposing bird only gave me an insolent stare with its beady eyes. It didn't even blink. Really mad now, I picked up a chunk of wood and hurled it at the hawk. With my pathetic aim, I didn't expect to actually hit the bird, and sure enough, I didn't. But my flimsy weapon seemed to have worked. The hawk flew off toward the deep forest next to our woods.

I figured the chickens were safe, under the tree. So did John. Still, while I was away, he worked outdoors most of the day, so he could keep an eye on them. Near sundown, he knew that any minute now, the girls would be going into the coop for the night. So he headed into the house for a shower.

It was soon after that I found him outside, a shovel in his hands.

John's always been the conventional type, not inclined to cavort out of doors in his muck boots and undies. So the underwear alone was cause for concern. But the shovel...I felt a twist in the pit of my stomach. "The hawk?"

He nodded somberly. "I didn't get there in time."

Half-dressed, he'd looked out the dining room window and saw the hawk in the yard, standing over a hen. A dead one. John raced out, and threw a big stick at the hawk—and at least had the satisfaction of running off the hawk before it had a chance to eat its kill.

The dead chicken had been the one we'd never named.

When I got home, John had just settled the last shovelful of dirt on her mangled body. For two days afterward, the traumatized hens wouldn't leave their coop. Feeling sad and guilty, John and I vowed to protect our five remaining girls a lot better. No more unsupervised roaming around the orchard from dawn 'til dusk, whether we were home or not. From now on, we would only let our chickens out of their fenced-in safety zone when we were outside too.

The hawk didn't come back. We like to think that since John prevented it from enjoying that delicious chicken dinner, it figured, why bother returning for another try? I suppose in the larger scheme of things, we'd been lucky. The hens hadn't been molested by your usual chicken predators, like foxes, raccoons or coyotes—and we'd lost only one. Still, I started a habit of scanning the sky as I did my chores, and checking the compost area for animal sign. And life, as it does, went on.

12 🐓 Kickin' It Up a Notch

After releasing my first Irish novel, *It Only Takes Once*, a romantic coming-of-age tale, I was inspired to double-down on our place. A few county growers were trying new crops to expand local food system, especially grains. I said to John, "Let's raise grains for chicken feed!"

John, never averse to experimenting, was game. Once the soil was warm enough for planting, I surveyed the spring seed offerings at our food co-op. Grain seeds were few and far between, but spying a packet of wintering-over barley grown in the neighboring county, I eagerly tucked it in my shopping cart.

The price made me blanch a bit—$4.00 for a very skinny package—but hey, this was organic, local seed, raised on a pristine island off the coast. Plus the description indicated that this variety was easy to thresh, the grains readily separating from the seedheads. Once home, I sowed a long row, and happily discovered the voles weren't eating the grassy shoots.

While John and I were set for apples, we visited a blueberry farm every August to pick berries to freeze. With self-reliance in mind, we decided to raise a bigger berry crop for winter eating. My overrun-with-voles potato bed had taught me not to try any more root or annual crops in that spot—maybe we'd have better luck with perennial plants. Surely with all our hole-digging, which would destroy lots of vole tunnels, the new plantings would be okay.

Ever optimistic, John and I set in six new blueberry shrubs, plus transplanted two more that hadn't been doing well in the main garden. An added vole safeguard: with the chickens free-ranging on the other side of the fenced berry patch, we had five built-in, soil-disturbing, rodent deterrents.

Still, we had the rest of our crops to worry about.

John and I were pondering the coming growing season with dread. It felt like we'd been fighting a losing battle—and our dream of living off the food we raised was at stake. I mean, you couldn't live on apples, now could you?

One thing was clear: if we wanted to grow annual crops, we'd have to take drastic steps. We'd admired the raised and screened beds we'd seen in our favorite homesteader magazines, and decided if that's what it takes to grow food in the Foothills, so be it—even if it meant we'd have to basically rebuild our entire vegetable patch.

Flush with this spring's income tax return, John and I visited the building supply center in the small town fifteen miles away. Back in the city, he'd built raised beds out of treated wood. To go organic, though, and avoid the toxins in treated products, we settled on untreated, kiln-dried lumber. For the boards, our first choice was cedar, since it was long-lasting, but the cost was more than we could afford. For an alternative, the store owner recommended Douglas fir. "It should last you five, maybe ten years."

Next, we purchased a quantity of what's called hardware cloth: ½ inch screening material to line the bottom of the beds. The bill for our anti-vole campaign? Let's just say it took a big chunk of Uncle Sam's refund.

Now that John and I were set for materials, he started building the boxes: nailing together a 3' x 8' rectangle of fir planks, ten inches deep. The boxes were heavy too—it took both of us to carry one. After John cut a right-sized length of the hardware cloth, I would hold it in place while he stapled it to all four edges of each box. It was laborious work, cutting all that wire and wrestling it into place, plus the stapling. And the cut ends were lethally sharp—we had the scratched hands to prove it.

By this time, it was April, and the ground had dried enough to work in. The next step was to dig a same-sized rectangle about six inches deep and "plant" your box,hardware cloth-side down. Since after a few rainstorms, the soil will settle several inches, you've got to fill the box to the tippety-top with soil. And let me tell you, a 3'x 8' bed holds a *lot* of dirt.

A thousand shovelfuls and five boxes later, we were ready for spring planting. We didn't transplant any fruit trees or blueberry shrubs into the boxes—moving them would likely set any harvests back for several years. They'd just have to hang in there. As for the rest of the garden, John and I had to wonder: had we wasted hundreds of dollars on this experiment? Would these raised beds save our crops from voles?

13 ✆ Spring Fever

The first of May marks the ancient Celtic festival of Beltane, which celebrates the bright half of the year. Inspired by the song in the movie *Camelot*, John likes to call this month "the lusty month of May." There's actually some historical basis for the "lusty" name: way back in the day, on Beltane it was customary for unmarried couples to go off to the woods for...well, use your imagination. In any event, when May Day finally arrives, it seems like the earth is brimming over with vibrant, lusty life!

While May first in the Foothills generally promises lots more chilly, overcast, if not downright wet days, it's exactly two weeks before our average last frost date. Which means we can get serious about planting Berryridge Farm staples: carrots, beets, parsnips and potatoes. Some folks in the Pacific Northwest say you can plant these root crops in April, but I'm sorry—after several growing seasons in the Foothills, I've discovered April is too undependable for anything, even peas. This April, the weather gods had brought upwards of five inches of rain, with nighttime temperatures in the low 40's or even down into the 30's—few seeds will germinate when it's that cold, and will simply rot in the wet ground. So postponing your seed sowing for several weeks may actually give your garden a head start.

When you get down to it, though, there's no such thing as hard and fast planting dates. Or harvest dates either. Both can vary tremendously year to year, depending upon temperatures, rainfall, and sunshine. Wherever you live, it might take a few growing seasons to figure out the best times to plant. If you aren't sure about the first and last frost dates in your area, you can consult your local university Ag extension program or check the NOAA (National Oceanic and Atmospheric Administration) website.

Back in the city, having only a small back yard, John and I played it safe—we'd buy the same basic tomato and zucchini starts we did the year before…and the year before that. But once we got our country acreage, we had a veritable gardener's playground. We could try all kinds of new plants!

With our expanded garden areas, we decided to go for a crop we'd never tried in the city, one you could plant any time from late fall to early spring: Easy-Peasy Garlic.

Garlic is one of the simplest short-season veggies you can raise in this corner of the Pacific Northwest. Since I call it easy-peasy, I wish I could tell you we mastered garlic-growing right out of the gate…but I can't.

The fall of Carrie's family relocation, we got a head start with our garlic. John was *on* it: he ordered a supply of garlic starts, two rather exotic varieties, and had them in the ground by early October. The first, tender shoots emerged in December, soon followed by a vigorous Northeaster. Not surprisingly, the garlic tops shriveled away, and there went our crop. It turns out, there *is* such a thing as being too organized.

So far, all the garlic I'd raised had been marginal at best. This year, I'd tossed an abundance of shriveled, unusable garlic heads into my compost pile, and what do you know: those shrunken cloves started growing in the compost. I thought, *Oh, boy, free garlic starts!* So I pulled out the sprouts and planted them alongside the fall-planted garlic. And while I was at it, here and there all over the garden. Well, guess what. The transplants were a total wash. I didn't get any mature, multi-cloved garlic heads, only slightly swollen roots.

Some folks swear by spring-planted garlic. I'd also tried setting my garlic in the ground around March, but the heads never grew that big. I concluded that the bulb structure needs many months to develop—and that means fall-planted garlic. You only need to get it in the ground before the soil freezes.

Here's what's worked for me:

You want to time your garlic planting strategically: after fall temperatures have dropped way down, but before the first hard freeze, in which case the ground is too frozen for planting. In late September, I go to the nearest food co-op for locally-grown, organic hardneck garlic and buy seven or eight of the biggest heads I can find, with the largest cloves. I keep my seed garlic in a paper bag in the mudroom—a cool, well-ventilated place—then plant in mid-November.

You separate the cloves and set each one into fertile, well-drained soil, about two inches deep, and they seem to do best at least six inches apart. And make sure the pointy end is up and the rough, flat end down, which is where the roots grow from. Cover your bed generously with mulch—in our area, we have many freeze-and-thaw cycles during the winter, so several inches of mulch will protect the garlic from the worst of the soil-heaving caused by temperature variations. Many people mulch with straw; I cover my garlic beds with a variety of materials like maple leaves and brackenfern fronds topped with compost. Keep your bed weeded and well-mulched and you're good to go!

In our area, you'll see the first green shoots around March.

Seeing that early bit of greenery is inspiring, and I like to think it gives you faith that yes, winter is indeed over, making way for the miracle of your garden bursting with life. Garlic foliage will grow nice and tall through the season. Not long after the summer solstice, you'll notice the lower leaves are starting to die. This is good: it means harvesting isn't far off. Wait until you have about five dried-up leaves, then you can pull out the garlic bulb. If you wait too long, and let the leaves higher up the stalk die, the cloves start to separate from the heads. Moisture will get into the bulb—and your garlic will spoil during storage.

With luck and fertile soil, your heads will be every bit as big as the original heads you planted. Brush the soil off the roots and set your harvested crop in a shaded, well-ventilated spot (I park them in our shop with the garage doors open all day). Let your garlic sit for a couple of weeks until the green parts have dried up. Cut off the stem, and your crop is ready to store. One last tip: don't be shy about using your garlic as soon as you harvest it. Fresh garlic has a crunchy texture and delicate taste you won't find in stored bulbs—perfect for summer pesto and vinaigrettes!

In spite of the voles eating practically all our favorite vegetables—savoy spinach, broccoli, snow peas, Nantes carrots, rainbow chard, beets, Yukon gold potatoes and our latest yummy discovery, parsnips—with our new protected raised beds, we were determined to raise them all. Besides, John and I felt like seasoned food gardeners: we'd gained a working knowledge about our soil, climate, and what we could grow out here. So we started testing some tried-and-true garden rules.

Take store-bought potting mix: one of our first experiments was starting seeds in plain garden soil. To many experts, this is blasphemy, even for the free-thinking folks you'll find in *Mother Earth News*. In one article, the writer admitted that yes, you can make your own potting mix. But her recipe seemed insanely complicated. And after you've put together your plethora of ingredients, you have to screen the soil, then bake it in your oven to sterilize it. I'm sorry, but I'm not going to put dirt in my oven—

what with processing so many root crops, I have enough dirt passing through my kitchen, thank you very much.

Besides, to me, potting mix seems a little creepy. As far as I can tell, it doesn't decompose—years after planting nursery starts, I'll still find clods of potting mix, with the tell-tale black color and white particles. If the material isn't breaking down after all this time, what the heck is this Franken-dirt doing in my garden?

So despite our misgivings, we took the risk, happily discovering that seeds start perfectly well in good ol' Berryridge earth.

Emboldened by these successes, John and I figured, no guts, no glory, right? So we really started pushing the food-grower's envelope.

John and I read that radishes are super-easy to grow, and if you plant a very slow-germinating crop like parsnips, it's a great idea to sow a fast-germinating item like radishes alongside them. The reason is 1) you'll know where your parsnips seedlings will show up (because you won't see any evidence of them for what seems like a really long time), and 2) the radish foliage will shade the delicate parsnip sprouts.

Now, although John and I love our veggies, neither of us had ever developed a taste for radishes. But then, we'd never eaten any home-grown, organic ones, which would surely make all the difference. Besides, since local chefs were all over radishes—using them in cooking demos at the Farmer's Market and featuring them at the area's finest restaurants—radishes *had* to be tasty!

I bought a packet of organic French breakfast radish seeds for $3.99, further encouraged by the label's enticing photo of the loveliest, rosy-white roots you ever saw. With the cold spring we'd had, even the peas were late. Both of us hungry for our first vegetables, John cast the radish seeds in the ground with great hopes.

We discovered radishes did indeed live up to their reputation as quick germinators. Within a few weeks, we were harvesting armfuls of these rose-red beauties. Really, they were the prettiest vegetables I'd ever seen! After a scrub, I sliced some up for a raw, Zen-like garnish on our dinner plates—and was prepared to be amazed.

I took a bite. So did my notoriously not-picky husband.
"Um, these don't taste very good," I said.
"They don't do much for me either," said John. (His nice way of saying, "Yuk!")
I decided radishes needed a little more preparation. I tried them as refrigerator pickles, even added some sugar that wasn't in the recipe, and took a bite. Nope, still unpalatable. Then I put radishes in a stir-fry with broccoli, carrots, and other delectables. No way. We ended picking them out.
Okay, it was time to get serious. John and I had never met a root vegetable that roasting wouldn't render into mouth-watering delicious-ness. So I drizzled a panful of radishes with extra virgin olive oil and roasted 'em.
It turns out I'd wasted the EVOO, electricity, and the time and water I'd used washing both the radishes and the roasting pan. Since the hens love people food, I took the roasted radishes out to their run, but not one of the girls would touch them. I ended up tossing the whole shebang onto the compost pile. Then I tromped over to the radish beds and pulled out the fifty or so still in the ground and threw them on top. That's one experiment we wouldn't repeat.
While the radish fiasco was all my fault, John's been known to take a few wrong turns in the seed-selection department. One of his favorite winter activities is perusing the dozens of seed catalogues that arrive in our mailbox. With this dizzying assortment of veggies to choose from, he always orders more seeds than we have room for. This season, he decided he'd go for something really new: purple carrots. Now, I'm a real carrot lover, but I wasn't too keen— purple produce kinda turns me off. But John was determined to sell me on the new variety. "Purple food like grapes is full of really great antioxidants—you know, like in red wine," he said. "These carrots'll be especially nutritious." Since we only had five protected raised beds, these purple guys would go straight into the ground.
Overcome by enthusiasm, John ended up planting not one bed of this purple variety, but three. Even after the voles had helped themselves, surely we'd have enough carrots to last well into next winter.

14 🐾 A New Varmint

The strawberry beds were a mess.

After a wet, chilly spring, the strawberry season had been several weeks later than usual. When I spotted the first perfect, plump red berry on June 21st, I was eagerly anticipating my first taste. I had to spend the day in town to present a workshop, but I knew this luscious berry, under the netting, would be safe from robins.

Early the next morning, I hustled to the bed to pick the berry, but it was…gone. It was then I realized robins were the least of our strawberry problems.

In the last year, chipmunks had become regular visitors to Berryridge Farm. I admit, they were fun to watch, scampering through the yard, fast as lightning. That was before John and I discovered where all that scampering was leading. During our previous strawberry harvest, I'd seen one run right through the netting, as if it wasn't there. I'd been pretty ticked off to find berries scattered here and there, some with bites in them, some not. But this year, after that first strawberry disappeared, I realized Chip had become much more destructive. I would go out to pick, and find smashed berries covering the large rocks ringing the bed. Half-destroyed berries were strewn all over the yard, mostly the biggest, ripest ones. John and I even found strawberries littering the woodsheds, where a chipmunk had obviously set up housekeeping.

You may be thinking, c'mon, what's the big deal? How much can a chipmunk really eat?

As it turns out, a *lot*. A chipmunk was eating our berries as fast as they were ripening. Remembering the time John had captured a bunny in his sweatshirt, I thought, if only chipmunks were this easy to get rid of. Since they weren't, and we were counting on the berries for both summer eating and freezing, we had to go on the offensive.

"Chip," I told John, "is ruining our crop. We've got to do something."

A friend had recommended baiting traps for chipmunks with peanut butter. John dutifully set out a couple of rat traps, all of which Chip ignored. This critter had also grown bolder, scurrying through the garden beds, always leaving smashed berries in his wake. In fact, when we'd get close enough to try to shoo him back into the woods, he'd give us a look like we were bothering *him*.

After a week or so of trap-setting, we were once again trying to shoo Chip away. But instead of darting into the woods, he clambered up our house foundation, and disappeared behind the siding—this critter could be moving his household from the woodpiles to inside our walls! That was it. The. Last. Straw.

John came up with a new trap bait: supplement the peanut butter with a ripe strawberry on the top. Could Chip resist this confection? Soon after, I saw a chipmunk racing into the garden. It halted mid-stride and did a somersault, tail switching, its whole body flip-flopping madly. "John," I called, "there's a chipmunk in the yard, acting very weird."

Outside weeding, John found it immediately. The animal was still caught in the rat trap, obviously suffering. As I watched, John speared the chipmunk with his handfork. I turned away, wincing.

You may think I'm a wuss, but while bike riding, I see so much dead wildlife up close. On my usual route, a winding country road bordered by fields and woodlands, with only a modest amount of weekend traffic, I find new corpses every day. Crushed butterflies. Flattened mice and moles, snakes and toads. Smashed opossums and squirrels. Battered songbirds, hawks and owls, and the broken bodies of deer.

The heavy exposure to dead creatures has turned me into someone who cannot watch even the mildest TV or movie violence (if there is such a thing). So my relief at catching our resident thief was tempered with regret—that John had to kill it, practically with his bare hands. After he'd buried the chipmunk, I met him out in the yard. "You okay?"

"The chipmunk looked like its back had been broken." John looked down. "I had to put it out of its misery as fast as I could."

"Oh, Honey," I said, feeling a little sick. "That must've been grisly."

"It's hard to kill something when you're looking 'em right in the eye," John said heavily. "I mean, I always liked chipmunks—I grew up watching 'Chip and Dale' and 'Bambi.'"

"I hear you," I said, patting his shoulder. Back in the 60s, I'd watched "Alvin and the Chipmunks" myself, so I'd been fond of these little woodland critters too. At any rate, Chip was gone. Our problem was solved.

Or was it?

You've probably guessed it by now: Berryridge Farm had not only one Chip, but many Chips.

After this first chipmunk death, the pillaging in the strawberry patch continued unabated. John set up more traps, including one just outside our bedroom window, where the chipmunk had climbed behind our siding. A couple of days later, I was in the bedroom when I heard a sharp *Crack*!—then some mewling cries. I couldn't bear to look. I knew it was another trapped chipmunk, in its death throes. Luckily John was nearby, and he once again had to end its suffering.

The next day, I was near one of our woodsheds when I heard another *Crack*! I turned toward the sound, and saw a trapped chipmunk, flipping in agony. It died right before my eyes, before John could do a mercy killing.

He continued to set traps, and within ten days or so, the body count had reached a dozen. "I'm starting to feel like a killing machine," he said sadly. I couldn't blame him. Neither of us object to hunting, but this war on wildlife was feeling pretty merciless. Still, John and I told ourselves we didn't have any other choice.

John, always fair-minded, pointed out the problem with fighting nature: Chip, or the many Chips, had been here first. And they'd only been doing what came naturally: eating the best food available. Here in the woods, we were the real intruders. *We* were the ones doing harm.

When John and I first moved to the Foothills, carving our one-half acre clearing out of the woods with a bulldozer was a given. Yet we didn't understand until the following spring how much collateral damage bulldozing would do. It was a year before John and I saw our first earthworm. The dozer, we slowly realized, had not only wiped out the brush, saplings, trees and stumps, but the worms, the toads, the salamanders and snakes. All "good garden friends," as John would say.

If it took a year for an earthworm to show up on Berryridge farm, it took two before we saw a toad, and months longer before we found any snakes. Even the mere presence of our house constituted a wildlife hazard: in the midst of their dogfights, our resident hummingbirds regularly crashed into our front windows. Sometimes they survived. Sometimes not. John holding a tiny dead bird in his palm, before burying it in the woods, was about the saddest thing either one of us had seen on our place.

By now, the hens had created a virtual desert in their scratching areas and needed a real pasture. John and I were set on creating one, but we'd held off on hiring out the job, since a good-sized productive pasture would involve more dozing. More death. We ended up cutting down some saplings and brush so the hens could venture past their fence—more grunt work. Yet that task was our penance. From now on, we would try and give back to nature what we'd taken.

15 🐚 Wild Thing, You Make My Heart...Sink

Lest you think John and I are hardly better than reformed murderers, even after the sad chipmunk episodes we still had plenty of wildlife around our place.

Our first night on Berryridge Farm, we realized deer and rabbits weren't the only untamed critters around when a pack of coyotes serenaded us in the wee hours. After reading about other wildlife incursions around the U.S., like deer turning up in motel rooms, bears in rural kitchens, and alligators on front porches, I feel pretty lucky our wildlife encounters have pretty much been confined to the outdoors.

Down the slope from us lived the neighbor who'd so kindly plowed the lane our first winter here, when John and I were snowbound. He and his wife were definitely an Odd Couple, though, the way they kept to themselves. They also kept...other things. Like a raccoon. During our only visit to their place, the raccoon waddled into sight, and our neighbor caught it by its tail. As the 'coon struggled furiously, he shoved it back into its pen.

Fortunately, the raccoon didn't seem to stray from their place. Apparently (and lucky for us), the critter had never found a pal to mate with, since we never saw any others. This oddball couple also had a wolf-dog, bred with what appeared to be a German shepherd. This animal freaked me out to no end. Fortunately, every time I encountered it on our lane, the creature would quickly run away.

John and I soon discovered that bigger animals made regular visits close by. Our new neighbors, a young mountain-man kind of guy partnered with a gal who looked like an REI model, reported seeing a black bear on their property, calmly munching on blackberries. I could tell Mountain Man thought the bear was more of an interesting sight than a worry. Taking our cue from him—and the fact that Mountain Man and his girlfriend lived over a third of a mile away—John and I decided we wouldn't get overly concerned about one bear. Especially if it stayed out of sight. Our sight, I mean.

Soon after, those same neighbors told us they saw a cougar next to the lane. The big cat had left incriminating evidence that what Mountain Man's girlfriend called (excuse my slang) "a big hairy turd" on the road. Now *that* worried me. Upon telling my Foothills friend Lori (keeper of all Foothills lore), she advised me that if you encounter a cougar, you follow one rule of thumb: "Don't turn your back on them." She paused for a moment, then added, "And whatever you do, do *not* run away." Apparently, fleeing a cougar will make it think *you're* the prey. So while you're shaking with terror you keep your eyes on the cat and do what the sheriffs of yore told the gunslingers in the Wild West: just back away slowly.

You might find it strange that although we had ten acres, John and I rarely ventured outside our yard. I certainly never strayed far into our wooded acreage by myself. I'm not trying to be a weenie or anything, but if I anticipate any chance of a bear or cougar encounter I want reinforcements along.

To get a good look at our woods on a regular basis, John and I started a tradition of walking the perimeter of the property in mid-spring. This is the time of year when the alders and understory are just beginning to leaf out, and before the brackenfern sprouts. In the Foothills, this fern species grows so densely that by early summer, the woods are all but impassable.

For some weeks, John and I had been hearing an odd, mechanical wheezing from what appeared to be our west boundary. Problem: no one lived anywhere near there—beyond our property line was an old, dense forest. A week before our hiking date, the noise seemed even louder than usual, so John decided to check out the situation.

Sometime later, when he met me in the garden, he was out of breath, his color high. "Everything okay?" I asked.

He shook his head ruefully. "You wouldn't believe what I just ran into."

Surprise in the Woods

One day in early May, I returned home from visiting my mom. With a couple of hours of daylight remaining, I started a minor repair on the chicken coop. About an hour before sunset, off to the west I detected that strange sound Sue and I had been hearing for the last week or two. I grabbed my walking stick and went to see if I could find the source.

When I arrived at the northwest corner marker of our acreage, the noise had stopped. After looking around a little more, I decided to return to the house by cutting through the woodsy center of the property. Stepping carefully through the underbrush, I discovered we had some trillium growing in places. Finding trillium is sort of a special event. Only about six or eight inches high, this delicate native flower is easy to miss, blooming only a couple of days each year. Bending to get a closer look, I inadvertently flushed out a grouse. In case the bird had been sitting on a nest, I gave it a wide berth and continued onward.

Walking twenty five or thirty yards more, and busy looking for more trillium, I stepped on a twig, which startled something else. I heard a rustle, then saw a shape move off to my right, behind a birch clump. I peered at the clump in the dimming light, just as an animal turned and looked in my direction. It was a cougar!

My heart jumped in my chest. For a few seconds we made direct eye contact, the cougar and I, about fifteen yards or so apart.

I finally spoke to it—the cougar that is, something super-casual like, "Oh, hi there!" Then I started backing up—not easy, considering all the stumps and logging slash on our place—and didn't take my eyes from the animal. After several yards I turned and walked toward our cleared area, frequently looking over my shoulder to see if the big cat was following—reminding myself not to run, but to walk with purpose. After what seemed like forever but was probably ten minutes, I made it inside our deer fencing.

We never did discover what that odd noise was; I put it down to the way sound bounces off the hills surrounding our place. In any event, my cougar encounter was a stark reminder that Sue and I couldn't take our safety for granted. From then on, I tucked my .380 into my belt for our woodland hikes.

Other than that one cougar encounter, the only big cats John and I had actually laid eyes on were bobcats. We'd spot them occasionally, padding along our fence line. Shy, and not much bigger than a cocker spaniel, they didn't inspire the kind of fear cougars did.

Our nearest neighbor must have felt the same way we did. One day a moveable chicken coop appeared in her small pasture, and around the coop roamed eight chickens. I admired her spunk, to give chickens a go without a fenced area, but then, she had two dogs. And they were about the best insurance you could get to deter wildlife. Unfortunately, her dogs couldn't keep the chickens safe. We learned a bobcat, within days of the hens' arrival, had picked off four of them.

One day, I was up unusually early, and from the kitchen window, I saw a long, low shape stalking the fence line next to the chicken pen. A bobcat, I was sure. I ran outside, shouting and waving my arms, and it lit for the woods. The cat didn't leave our property, however. The same week, John and I saw the bobcat outside our fence not far from the hen compound, walking away from it.

Naturally, the cat had plenty of opportunities to check out our hens when we weren't around, but I had every confidence the sturdy compound John had built would protect them. For sure, all those layers of fencing and wire must have confused the cat enough so that he quit trying to get in.

A few weeks later, from our bedroom window, I saw the bobcat again, in our front (unfenced) yard. The cat must have detected my presence, because it turned and looked right back at me. It was an extraordinarily pretty animal, with features as delicate as a housecat.

It was hard for me to conjure up any dislike for it. Besides, from everything I'd heard, bobcats posed no threat to humans. So I put the cat firmly out of my mind.

16 🐾 You Win a Few, You Lose a Few

A freak summer windstorm blasted through the Foothills one afternoon, breaking off our little Honeycrisp apple tree at the base and blowing it halfway across the yard.

Shorter and more spindly than the other fruit trees we'd planted at the same time, that tree had never thrived. The spongy ground around it signified tunnels, so no doubt the voles had done a number on the tree's root structure from the get-go. But now that it was June, John and I were counting on our new screened planting boxes to keep our other crops from meeting the same fate.

Days after sowing our veggie seeds, we checked the boxes each day, watching for the first tiny "seedlets" to show up. They did, and soon became seedlings. Then viable plants. Peas, beets, carrots, broccoli, chard, you name it, it was growing! The raised box beds had worked—no vole predation! Even though these vile critters were still in our garden—they'd hit the nearby potato bed hard, since we didn't have enough boxes for taters.

The good news was, I could see that voles were very inflexible in their eating patterns, and apparently needed to tunnel up to eat from below. Not even one vole had figured out that they could simply climb the wood wall of the box and just nosh on the veggies from the surface.

There were still a few, less worrisome pests around. I found cabbage worms on the broccoli, but discovered if you washed your pickings carefully, you could feast on the broccoli without worries. If you cooked it, that is. Then came the day I found a green worm not in the rinse water, but in the water I'd cooked the broccoli in. I got so grossed out I made a vow: we were done with cruciferous vegetables. Store broccoli, which was inexpensive and available year round—would have to do.

The wintering-over barley was ready to harvest. My romantic notions of hand-threshing grain—that I'd enjoyed in historical movies—soon evaporated with the reality of bashing stalks of barley over a tarp. Then a new kind of grass, that suspiciously resembled barley sprouts, seemed to be invading the whole area. The roots of this grass had long runners with extensive sprouts, and were hard as the dickens to pull out. I guessed that with my barley adventure, I'd succeeded only in introducing a new and pernicious "weed" to our garden.

Then there were our purple carrots. As with the rest of our experiments, I had great expectations. A few weeks before the carrots would mature, I poked at the tops to check the roots' circumference. To my dismay, the foliage easily detached from the roots. Were the voles going after them? I told John, "I'd better pick 'em before the voles get the rest."

Instead of letting the purple carrots grow a full season for maximum size, I started pulling them out…and yep, the purpleness was pretty strange. But what was really weird was that there wasn't a trace of vole damage to the roots—the voles had completely ignored them. And why the tops were wonky…apparently, the tops of these carrots are simply weak.

If the voles had ignored these carrots, other pests had not. On closer inspection, it turns out the purple color cleverly disguised the serious insect damage on just about every carrot. Rot had affected the bottom third of the root too. Then, when I tried to rinse the soil off the carrots, holding them by the foliage and hosing them down, the tops simply broke right off. The compost pile was once again the beneficiary. Even though I didn't toss out the entire crop, but kept a couple of big bagfuls, I still had to cut off the gnarly root ends.

When it came time to peel one, I discovered two *more* drawbacks: 1) the insect damage wasn't only on the ends, but all over, and 2) only the peel was purple! Inside, these carrots were mostly orange, in varying shades from yellow to a variegated purply-orange, that is. Worst of all, in my opinion: they didn't even taste very good. My purple carrot takeaway: if you're going to end up with orange carrots anyway, you might as well go with your "normal" varieties and skip the grief.

In our ongoing war against pests, it looked like the raised boxes may have been our only "win." Especially after we found another, very destructive (if invisible) predator—one that lived freely all over our property.

17 🍠 Dud Spuds

When it comes to growing potatoes, I am the kiss of death. I realize that's an unfortunate allusion, given the Irish Potato Famine back in the 1800s. And no disrespect to our deceased chipmunks, either. But whether my problem is ignorance, negligence, bad luck, or out-and-out stupidity, as the Berryridge Farm potato manager, I have overseen the ruin of more potato crops than you can shake a hoe at.

Early on, I took charge of our potato crop—and that's Irish potatoes, as opposed to sweet potatoes—because 1) I love potatoes, and 2) since I'm Irish on both sides, I should be a champion spud grower. But it hasn't turned out that way. I pretty much lay the blame on that aforementioned invisible predator.

This plant-killing perp is not of the animal variety. It's fungus. And in the Foothills' moist climate, a host of funguses, many of them known as blight, are the archenemy of tomatoes, potatoes, and fruit trees. While our area is famous for raspberry and blueberry production, there's another local crop that a lot of people don't take much notice of: many acres of seed potatoes grown on the western side of the county. And apparently, spores of the funguses that prey on potatoes drift with the prevailing winds. Which come from, yep, the west.

Blight was the disease that killed the Irish potato crop for three years in a row in the 1840s—Ireland has a damp climate similar to our region, only the summers are cooler. In the Foothills, you can almost tell time with the blight. In mid-August, when the nights cool down and the dew grows noticeably heavier, you can figure that the first, yellow-brown spots on your potato foliage won't be far behind. Within days, the green parts start wilting, and a few days after that, your potato beds turn into a brown-black mess. If you harvest at the first sign of blight, the tubers won't be spoiled, but likely won't have had time to mature. So that means all you get for your trouble is undersized potatoes.

Tomatoes, being a nightshade plant like potatoes, are also prey to blight. It's the same drill. With fall approaching, you'll get yellowing foliage starting on the lower leaves, and the discoloration quickly marches upward. Then brown-black spots appear. Unlike with potatoes, it's not only the tomato leaves and stems that are affected. The fruits develop shiny brown spots, decomposing so swiftly they seem to be rotting before your very eyes.

After several summers, I got used to slinging buckets of rotten tomatoes into my compost pile, regretting all the pasta sauce I wouldn't get to make. Or eat. Still, I was philosophical about the tomatoes—any crop loss was due entirely to weather, not me. But I took my potato failures personally.

Those tater fiascos have been legion. Between early and late blight, vole destruction and storage stupidity—especially the time I stashed my bumper potato crop in our uninsulated shop before a Northeaster blew in—you may wonder why I just don't give up. Yet each year I'm doing it again, kneeling in the chilly spring soil to plant potatoes, daring Mother Nature to *bring it on.*

The summer after the frozen spud episode, despite the vole predation, I ended up with a small potato crop—and I was determined to follow sensible storage protocols. My book royalties had paid for a new kitchen fridge, so we put the old one in the shop, where I stored my taters. With my extra produce tucked safely away for the season, I had the situation covered. Until one day, after another Northeaster, I went to the shop to fetch more potatoes. I discovered my bags of spuds were full of frost: foiled—or should I say frozen—again! I'd forgotten one small detail: to take into account how much colder that outdoor fridge will keep your food. If I'd been thinking, I would have adjusted the temperature to the warmest setting. I immediately turned up the fridge temp, but of course it was too late. This year's tater crop went the way of the previously frozen one: the compost pile.

You may wonder, why bother growing potatoes at all? Well, if you compare the taste difference between the spuds you buy at the grocery store, even the organic ones, and the potatoes you grow yourself, you'll know there's no comparison: hands-down, home grown tastes best! Happily, since potatoes will continue to be my must-grow crop, each year I discover a new bit of tater-raising wisdom, which invariably improves my harvest. Here's what I've learned:

• PLANT HIGH-QUALITY SEED POTATOES.

Some homesteaders use their home-grown potatoes for seed. Early in my potato-growing career, I tried it and ended up with edible, if undersized spuds—if you don't mind lots of scab and worm holes. However, for quality control, most gardening experts recommend that you obtain certified seed potatoes. This seed is reasonably free from disease, funguses, and nasty pests. Conventionally-grown seed potatoes are generally dosed with fungicide to retard spoilage, so I use organic seed.

Whether you go organic or not, when you plant your seed potatoes, be sure to cut them into smaller pieces (say, two inches in diameter), and make sure there are at least a couple of "eyes" in the piece. If your seed chunks are too large, you'll have a big old hunk of decomposing potato right next to your developing tubers.

• PROTECT YOUR TATERS

Since voles are our greatest challenge, I now plant my crop only in one of our screened beds. Despite the expense and effort of building the raised boxes, they've proved their worth every season. With no vole predation, our harvests have quadrupled. Quintupled! At least!

• TIME YOUR PLANTING STRATEGICALLY

Some old-time garden advice tells you to plant your potato hills on St. Patrick's Day. I concluded years ago that with the sopping wet springs in the Foothills, planting *anything* in March is a big mistake. So when is the optimal time to plant your spuds? The potato experts in Mother Earth News advise that you go with soil temperature: 50 degrees minimum. Otherwise, your seed taters may simply rot before they can send up their leaves. (Been there, done that.) Preferring to rely on my experience and observation, I don't use a soil thermometer, but I generally plant my potatoes the first week of May, and that seems to work well in our climate.

• CREATE OPTIMAL GROWING CONDITIONS

I rotate all my vegetable beds every year. Some beds get more sunlight and warmth; the planting areas south of the house and shop can get downright tropical in the summer. While potatoes don't like wet, cold soil, they also won't thrive with a lot of heat. Which explains why one season, after planting my spuds in the warmest bed in our garden, I had about a 20% sprouting rate. In particularly hot summers, my tater greenery has died back in mid-August. Now I make sure to select beds in the cooler parts of the yard, a distance from the heat radiating off the buildings.

As for soil pH: Since this area of our state has very acidic soil, I used to apply a generous amount of dolomite lime to all our veggie beds, to "sweeten" the soil. Then I learned that potatoes like slightly acidic dirt. Whether you're growing potatoes or not, it's a good idea to find out if your soil tends to be acidic or alkaline. Even if it is acidic, apply dolomite lime with care.

• AVOID POTATO "SUNBURN"

Potatoes in the ground that are exposed to sunlight will develop green areas that make your taters bitter. They not only taste bad, but the green parts are poisonous! However, I've discovered an easy solution: mulch, mulch and more mulch. Cover your hills with an ample layer of soil plus several inches of leaves and compost, and you'll no longer see your spuds with "the wearin' of the green."

• FIGHT BLIGHT

Season after season, blight has marched through my tater crop as relentlessly as Sherman's March through Georgia. Then the light finally went on: I was mulching my potato beds with home-grown compost. And what was wrong with my compost, you might ask? Well, I was throwing all our blighted tomatoes into the pile. All that fluffy, nutritious compost was probably rife with fungus! Once I realized my error, I didn't use my previous year's compost on my potato beds, and guess what: my spuds were as blemish-free as babies. I also began tossing any spoiled tomatoes into a separate weed pile, far from my regular kitchen compost.

Despite my newfound knowledge, I'm still not raising perfect potatoes! But with the quality of my potatoes being a *leetle* more consistent, I'm angsting less.

18 ✎ As the Compost Turns

Food-growing experts confirm what I've learned from experience: compost is the best fertilizer. After researching all kinds of store-bought fertilizers and soil amendments, as well as the pros and cons of each, I've found the simplest, most elegant path to productive soil: rely on Mother Nature. You don't need to buy compost—you can make it at home for free, with material right from your own kitchen and back yard.

With all the undesirable carrots, radishes, and sundry other garden failures at our place, my compost pile is often packing on the pounds faster than a contestant at a pie-eating contest. Fortunately, the nature of a compost pile is that it's better to give (to it) than receive.

Harvest time, when you've got a lot of veggie trimmings, is a great opportunity to start a compost pile. Still, you can do it any time of year—even in winter, provided your ground is fairly workable.

When it comes to creating compost, you'll find lots of techniques and schools of thought. Some gardeners go at the process scientifically; in the book, *Gardening When it Counts*, author Steve Solomon outlines the precise ratio of carbon to nitrogen-containing materials for optimal compost. Upon reading Solomon's detailed directions, I got pretty overwhelmed—you know that feeling of *You're Doing it Wrong*. However, I did learn from him that sawdust isn't the best compost component—too much carbon. Once I stopped putting sawdust in my pile, my garden fertility improved.

You can create your compost in a bin, a hole, a trench, inside a small, above-ground fenced spot, or buy a fancy compost container at a gardening supply store. I keep my process super basic and not terribly scientific: I balance green veggie waste (which is nitrogen-rich) with brown, crunchy stuff (the carbonaceous element) and keep the pile mixed up. I recommend feeding your compost pile year-round—even in a moderately chilly winter climate like the Foothills, when the ground freezes frequently, the pile itself won't freeze solid if you turn it once or twice a week.

Here's my process: I begin with the composting site I created years ago, a shallow hole about three feet across and 18 inches deep—it's more like a wide trench. Into the trench goes a bucket of soil, as weed-free and rock-free as possible. To the soil I add a bucket of kitchen scraps like raw veggie peelings and apple cores (again, the green stuff) and another bucket of dead leaves (the brown stuff). Mix/turn well, and let nature do its magic. Every time I add food scraps to the pile, I also add old leaves or dead brackenfern. In the summertime, when I might be putting lots of strawberry tops or other fruit scraps in my compost, the pile may grow acidic, so I make sure to add extra brown material. I recommend that you avoid adding your discarded tomatoes, potatoes, or their peels into the pile—even if the vegetables look perfectly healthy, keep in mind blight is invisible before it hits.

During dry periods, keep the pile moist. Turning your compost every time you add green material will help keep the decomposition process more active. An added benefit to frequent turning: it prevents recognizable food chunks from sitting on the pile, thus deterring rodents and neighbor dogs!

Let your pile "cook" for a couple of months, until the food scraps and dead leaves have "digested" into a fairly uniform, rich, dark substance. At that point, the compost is ready to spread on your garden beds. The secret to a swift scraps-to-finished-compost process lies in a couple of things: keep your kitchen scraps and peelings fairly small, and as I've said before, turn your pile often and well! There's a world of microbes doing their thing in there, and every time you turn your compost, you're introducing fresh oxygen into the pile. Without frequent turning, you may not get enough oxygen into the mix, and it will soon get a sour smell. That can mean the decomposition process is turning anaerobic, and all your microorganisms aren't getting the oxygen they need.

In terms of other high-nitrogen materials beyond fruit and veggie material, some gardeners might add grass clippings to the pile—a great choice, as long as you don't use Weed n' Feed or moss killer on your lawn. Others hold the "everything and the kitchen sink" philosophy, tossing in stuff like hair clippings, weeds, and newspaper.

Not me. For one thing, hair's just gross. And any discarded hair could contain sulfate residues from shampoo. Newspaper? Well, there's all the ink. I don't know what's in it and what I don't know might hurt my pile. Some composters use weeds, but as for me, no way. Weeds are survivors that can grow through the cruelest winter plus through drought, and don't even *need* soil—how many times have you seen weeds growing through cracks in asphalt?

Besides, in our rainy climate, I don't trust the deadest of weeds to stay dead. I've noted lots of pulled weeds re-rooting in my garden beds—why give them a nutritious medium like compost to live in? To me, food leftovers are another red light, with the exception of brown stuff like dry toast. You don't want any material with fats, oil, meat or dairy in your pile or you might find the grossest of gross-outs: maggots.

And there you have it, an easy way to create and maintain healthy soil. Keeping up a regular compost-turning schedule is a great way to stay active too!

The techniques I've described cover vegetarian compost—which I figure is safe to apply at any stage of the decomposition process. I've even heard of gardeners who lay fresh veggie scraps on their beds. That's not necessarily the case for manure-sourced compost. With the advent of our chickens, John and I had a whole new source of fertilizer. Although long ago, I'd gotten past my fastidiousness about manure in general, I was still too much of a germophobe to put chicken poo in my compost pile. So I started two separate operations: vegetarian compost and composted manure. For one thing, chicken manure is highly alkaline, and it takes longer to break down to safely use on a garden bed. But in the spirit of full disclosure, I also separated the piles because I'm well...picky.

For my chicken compost, I mix the manure with some kind of amendment, like straw, sawdust or woodchips to keep it from being a big old gloppy mess—and I don't worry about the scientifically-recommended carbon-nitrogen ratio. Whatever you add, make sure to turn your manure mixture every once in a while, and when your pile gets too heavy to turn, start a new one. Let the manure pile sit twice as long as the veggie compost—at least six months.

Despite all my time dealing with chicken manure, I confess I'm still too persnickety to put manure on root crops, or above-soil plants we'll be eating later in the season. But manure compost is perfect for asparagus. After the manure is well-rotted, I'll spread it on the beds in late fall. This more robust kind of compost can take all winter to safely decompose, and at the same time, feed the asparagus roots. And come late April, you'll be harvesting the plumpest, most tender spears you can imagine!

19 ☞ Seasonal Self-Reliance

While our dedication to food-growing was really starting to pay off, John and I were becoming even more committed to eating seasonally.

Hewing to a local mindset, you often have a *long* wait to feast on your favorite fruits and veggies. But I'm convinced waiting to eat produce until it's in season in your area is totally worth it, especially a crop like asparagus. You can get it any old time of the year, of course, grown outside the U.S. The out-of-season spears are often skinny, a little desiccated, and the rubber-banded bundle is often sitting in a puddle of gray water. And you'll pay dearly for the privilege of eat-it-anytime asparagus.

Each spring, our food co-op always stocks organic, locally grown asparagus. Prices generally start around five bucks a pound, and I've seen it as high as $7.99! When you factor in the inedible bottom one-third of the spear that you snap off, the real cost is even higher. I could *never* bring myself to pay that kind of money, no matter how wonderful it tastes. Which is why John and I pat ourselves on the back every spring, for planting four rows of asparagus early in the game.

However, through the years I have fallen down on the asparagus job like I have on so many others. Too often, I allowed the weeds in the bed to have the upper hand; some years, I let the weeds grow one to two feet high, thereby siphoning water and nutrients away from the asparagus plants. Worse, I let the weeds go to seed! As a result, I had only myself to blame when all that greenery gave the voles plenty of cover. They managed to destroy about twelve crowns total, but despite their damage we still produce enough asparagus for John and me to roast or stir-fry an ample serving nearly every day during the harvesting season.

If you want to grow your own, all you need is a decent sized space, maybe twelve by twelve feet...and lots of patience. John and I put in our first row of ten asparagus crowns our second year here, and three more rows the following spring. The crowns can fool you—they're sort of pale, brownish, dried-up looking things that you plant in a trench around a foot deep. You've got to wonder, how will they push up beautiful green spears?

The amazing thing is, they do. Here's where your patience comes in: the first year the spears show up, it's hands off the merchandise—you've got to give your crowns time to develop a strong root system. The second spring, you can harvest a spear here or there, and give yourself the merest taste. But you still need to give the plants an opportunity to build up their strength. But Year Three, it's showtime! When the spears emerge in mid-spring, and reach about six to eight inches tall, you can start cutting.

I use a cheapo, serrated knife with a super-skinny blade. One of John's former police colleagues, who picked asparagus as a farm kid, gave us a tip: you insert the knife into the soil at a diagonal, cutting an inch or two under the surface. The slant helps keep you from nicking any other spears that are still underground. Be sure to check your beds every day in hot weather, because the spears can grow several inches a day. The harvest period lasts from six to eight weeks. I tend to play it safe, and dial down my cutting at around six weeks, harvesting about half of what I picked at the start. At any rate, when the emerging spears are pencil-thin you quit.

If, during harvest-time, you leave your garden over a warm weekend, or otherwise neglect to harvest your spears, you'll return to the bed and find some have gotten fourteen or more inches high! Well, my friends, you'll have to let them go. The good news is, in addition to the super-skinny spears you left in the bed, the big ones that got away will keep building up the crown's roots for next year. As summer progresses, the spears will grow five feet high or taller, and all the little "scales" on the stalks grow into ferny branches. Soon after, the ferns will flower—a big draw for bees. The plants are often so tall you've got to stake them or otherwise string a rope around your bed to keep them from getting blown over.

The ferns begin dying back with the first frosts, and by late December, you can cut them to the ground. Keep your bed well-watered and deeply mulched, and you can count on fat, yummy spears for up to fifteen years.

The one problem with mulch on your asparagus is the one, big, and utterly inescapable Grow-Your-Own Catch-22: mulching your beds only provides more cover for voles. Sometimes, you just can't win.

20 🐀 More Spores

Blight on your annual vegetable crops are small potatoes, pun intended. Blight in fruit trees, however, will cost ya. I talked to a local apple grower who said that given the copious rainfall in our county, "You can't grow organic commercial apples in this climate." At least, not if you want to produce the gorgeous apples you see in grocery stores. The funguses and pests you have to fight with various sprays are just too overwhelming.

John and I had already viewed with concern the conventionally-grown raspberry fields in our county. Growers will post notices at the edge of the fields when workers are spraying. To me, seeing "Danger—Do Not Enter" signs for so much of the growing season is alarming. If the spray is that dangerous, I wonder why it's permitted at all! Anyway, considering the health hazards of spraying our orchards, we made a decision early on: even if sprays would give us scab-free, blight-free, earwig-free, and every other kind of yuck-free fruit, we'd go organic.

While we refrained from spraying our apricot trees, the manure that our chickens deposited free of charge around them didn't provide the benefit we hoped. After several years, they were still stunted. No surprise, because each winter, the new growth from the previous spring and summer would turn black from fire blight. The European pears were growing, but the trees produced very few blossoms—and consequently, not even one measly fruit—plus the leaves turned an unsightly brown every summer.

Our apple trees showed various signs of fungal pressure, most of it cosmetic. Not so for our two heirloom trees, the Ashmeads Kernal and De Sonnaville trees. Their height gain was nearly nonexistent, and the leaves turned ratty almost as soon as they emerged in spring. Our two European plum trees seemed to languish, despite appearing unaffected by fungus, but the other two plum trees were thriving.

Especially the Japanese plum. Planting the plum trees in our second orchard space, we sort of ran out of room. We ended up siting this variety in the middle of our garden, to provide a bit of shade. Also, this little tree would add some vertical interest to the flat berry and vegetable beds. Well, that tree did not stay little.

It seemed to grow three times as fast as every other fruit tree in the yard. Before long, the trunk had a nine-inch diameter, and the foliage was shading two strawberry beds. Out came the pruning loppers, and John tried to bring that bad boy under control. He was dismayed, though, to discover this particular plum variety had needle-sharp, one-inch spines on every branch and twig. However, even with a thorough pruning, the tree bore fruit like a champ.

Given the challenges with our existing fruit-raising, John and I decided to fast-track more fruit production. We'd been blue after the loss of the Honeycrisp tree, so with the advent of fall, the best time to plant, off John went to the Foothills nursery to buy a replacement. He must have been especially sad, because he returned with not one but two Honeycrisps and another Asian pear tree. Dismayed, I stared at the three giant pots in the back of his Ranger. "Where will we put them all?"

John shrugged. "We'll find room." He opened the gate and entered our newest orchard, where we let the chickens run loose, and stared at the apricot trees.

I followed him in. "They've got to go, huh?"

We'd talked about taking out the apricot trees. They hadn't really grown, and this past year, with a cold, soggy spring, John had had to prune off even more blackened branches. Now, he nodded. "I'll get the shovel."

He hated waste. He couldn't even bear to throw old food out of the fridge, so digging trees out of the ground was really painful for him. And I'm a Taurus, stubborn about giving up on something. But it was time for both of us to cry uncle: the chances of those apricot trees thriving, much less bearing, were zilch.

With an afternoon's labor, John had both trees removed, opening up a space for a new baby Honeycrisp. Not far away, he planted the second Honeycrisp and the new Asian pear. Despite digging up the two apricots, Berryridge Farm still had twenty-four fruit trees.

As I helped John put away tools, I said, "Please tell me we're done putting in fruit trees."

"I think so," he said, then he grinned at me. "At least, until we clear more orchard space."

Halfway across the yard, the Japanese plum tree's vigor seemed like a good omen. It wasn't.

One day, at pruning time, John set down his loppers and gestured to me to come over. "Look at this," he said. The tree had black, knobby growths on every bough and branch. Well, it didn't take a genius: black = fungus. I did an Internet search and discovered these growths are called black knot, and will eventually affect the tree's fruiting.

John got out his dad's trusty old pocketknife and carefully cut away the black parts. The tree wasn't at all fazed by his amateur surgery, soon producing a cloud of blossoms.

One midsummer afternoon, when John and I were weeding the strawberries beneath the tree, I looked up at the branches. "Holy cow, I think this guy has put on six feet of new growth."

John peered up at the tree, then examined its large roots exposed above the soil line. "Uh-oh," he said. "I think we planted this tree too close to our drainfield."

I eyeballed the distance from the plum's trunk to our septic field—hardly ten feet. I guessed that being so close to a source of water gave the plum some extra *oomph*. Because that tree wasn't only vigorous. It was swiftly turning into a monster.

21 🖝 A Passage

Winter was on its way, the second one for our flock of chickens. For John and me, the cold months generally mean staying close to home, making sure that any Northeaster knocking out the power doesn't freeze our pipes, like one late fall storm did our first year in the Foothills. Now that we had our girls to look after, we were ready to pretty much hunker down for the season.

By November, we felt like old hands at chicken-raising, and wouldn't be taken off guard by this season's molting. That's when a hen's feathers gradually fall out, and a new set grows in. At the same time, egg production drops. The previous winter, our six girls had gone from producing three to six eggs per day between them, declining to one or two each day. Sometimes two or three days would go by with no eggs at all. Now, with one less hen after the hawk attack last spring, we figured the egg numbers would dwindle a bit further over the winter months—maybe a few more days with no eggs.

As Thanksgiving approached we were prepared for this break in the hens' laying cycle, and the three dozen eggs stashed in the fridge would provide a nice cushion for holiday baking. I didn't mind fewer eggs; I was actually looking forward to a respite from trying to figure out what to do with all of them. Having made plans to visit family for the holiday, however, I had one minor worry.

"The bobcat's back," I told John a couple of days before Thanksgiving.

Turning on the coffeemaker, he asked, "Where'd you see him?"

"He was pacing along the west fence line," I said. "And here we've got our trip this Thursday."

John peered out the kitchen window toward the hen run. "We'll only be gone one day," he reminded me. "The hens'll be okay."

I let out the breath I'd been holding. It was true—the chickens would be perfectly safe inside their safety zone. No bobcat, however determined, could squirm through our girls' secure, steer-wired cage.

The holidays felt more special this year. My daughter Carrie had modified her employment contract, and she, her husband and Little Megs had moved back to the Seattle area. My younger daughter Meghann was slowly finding her feet after a divorce, and her two sons seemed to be adjusting to the big change.

John's mom Wanda seemed to be ticking right along too, despite my sister-in-law Becky's absence. Confined to her 50s-era split level in the lovely, tree-lined suburb, Wanda was always pleased to get John's phone calls, and would fill him in on family news, her mind as sharp as his favorite Bowie knife. At the convivial Turkey Day celebration with the Browne extended family, Wanda seemed a little subdued. She even stretched out on the couch for most of the afternoon. But then, she was eighty-eight. Surely entitled to some extra rest!

Actually, Wanda needed more than a nap. Because she had been hiding a secret.

The night of Christmas Eve, a high wind knocked out our power. Waking up on the big day with no electricity, John and I had an even better reason to stick around Berryridge Farm—so he could fire up the generator.

As soon as the power was restored, John called his mom to wish her a Merry Christmas, but Wanda didn't pick up. He phoned her again that evening, but still, no answer. Very worried at this point, John decided first thing in the morning, he'd contact his brother Sid to see what was going on, and make plans to visit.

A Downhill Spiral

The day after Christmas, before I could call my mom, the phone rang. It was Sid's son. Checking on his grandma, my nephew had found her in bed. Mom had been there all day, too weak to get up. In spite of her protests, he carried her to his car and took her to the hospital.

By the time my brother and I arrived, the doctors had diagnosed Mom's condition: congestive heart failure and atrial fibrillation. Her lungs were so filled with fluid she could hardly breathe. And what she'd known for months but had kept to herself, was yet another serious ailment: Stage III kidney failure.

Her doctors, along with me, Sid, and his son wanted her to pursue treatment. "No," said Mom, quite emphatic. "I just want to go." During her hospital stay, Sid and I spent our days in her room with her, and our nights in our childhood home. Despite our encouragement, as the days passed, Mom continued to decline. After she'd been hospitalized less than a week, she did consent to having the fluid siphoned out of her lungs, to make her more comfortable. She would not, however, take any medicine of any kind.

Since hospitals don't want to keep patients who are refusing treatment, and Mom was far too weak to be home, her doctors recommended that Sid and I have her moved to a care center. The center was a friendly facility with a compassionate staff, and two cuddly cats roamed the halls. It was also a place we all knew she wouldn't be leaving. She would say it again, and again: "I just want to go."

John and Sid had seen the writing on the wall: Wanda had lost the will to live.

The Browne clan gathered at her house. I traveled to Seattle to join John, his son Collin and daughter Sasha with her two little girls. Sid's family came too, along with John and Sid's cousin Cyd who'd been close to her aunt Wanda since childhood. Cyd, a registered nurse who worked with the elderly, was a comforting presence, especially when she took John and Sid aside. "You made the right choice," she told them, "to respect Wanda's wishes."

That evening, sitting between John and Sasha, I looked at piles of old photos, marveling once again at the lovingness of the Browne's, and the rarity of John's unusually functional family.

John and I slept in Becky's old room. She'd moved out nearly two years ago, but the room held a poignant impression that she'd left only yesterday. A hairbrush with short gray hairs sat on the vanity table; the hairdryer was still plugged in. The closet was full of clothing Becky hadn't worn for over a decade.

At dawn the next morning, a nurse from the care center called. "I think you'd better come."

Wanda lay on a hospital bed in an impersonal room. White walls, white sheets, white blankets, without any photos, mementoes, or personal items around to make the place homey. All that long day we—the whole Browne family—kept a vigil. Swathed in blankets in the overly warm room, Wanda had stopped eating and drinking, and was barely conscious. When she did speak, it was only the merest whisper, in a repeating refrain. "What's taking so long?"

Becky called to say goodbye to her mother, weeping over the phone that John held to Wanda's ear. She hadn't seen her mom since she left the family home. Now she never would again. Still, I knew that like Wanda, Becky believed that something greater, and much more beautiful would be waiting for her mother on the other side.

By late afternoon, as Wanda's breath turned fainter, the nurses didn't have to tell us that the time was drawing near. When it was my turn to say goodbye, I took her hand, keeping my touch as light as I could—my experience with my dad's passing made me extra mindful of the sensitive skin of the dying. I whispered all the loving things I'd never said aloud before. Her eyes opened a bit, and I felt a tiny pressure as she tried to squeeze my hand. I kissed her forehead, then left her side to make room for John's daughter and son, their faces pinched with grief.

By early evening, Wanda's breathing was almost negligible. I left the care center, as did most of the family, taking hungry children back to the family home to put them to bed, and to allow the weary travelers to get some rest. John, his cousin Cyd, and her husband stayed behind.

A couple of hours later, John called the house. His mother was gone. Yet despite this sad event, I sensed his relief, and even a tremulous sort of joy in his voice. "At the end, there was the most amazing thing."

A Soft Purring

After everyone else left, my mother grew agitated. Cyd spoke to the attending nurse, and asked her to administer a sedative. Mom's restlessness ceased almost immediately, and soon after, one of the care center's cats crept in. It jumped up on the bed, and curled next to Mom's legs, purring in the quiet room. After a time, the cat stretched and jumped off the bed, then padded out the door.

Everything was silent. After a long moment, Cyd said, "I think she's gone."

The cat, I'm convinced, had eased Mom's passage. After the two short weeks since we'd discovered her illness, the ordeal was over. Mom had left instructions that she wanted no funeral, or service of any kind. Although in a way, our family had celebrated her life in the stark white room with her, as she drew her last breaths.

I came home by myself, leaving John to help Sid with the necessary tasks following a loved one's passing. The family respected Wanda's wishes about the service. Without any sort of memorial, though, I felt like my mother-in-law's life had been somehow unfinished. That her extraordinary patience and calm, her sharp intellect, and her devoted parenting and grandparenting had gone unrecognized.

Grief heavy in my chest, and missing John, I tried to keep up my own routine. In the olden days, ladies of leisure could spend a mourning period or any other kind of setback lying on a daybed with their smelling salts and a lace handkerchief. While the idea of a rest sounded tempting, I didn't have that luxury.

The chickens had to be cared for, and the burning maw of the woodstove had to be fed. Fortunately, the winter was unusually mild, so keeping the stove going wasn't as time-consuming as it could have been. I was tempted to take a break from writing, but my work was the one thing that took my mind off my sadness. Besides, to prepare my second novel for publication, I had a deadline to meet. I kept up my usual afternoon walk, usually pushing the envelope to get outside before dark.

One balmy evening—well, balmy for January—walking up our private lane as twilight fell, I experienced a first. And I got the scare of my life.

22 ⟰ Bear-y Ridge

Just ahead, I saw a big, black *something*.

I froze in terror, hardly able to breathe. I didn't call for help, because there was no one within earshot. I'd seen black bears before, on the main road, and from a distance. But never when I was completely alone. Or in the near-dark.

I tried to tell myself I'd seen a deer. But who was I kidding—this creature had a huge, dark, rounded mass, not a slender silhouette. And deer generally either saunter, trot, or spring into their distinctive ping-pongy gait. This animal *lumbered*.

And here I was, with nothing more than an umbrella to defend myself with. The bear stopped in the middle of the road, as if assessing me. It must have decided I didn't pose a threat, because it crossed to the other side of the road and disappeared into the brush. I didn't move a muscle for several moments—minutes that felt like hours, waiting for my heart to stop pounding, for my stomach to unclench, and hoping the bear was making some headway toward wherever it was going. But there was no way around what I had to do next. I wasn't going to return home by teleportation, like on *Star Trek*—no chance for a "Beam me up, Scotty," to get me back safe. I'd have to walk.

For me, three-fourths of a mile is a fifteen-minute jaunt. But now, it was a formidable distance. You might be wondering, why didn't I whip out my cell phone and call for help? Surely no one would be dumb enough to take a walk on the wild side without a phone! Actually, in the interests of living a simpler life, I don't have a cell phone. Besides, there's no cell service in this part of the Foothills. I really was on my own.

So I forced myself to move forward, one cautious step at a time. Then I started walking faster, peering right, left, and behind me— I'd never been so vigilant. And I was *never* so glad to make it to our driveway, then inside our fence.

A couple of days later, I encountered my neighbor Roberta, the REI model, walking her dog on our lane. When I told her about the bear, she said, "I've heard about a bunch of sightings lately—the mild winter is bringing black bears out of hibernation early."

"January really *is* early," I said. "You be careful out there."

"You too," she replied, and I went on my way, keeping my eyes peeled.

If I'd seen a bear while hiking on the many remote trails in the Foothills or up in the Cascade Mountains, I would've been just as scared, but I wouldn't have been shocked. Black bears in the Pacific Northwest wilderness are about as common as wild mushrooms. This bear sighting, however, did take me by surprise: this critter was maybe a couple of hundred yards from our house, as the crow flies. After talking to Roberta, I was now sure about one thing: we might not see bears in our *yard*, but they were definitely around. And closer than we'd ever thought.

A week after Wanda's passing, John returned to Berryridge Farm, looking drawn. He was extra quiet too—although I knew he didn't regret his mother's death, not exactly. With no desire to keep going through illness and pain, she had been more than ready to go of life. Still, he retreated to his world of books, spending the January afternoons on the couch, tending the woodstove in between turning pages.

I didn't ask him to do any chicken chores; I knew he needed time to regain his equilibrium. And neither he nor I were paying much attention to the weather forecast. When a frigid Northeaster blew in mid-month, bringing a foot and a half of snow, we were caught off guard. Later that afternoon, we had more than the neighborhood bears to worry about: the power went out. John put his book aside, looking grim. "Before it gets dark, we've got to get the generator out to the pumphouse."

A power outage at our place is not much fun; after night falls, even less so. Country dark seems more daunting than in the city; with no lights from passing cars, I mean, it's *dark*. Too, time seems to slow to a crawl, with no lights, no TV, and no Internet, and you've got to fumble around with a flashlight. And whether it's daytime or nighttime, you open the fridge only when necessary— and the same goes for flushing the toilet. Most disheartening is when you know the water tank in the pumphouse will soon be empty. You've got to gird your loins to face the snow and freezing cold, so you can hook up the pumphouse generator and keep the water flowing.

One of our county friends has a skookum protection against power outages: a 10,000-watt generator that's hard-wired into the home's electrical circuits. It's set up to automatically kick on when the power goes out, so he's never without lights, heat or TV.

On the other hand, John and I were not (nor would we ever be) able to afford a system like that. Determined to never again experience a frozen water system, we had no choice but to face the elements. As we bundled up, I could tell John was cross with himself for not being better prepared.

My heart ached for my husband, losing his mom, only to face what had to be the worst winter storm we'd had in four years. But since there was no avoiding the chore ahead, John grabbed our heavy, flat-bottomed shovel. I found the lighter snow shovel, and stared bleakly at the long, snowbound driveway. "Where do we start?"

"Anywhere," John replied. "You just start."

We began shoveling, heading into the wind toward the pumphouse. Nearly two hours later, as darkness fell, we had a eighty-foot long passage just wide enough to accommodate the generator. Then, hands numb with cold, John and I dragged the heavy machine out of the shop, and alternately pushed, dragged, and cajoled it along the bumpy, snow-laden path.

After John got the generator started, once we were inside he said, "I'm never doing that again." He drew up a sketch of a small cubby along the south side of the pumphouse. "We can keep the generator in here during the cold months." As soon as the snow melted, he was on task.

I couldn't help thinking that this Northeaster might be good for one thing: maybe the cold would send the bears *back* into hibernation. In any event, during the worst weather, the chickens had mostly holed up in the coop, which you'd expect. Yet they didn't seem quite...right. Perhaps our hens were also feeling the sadness emanating from their humans, because they, like 19th century Victorian ladies, went into a decline.

23 🐾 What Happened to the Girls?

The hens stopped laying.

John and I had expected a decrease in egg production, like this time last year. We weren't dismayed by our molting birds' scraggly appearance either, as we'd been before. But this winter, they weren't only looking strange, they were acting strange.

Instead of scratching around the yard no matter what the weather, the hens, like John, went into retreat, spending most of their time in their safety zone. With snow on the ground, you couldn't coax the chickens into the yard for love or money. The scratch we tossed out for them got ignored—okay, I could understand that. Plain ol' grain wasn't much of an incentive—the girls could get that any old day. But it was downright bizarre when I got the same reaction with leftover salmon bits—a treat that had previously sent the hens insane with chicken food lust.

Even more puzzling was that the hens were so...subdued. No brassy cackling and complaining. They spooked so easily you'd think they were purebred racehorses. What had happened to our feisty, active girls?

Even after the snow melted, they abandoned the outdoors to spend the days inside the coop. They'd venture out to peck at their feeder every so often, then back inside they'd go. Were our girls chilly? Still freaked out by the bobcat that had lurked around the pen a couple of months ago? Or simply bummed out by winter? By now, with the hens hanging out in the coop practically 24/7, the small space was awash in feathers—clearly, molting was still going great guns. But how could the girls lay if they weren't getting any natural light, sitting around in the dark all day? (I guess if I lost my clothes during the coldest time of the year, I'd be staying inside too, but still.)

Fleetingly, I wondered if the chickens were sick, but they were still eating like troopers. Whatever ailed them, by mid-winter they were not only producing fewer eggs, they'd given up laying altogether.

Three weeks into the egg drought, I was getting concerned. "They're only a year and a half old," I said to John one day. We'd read that laying hens' output decreases a little bit each year. "They can't be too old to lay, can they?"

"I always heard they'd be good for at least four or five years," John said, looking thoughtful. "Must be something else going on."

Soon after, I met a young gal at a writers' meeting who kept a home flock, and asked for advice. "Oh, they're just cold," she said. "Put a heater in the coop, and they'll start laying like that!" She snapped her fingers.

As soon as we got home, John re-installed his coffee-can heater from the previous winter and plugged in the light bulb. The next day, with high hopes, we checked the nest boxes, but they were still empty. And the boxes stayed that way.

"Maybe the girls need more light," I said to John. "Didn't we read somewhere that having the coops lit up, day and night, is how commercial egg producers keep hens laying?"

"Seems worth a try," he replied, so I went straight out to the coop and re-positioned the light bulb, fully illuminating their roost. Now, with the inside of the coop as sunny and warm as the tropics, I figured we'd see eggs within hours…

But no. With our stash of eggs nearly gone, I broke down and bought a dozen from our local drive-through dairy stand. I hoped my purchase would somehow prompt the chicken gods to send out some egg-laying vibes, but still no action. Two additional weeks passed with that 60-watt bulb burning night and day. The girls must've liked it, since they continued to hole up in the coop most of the daylight hours—even the fully-feathered hens.

Okay, maybe the chickens were simply being stubborn. Time for tough love.

Every day, I filled their feeder with no-soy, balanced organic feed. "You slackers are getting this expensive food," I scolded. "We want a return on our investment!"

John's warnings to the hens were even more dire: "Come on, girls, let's see some eggs or it's the stew pot for you!"

Joking aside, John and I actually began some soul-searching. What would we do if the hens really *had* stopped laying for good? Would we look for a new source for buying pullets? Or did we want to give up keeping a flock entirely? We grew so discouraged we even quit checking the nest boxes.

It had now been six weeks since we'd seen an egg. I don't know what took me so long—trying to figure things out for ourselves, maybe?—but I finally Googled our no-egg problem. With the search prompt, "When chickens stop laying eggs," the sites I pulled up pretty much told me what we already knew:

> Hens might be chilled
> Hens might be afraid
> Shorter days = fewer eggs

Then we came across something new:

> Feed wasn't balanced.

Uh-oh. "Maybe that's our problem," I confessed to John. "I've been cheating, mixing a lot of scratch into their feed." Apparently trying to stretch our organic layer mix with generous amounts of grain was a big no-no.

More discouraged than ever, I was ready to leave the site...then I saw the word *Molting*. Reading on, I discovered the process wasn't simply to grow another set of feathers, but to give the hens' reproductive systems a break. Once their egg-producing innards were rejuvenated, they'd get back to laying. Could there be hope after all?

The next morning, the last day of February, I went out to feed the chickens (with 100% feed, by the way). Just for the heck of it, I checked the boxes. And what do you know: in a nest lay one medium-sized, lovely brown egg. "John," I called, bursting into the house. "We got an egg!" We were as proud as if we'd laid it ourselves. The next day, there was another egg, and two days later, a pair more.

For insurance, we kept the light running another week, but clearly, we were back in the egg game.

24 ✎ You Can Take It with You

S oon we were getting two to four eggs a day, and I returned to powering down omelets and egg salad. Along with their egg-laying talents, the hens also regained their mojo—back to scratching rain or shine, cackling and squawking whenever they heard John or me outside. I occasionally longed for the serene weeding sessions I had B.C. (Before Chickens), but the girls brought some liveliness that Berryridge Farm was lacking.

Wanda's death had taken a lot out of John. The one activity that seemed to give him his former energy was spending time with his brother Sid, as they fixed up their mother's home for selling. And in the next months, facing the monumental job ahead of them, the two brothers would be hanging out together a *lot*. Although many of the repairs, both exterior and interior, were a decade overdue (or more), John and his brother weren't afraid of hard work. Keeping one of their dad's favorite sayings in mind, "You can't eat an elephant in one bite," they planned to take several months for the job.

The *really* overwhelming part of the whole project, though, was clearing out the house. It had been in the family for over half a century, so the place had fifty years of stuff living in it. And you have to understand, this is a family that *didn't like to throw anything away*.

Despite the sad task of going through Wanda's things, the guys shared a light moment. As executor of Wanda's will, Sid had had some practical conversations with his mom during her hospital stay. She told him she'd set aside some money so he could pay her final bills. And where was this money? Not in the bank: Wanda had stashed several thousand dollars in two pairs of undies, in her lingerie drawer!

As John told me later, he and Sid both had to chuckle. He added, "Mom obviously didn't realize the first place burglars look for cash is in your underwear drawer!"

The brothers' shared jokes did help lighten their load. John and Sid also had to clear out their deceased dad's possessions, which Wanda had never disposed of in the eight years since he'd passed away. Adding to their cleaning burden, their sister Becky had left almost all her clothing and personal items at the house when she moved across the state.

John and his brother would go on a work binge, then each would go home with any family memorabilia and possessions they'd chosen—knickknacks, housewares, and tools, especially items with sentimental value. (And my husband is a sentimental guy.) The guys would rest up for several days, then meet back at the Browne home.

As a tidy person, I could only imagine the disorder of an old house in the middle of fix-ups, rebuilds, and upgrades, plus five decades of everyday clutter. Still, after a few days in his brother's company, John seemed livelier when he returned to Berryridge Farm. I wondered if, during those weeks of working and reminiscing together, John and his brother actually *did* give their mother a celebration of life.

As our shop got more crowded with Browne family items, John decided to create another small structure, for storage this time. Our neighbor Jake had given us eight or nine trusses left over from his last building project, inspiring John to construct his biggest shed yet. To that end, John headed to the building supply store to lay in a supply of more lumber. Once home, he stacked all his building materials upright inside the shop, against the south wall: treated 2" x 4"s, sheets of plywood and a dozen or so eight-foot orchard stakes.

Going inside the shop, I'd look askance at all that stored lumber. Once I protested mildly. "You won't be starting the shed for weeks. Or maybe months." John and his brother were far from finished with the family home. "Do you have to buy all that *now*?" (You may have concluded this wasn't the first time I'd asked this question. You would be correct.)

"I like to have all my lumber on hand, so everything's ready when I do get the time," John said. "That's what my dad always did." And having been a Boy Scout, John firmly believed in the motto, "Be Prepared."

Preparation is all very well, of course; like the adage says, "Well begun is half done." But if the shop walls could talk, they might have said, *Bet you'll never be prepared for what's coming next.*

25 🐾 Warning Signs

The spring rains lingered. You'd think after all our years in the Foothills, we wouldn't mind a slow start to the season. But as the gray and sodden April days dragged by, I'd check the little bluebird thermometer John had brought home from his mother's house. Still hovering near 40 degrees, those temps meant the soil would be far too cold and wet to plant anything.

The hens seemed pretty miserable, two of them looking especially peaked. When chickens aren't feeling well, they stop scratching. Instead, they'll hunch up, motionless, with their feathers fluffed out. I'm guessing it's kind of like when you curl up on your couch with a fuzzy blanket. Anyway, the girls went back to huddling under cover, instead of running around the yard.

With the rains, multiple kinds of fungi sprouted all over our place: mushrooms in white, gray, brown and even bright orange, growing on soil, wood chips, beauty bark and old logs. When we first got the hens, John and I had set several rotting logs horizontally along the fence line of their safety zone to keep the chicken from scratching an opening beneath. One afternoon John came into the garden, looking downcast. "One of the hens died."

I dropped my trowel. "What happened?"

"I wish I knew," he said. "I only saw four girls, so I went into the coop and there she was, lying on the coop floor. Maisie or Daisy, I couldn't tell which."

"Oh." Feeling a twinge of sorrow, I sat back on my heels. Hens could sicken from any number of causes, like parasites or disease. But it could be there were other reasons they died, that you couldn't necessarily prevent. We'd seen the dead chicken at our hen lady Shannon's homestead; at the time, Shannon had offered nary an explanation or diagnosis. Now, I drew the same conclusion I had then: a chicken just up and dying could be nature's way of culling out the weaker organisms.

"I did see a hen pecking at some mushrooms a couple of days ago," John said. "I wonder if they were poisonous." He heaved a sigh. "I'd better go bury her."

"At least it wasn't Chloe, Marilyn or Dottie," I said, my heart heavy. That our favorite girls had been spared was cold comfort. As John turned to fetch a shovel, I added, "Maybe it was just her time to go."

You can hardly compare your mother's passing with the death of a hen. Still, I knew this new Berryridge loss was yet another challenge my husband had to face.

To combat the cold spring malaise, John got back into walking regularly in between his trips to work on the Browne house. One May day he was gone about twice as long as usual. When he strode into the driveway, I asked, "Did you take an extra-long walk?"

"No," he said, looking a little cross. "I've been knocking caterpillar nests out along the lane. There's a lot of them this year."

Tent caterpillars were a common enough sight in our region, and we'd seen plenty of them in the city. The tent moths lay eggs mostly in alder trees, and when they hatch in spring, a creepy-looking webbed nest, or "tent" develops. About eight inches across, the tents are hard to miss. The caterpillar (larvae stage) eats the leaves close to the tent, and after a few weeks, spins a cocoon to prepare for the moth stage. Every few years, you'd see infestations here and there, but within weeks, the caterpillars would be gone.

Like John, this year I'd seen more tents than in previous years. We even found an active one in the Ashmeads Kernal apple tree, which John cut out immediately. No big deal.

What had me more twitterpated was closer to home. Right next to the house, in fact.

One mild June afternoon, weeding my biggest strawberry bed, I caught a funny smell. The merest whiff of...manure?

I looked across at the chickens, pecking away in the orchard. We didn't let the hens into our main yard, although we heard they were great for your garden—fluffing up the soil with their scratching, and of course, "nutriating" (as sustainable farmer Joel Salatin would say) the soil with their droppings. We did let them in—once. After only a few minutes the hens had torn up a spot I hadn't wanted tearing up. When John and I tried to catch them, all four proved to be masterful escape artists. After a half an hour of bird-chasing, we finally caught them all, never to repeat the experiment again.

Now, I meandered over to John's new shed site, where he was framing in a wall. "I'm smelling something strange, near the septic tank," I told him. "Do you think we should like...get someone out to look at it?"

"I'm sure it's fine," he said. "We've got that extra-large tank— it'll be good for *years*."

Well, what did I know about septic systems? John's first home with his former wife had a septic tank, and their system never gave them a problem. Besides, this aroma was really faint. And I tend to be a *little* sensitive (a nice way to put it, John's thinking!) about smells. Chemical odors, fragrances in personal care products, vehicle exhaust—not to mention the tiniest waft of wood smoke inside the house—makes me cranky.

Taking a page from John, I decided not to take the odor too seriously—it was the middle of strawberry season. Between picking and putting up fruit, and trying to maintain the rest of the garden with

John away so often, I decided it was a waste of energy to dwell on either the smell or its source.

After all this time, however, I was still concerned about the contents of the 50-gallon drums on the junkyard property down the road—even if the donut smell was more puzzling than worrying. Interestingly, on my bike rides I'd be passed nearly every day by a flatbed truck, trailing a cloud not of diesel fumes, but the scent of popcorn. Seeing the truck with such regularity, I concluded these folks lived close by.

Then one day, I saw the flatbed turn into the junkyard driveway. Putting two and two together, I realized the property owner was running a small bio-fuel operation, and drums had to contain leftover restaurant fryer oil! Then and there, I had to admit that too often, I *look* for problems—and that's why I'd reacted to the odd odor at our place. Having solved the mystery donut aroma, I saved my energy for our strawberry crop.

Funny smells aside, John had plenty on his plate these days, trying to keep up with his chores here at home between the fix-ups down south. His walks, while batting around caterpillar nests, must have been especially motivating, because he started on a bunch of tasks he'd postponed. And one day, he steeled himself. He would be ruthless. He would be deadly. Like a Samurai warrior, he would wield his "sword"...er, saw, and eliminate several fruit trees neither of us wanted anymore.

The two European pear trees were the first to go. For years, we'd been gazing balefully at them, taking up valuable real estate near our prime bearing apple trees but without producing. The previous winter, in the spirit of giving the blighted pear trees a new lease on life, John broke our organic vow: he bought some fungicide and sprayed them. I wasn't happy about it, especially since the spray had drifted straight over to our raspberry patch. Not that the spray did any good. Like the previous years, the trees pushed out a few marginal blossoms, with the same result: zero fruit set.

The next tree to get the ax was the Karmijn de Sonnaville apple. This tree hadn't really grown in the years since planting; in fact, it seemed to have shrunk. Each spring, ol' Karmijn eked out some sparse leaves that would promptly turn dark and curl up. Nearby was our other heirloom apple, the Ashmeads Kernal. Its performance wasn't much better, but I loved the variety name so much, I said to John, "Let's give it another year." Already sick of killing trees, he readily agreed.

Along with all the home improvements at Wanda's house, John was inspired to upgrade the chicken lodgings. For two years, the girls' safety zone had been covered by a tarp, but by now the plastic was full of holes and leaking everywhere. The whole area was getting muddier, and wet chicken manure littered the ground. Which also meant our eggs were getting dirtier. Since I had no way to determine that whatever was soiling the eggs was dirt or poo, I was changing the straw in the nest boxes every couple of days.

John laid in a supply of steel roofing, and with a couple of short pieces of lumber, raised the roofline. After I helped him cut away the steer wire forming the top of the cage, he affixed the steel panels, and voila! A dry chicken run! The improvements left a gap of several inches on two walls, between farm fence and the new roof, but a small patch of wire would take care of that.

One last to-do was a project John and I didn't get around to: hiring a plumber to install the toilet in the shop. We'd intended to do it for years, but our source of home improvement funds—our income tax return—was always spent within a couple of months. By the time the weather was warm enough to use an unheated bathroom, our money would be long gone. Still, there was no big rush. Thanks to John, the open toilet pipe was securely capped by his practical little duct tape "hat."

Just days after John finished the coop repairs, we hosted what was for us, quite the bash: a Berryridge Farm garden potluck and farm tour for our family and friends. John showed the upgraded hen compound to his handyman-leaning pals, and I escorted our visitors around the garden to nosh on raw pea pods and sample the cherry tomatoes. Thinking of that funny smell near the septic tank, I secretly fretted about all the extra flushes thirty or so people might do, but told myself not to be so OCD!

One couple, Micah and Dina, lingered after the other guests had left, to show us their 90s-era Volkswagen Vanagon, newly reupholstered in a vibrant Scotch plaid. Micah had twinkling dark eyes and a luxuriant brown moustache that twitched when he smiled, which was often. "With the van remodel," said Micah, "we're testing it out by going to Banff next week."

"We've been wanting to go there for years," Dina added. "We can't wait!"

"How exciting!" I said, while sighing inwardly—our place was so demanding time-wise, money-wise and every other kind of wise that John and I didn't travel, or even hit the road for a weekend to see new sights. We left Berryridge Farm only to visit family—end of story. As John liked to say, we lived where other people came to take vacations, so we didn't need them. Our little country paradise was worth every sacrifice, every bit of energy we put into it and more.

Yet as John and I waved goodbye to Micah and Dina, on their way to the rugged and picturesque Canadian Rockies, I thought, *Was it really?*

26 🖎 The Big Blowout

Two days later I saw a chilling sight, one I'd never encountered before: gray-brown water seeping beneath the closed garage door of our shop.

I had no clue what I was looking at, but what I did sense was that John and I were in *big* trouble. Hurrying to the man door of the shop, I stuck the key in the lock with shaking hands. It couldn't be a leaky gutter—we hadn't gotten any rain for two weeks. I threw the door open and nearly stepped into a small river of muck and gravel strewn in a path from the south wall, oozing from beneath the deep freezer and the lumber John had stacked next to it. A six-foot wide stream of muddy water flowed toward the garage doors, the air filled with a ripe odor. Shocked, I stared at the mess.

A busted waterline? Or…I cringed. The septic tank?

With a sinking heart, I remembered the thirty visitors we'd hosted last week—nearly all of them needing a pit stop after their long drive from town—and took a deep sniff. The wet material didn't exactly smell *bad*, but it was definitely a little fetid. Normally, the first thing I do in emergencies like this is yell, "John, come quick!" But he'd left for his mom's house the night before. It was up to me to figure this out.

Water was still streaming toward the doors, and I could hear the swish and thump of the dishwasher inside the house. My first move: run inside and shut off the appliance. If we did have a septic backup, I didn't want to allow more graywater down the drain. And though I *so* wanted to believe this brown liquid was something, *anything* other than sewage, it was flowing straight from the area where we'd had plumbing installed for our future shop bathroom— including the duct-tape capped toilet pipe. Whatever the problem was, the off-odor made my conclusion inevitable: let's go with a septic tank problem.

I rushed back into the house, feeling sick. I'm sure most people would be really dismayed to have to deal with a potential septic system failure. But as an avowed germophobe, I could feel my revulsion almost overwhelming me. Digging out the phone book, I called the most promising on-site septic outfit I could find. They couldn't come out until tomorrow, so I tried another company, and bingo! Choice #2 could work me in by mid-afternoon. Then I called John and described the mess. "I've got a septic guy coming out."

"I'll bet it's a broken water pipe," John said immediately. "Although how the line could have busted is a mystery."

"It's not just *water*," I insisted.

"I can't believe it's the septic system," John said. "It's only six years old! Can you call Garrett and ask him to come out?"

"Good idea," I said, and promised to touch base as soon as I knew anything.

I left a message with Garrett, the contractor who'd installed our water and septic systems. Then I returned to the shop to face the music.

The pole building we called our shop actually served three roles: a shop, a barn and garden center, and an all-around storage unit.

The south wall was completely obscured by the supply of lumber John had purchased for his new shed. Besides the treated 2 x 4's, plywood, and the oversized orchard stakes, the stack also included other pieces of wood he was saving for future, as yet unplanned building projects. The bottom edge of every piece was sitting in the brown slime. So I had a job to do: relocate all the lumber so I could see what exactly was behind it.

I pulled on my muck boots, waded into the goo and set to work.

Upon closer inspection, I could see what I was stepping in didn't look like mud and gravel after all. Once I'd moved the plywood panel hiding the toilet pipe, I found John's duct-tape cap askew, with an unmistakable brown substance oozing from the opening. Well. I was no genius, but I didn't have to be one to diagnose the problem: our septic system had indeed failed. And the sewage buildup had belched the cap right off the end of the pipe.

However, with only an hour or so to move the lumber outside before the septic guy arrived, I didn't have time to think about the sewage beneath my feet. To and fro I lurched with one load after another, propping the wood against the shop's exterior wall, the farthest from the scene of the crime. I was on my last trip when a large white pickup pulled into our driveway.

I quickly introduced myself to Mike, and immediately escorted him straight to the open pipe in the shop. "Oh, *yeaaah*," was all he said. Then I led him to our septic tank, which was concealed by a beauty bark-covered tarp. I fetched two shovels, and Mike and I quickly shoveled the bark aside.

He pulled up the tarp and pointed to the soil around the two tank covers. "See right there, the ground's damp."

"That's not a good sign?"

Mike chuckled. "No."

I guess when you're a septic professional, you can find humor in sewage matters. Next, Mike strode to the white plastic post some twenty yards away, which marks the far end of our drainfield. He pulled off the port top and peered down. "Everything looks okay here."

I breathed a sigh of relief. Still, the reprieve was short-lived.

Grabbing a cordless drill from his pickup, Mike headed back to the tank, loosened the screws from the outflow port cover and removed it. *Without gloves on.* Just beneath the cover was brown liquid, sort of burbling at ground level. Utterly revolted, I couldn't speak. "The liquid isn't supposed to be this high," he said. "It should be beneath the baffles."

I wasn't sure what a baffle was, but whatever Mike was pointing at was hidden by the brown water. "Got to get the filter outta there," he added, glancing around the yard. Spying the garden tools I had stacked outside near the shop door, he grabbed my potato fork. As I watched in horrified fascination, he dunked the fork into the brown soup, and fished around for a moment until he hooked his game.

He slowly eased up the fork, and at the end of it dangled a tube-shaped plastic net. It was completely clogged.

On the bright side, the level of the brown soup in the tank began lowering immediately. Mike grabbed one of our garden hoses lying nearby, and once I turned on the outdoor faucet he rinsed off the filter, again with gloveless hands. "You need to get the tank pumped," he said as he replaced the filter and cover, and recommended two local pumping outfits.

"I will," I assured him, making a mental note of his referrals. "I'll call right after we finish."

"I mean, *soon*," he said, smiling. Mike really was quite a jovial, good natured guy, considering his profession.

He disappeared into his truck to make out his invoice. Upon his return to the house, I got him a pen. "You need to get the tank pumped," he said again as he finalized the bill. Then he said it one more time as he added up the charges. "That'll be $240 for the service call, and the $35 county fee to file an inspection report."

"How about $25 on top," I said, overcome with gratitude as Mike signed off on the paperwork and returned my pen. Grateful as I was, I knew that was one pen I wouldn't be using again. "Because you came out here right away."

As I walked Mike to his truck, with more thank yous, he repeated his mantra. "I'd get that tank pumped right away."

I took his four reminders to mean that we really, *really* needed to get our tank pumped. I waved goodbye, then turned back to the yard. Donning my oldest garden gloves, I gingerly picked up the potato fork, and moved it away from the other tools.

Like the pen, that was one fork I wouldn't be using again.

27 🐦 Out of Sight, (Not) Out of Mind

So there I was, $300 later, with a river of sewage to clean up. I contacted a pumping outfit, and found a guy who could be out in two days. Then I called John back and gave him the story. "I'll be home tonight," he said glumly. I figured he was already imagining the damage to his shop, building supplies and beloved power tools. To prevent my husband from having to face the worst when he arrived at home, after we said goodbye, I once again got busy.

I found John's heavy, flat-bottomed shovel and two five-gallon buckets. Shovelful by shovelful, I filled one bucket with liquid, and the other with "solids." Still, I knew this would be the easy part. The germs were still there. The next step, then, would be sanitizing everything in the path of destruction, then mopping the shop floor.

However, this blowout could have been a *real* emergency—the septic system could have backed up into the house. (My memories of the sewer backup I experienced in the farmyard singlewide, portrayed in *Little Farm in the Foothills*, were still as fresh as if it had happened yesterday.) The other "could-have-been" was not *quite* as bad, but bad enough—if the blowout had happened two weeks earlier, the sewage would have completely spoiled my prized strawberry crop.

For the rest of the day, I used water sparingly—not wanting to add to the filled-to-the-brim tank. I was reluctant to even *drink* our water, although that was really irrational. Our house water line was a fair distance from the sewer outflow pipe, and the well and pumphouse were over one hundred feet from the backup site.

When John returned at dusk, he surveyed the situation with his usual Browne calmness, and said exactly what I thought he would. "You know, it could have been worse."

I always thought pumping septic tanks would be the world's nastiest job. I'd see the trucks with "Johnny on the Spot" emblazoned on the side of the tank, or others with equally colorful puns or logos, and feel *so* sorry for the driver. Yet, the pumping process turned out to be a surprisingly sanitary, straightforward process. Not revolting as I'd expected, the reason I hadn't pressured John to have the job done a long time ago.

Dirk the Septic Pumping Guy was a pleasant young man who wasted no time hauling his long hose through our gate. He opened one of the tank ports, and attached the hose. I thought there would be a stench to make your eyes water, but there wasn't. And over the roar of the truck's vacuum system, for about an hour we chatted with him as the powerful machine sucked all that sewage away. Dirk reiterated what Garrett had told us years ago. "Clean your filter every year."

"Right," I said, looking at John meaningfully. *That'll be your job.*

Dirk added, "And get your tank pumped every four years."

The damage: $488.25, plus another $30 for the county fee. I was sure it wouldn't have cost nearly that much if we'd maintained our system properly. The grand total for our septic negligence? A cool $800.

I thought our well going dry back in our first year was the worst thing that could happen to our infrastructure. But this—septic failure, through our own ignorance and procrastination, was much worse. You can buy water. You can even take a shower at a friend's house or the YMCA. But you'll never unsee a river of sewage in your garage.

Even if "all's well that ends well," our septic blowout taught us a valuable lesson. Actually several, so I'll share them here.

• If you're the proud owner of an OSS, you need to stay on top of your system's overall maintenance—i.e., follow your county's regulations or your septic professional's recommendations. 'Nuff said.

• If you're still resisting the idea of dealing with your septic system, and don't know the exact location of your tank, find out where it is *now*.

• Cover your tank with a tarp, then hide the tarp with a few wheelbarrow loads of beauty bark, advice we got from our site developer Garrett. That way, your tank's location will be obvious—especially if you have an OSS emergency and you're too stressed to remember where the heck your tank is. The added benefit to the tarp and beauty bark is that you'll have easy access to the tank for that regular maintenance you're going to do.

• For the best percolation for your septic drain field—the area of your yard where your liquids flow while your solids stay in the tank—plant grass over it. I sure wish we'd known that sooner! Various segments of our septic field are covered with weeds, gravel, rocks, vegetable beds, our old burn pile, and more rocks. Still, John and I decided we're not up for tearing out the whole works to plant grass.

Finally, I learned that when it comes to OSS ownership, "out of sight, out of mind" is *not* a good motto. Regular maintenance really *does* mean you need to rinse your filter annually. And as I learned, that job isn't all that bad. If John and I had taken care of this chore over the years, we could have saved ourselves the $300 emergency service call, for sure.

After the blowout, I figured I'd spent twelve to fourteen hours cleaning the shop and laundering the layers of clothing I'd worn for the job. I had no way to add up the cost of the sewage trauma to this germophobe's mental well-being, but one thing seemed clear:

two years of being up close and personal with chicken manure had prepared me for this moment.

Without this extended exposure to animal poo, before slinging my first shovelful of backed-up sewage into the bucket, I would have run for the hills. Correction: run *screaming* for the hills.

28 ☙ "Junk" Woods

The slopes embracing Berryridge Farm, thickly forested with tall evergreens, seemed unchanging. Yet the clear-cut surrounding our house and clearing was maturing.

The alders and red birch trees that had been mere saplings when we moved to the Foothills were easily thirty feet high now, and thick as grass. Alders reproduce as profligately as weeds, growing as separate trunks. Red birches reseed every bit as readily, only you get more bang for your buck: regrowth from the logged-off stumps, called "stools," emerges as a coppice. That means after you cut down the tree, several smaller trunks will start growing from the original stump—sometimes as many as ten or even twenty. And these birches are *survivors*—you can lop off a branch for a garden stake, and a few weeks later, find healthy green leaves sprouting from the stick!

I thought of both species as sort of junk trees. Although alders and birch are the first to leaf out in spring, creating a lovely green haze in the woods, by late summer, the leaves turn a mottled black-brown and down they fall. Easy come, easy go.

Yet these natives have their uses, alders especially—certainly more than being turned into planks upon which you can roast a salmon. Alder trees function as a kind of nursery for the forest. I understand that they provide shade for the baby conifers, and all that leaf mulch provides nutrients and maintains soil moisture too. Alders and birches serve as wind and snow protection as well— their trunks are fairly flexible, and can bend almost double in a high wind or heavy snowfall. Small firs, especially, are thus protected from being smashed by the moisture-laden snow of our region.

Yet by the time firs are gaining some height, say, after seven to ten years, both alders and birches are showing their age. These species often succumb to weather-related damage—the entire tree uprooted when the soil becomes saturated, or with snow and ice, the treetop might snap off. When that happens, water often gets into the interior, the guts of the tree so to speak, and it will start to decompose from the inside, speeding its decline. Another downside to alders is that they're prey to tent caterpillars. But there's a method to Mother Nature's madness: every alder that breaks, or dies young, means more sunlight for the firs growing beneath it.

Still, we had one "junk tree"—a birch coppice—that I'd allowed to grow close to the house, near my main pollinator garden. With its numerous trunks putting on six feet of height every year, the clump was starting to cast its shadow on two large vegetable beds and my most productive strawberry patch. I hadn't wanted to cut it down, though—the tree provided the sole source of shade for the back patio, and on hot days, just beneath it was the coolest part of the yard. After John and I gave the birch some judicious pruning, I felt sure we could keep our coppice for years to come. I often parked a chair under the tree, listening to the rustle of the leaves in the summer breeze.

The Japanese have a practice, called "forest bathing," that recommends strolls in the woods to lower stress and improve your overall health. Researchers have confirmed that staying overnight in forests, or even simply walking through them, can have therapeutic effects. As someone who is outside every day, either in the woods or close to it, I firmly believe this research is on to something. I've always felt a sense of calm and serenity in our yard, surrounded by woodlands, and when I venture deeper into the trees, that sensation grows even stronger.

One summer day, as I sat under my birch clump, the trunks swaying gently around me, I rose from my chair to lay my palm against one of the coppices. And I felt something. A quickening, a...life force. I sensed the spirit, even the *soul* of that tree under my hand, even of the woods surrounding me. Something infinitely precious.

We might've had nine acres of "junk" trees, but this birch wasn't one of them.

Even if you treasure your trees, you have to be practical.

Living in a dense stand of alder means you are the steward of your woods. Alders and birches can grow so thickly you can have dozens of saplings growing within inches of each other, mostly stunted trees that are tall but very skinny. A small fir only inches high among the mess has no chance to reach maturity. So if you want your conifers to thrive, thinning your deciduous trees is part of the deal.

For John and me, both alder and birch, growing so prolifically on our acreage, have been a boon—while growing our own food, we were also "growing" our own firewood! Since our move to the Foothills, John has been our on-site firewood harvester—although we did once hire a couple of professional loggers to fall a pair of ginormous, dying maples on the steep ridge adjacent to our house. Being the kind of trees old-time loggers called "widowmakers," and the fact that in a bad storm, one or both of them could fall onto the house, John and I decided to go with "better safe than sorry."

Once the loggers downed both trees, they started bucking up the maple trunks, a very *hard* hardwood, into four-foot logs. Before they could finish, one of the guys showed up at our door unexpectedly, looking stressed. "My buddy got stung by a hornet," he said. "He's allergic but he doesn't have any medication with him. I've got to take him to the doctor."

They left in a rush, though the un-allergic logger returned to finish the job. Since John and I were counting on that goldmine of firewood, the rest of the task belonged to us. Over the next months, John ventured down the ridge to split the logs into quarters, and I helped him haul the wood chunks up the slope.

Lucky for John and me, game but aging Boomers, alders and birches are a much lighter wood. And the extraordinary thing about red birches is that they don't coppice only once, but forever!

Meaning, you can cut ten coppiced trunks nine inches in diameter, and within a couple of months, you'll find twenty more saplings growing from the main stump. Prune off all but the bigger ones, and in few short years the coppice is ready to harvest again. John and I always thought of these birches as the firewood gift that keeps on giving.

Mostly.

29 🐚 Under New Management

B usy with his shed-building and the trips to his mother's house, John adopted a new firewood processing system: instead of splitting a big supply of logs in late summer, like people do who heat with wood, he would chop wood as needed.

I didn't blame him—with the Browne family house remodel, he had so much on his plate. Yet I did feel anxious as the days grew cooler, and the nights went down into the 30s without the comforting sight of a few cords of firewood ready and waiting for our stove. Still, why was I fretting? We had four sheds chock-full of dry logs. Why not "split as you go"?

To help out, I decided to learn how to split wood. We had all the accoutrements I needed: short-handled maul, splitting maul, wedges and hatchets. One afternoon when it was too rainy to dig in the dirt, I went out to the covered splitting shed with John for my first tutorial.

The hens clustered near the fence to watch. I wasn't too keen to have more witnesses to my amateur efforts, but the girls always liked to be as close to the action as possible—not to mention being available in case we had some treats.

Following John's advice, I selected a birch log—nice soft wood, not rock-hard like the maple we had stacked. Easy, I thought.

"Okay, so you place the wedge here," and John demonstrated, "then pound it in with the maul."

"Right," I said. Lifting the maul, I heaved it onto the wedge. The birch wasn't soft at all. How did John make it look so easy? "Now, you hit the wedge harder," he said, "'til the log breaks apart."

"Gotcha." I swung the mallet and Bam! I split the piece, but the impact reverbed into my wrists, shooting up both arms into my shoulders. Jeez, that really hurt! I tried five more logs, and each hit zinged through me harder than the last. I chopped a couple more logs, but by now my wrists were aching. "I'm calling it a day," I said.

"You did good for your first try," John said approvingly.

I had enjoyed splitting—that is, aside from the pain—and the chance to master one more self-reliant skill felt satisfying. That night, though, the tingling in my arms got worse, and my hands felt almost numb.

It took two days for the feeling to fully return to my hands, and in that space of time I made a decision: splitting wood was *so* not for me. Better to concentrate on the outdoor tasks I could do more easily. I was happy to run the food-growing side of things, clear brush, and stack, if not split our firewood. This sounds terribly sexist, and right out of the 1960s for sure, but as far as I was concerned, splitting wood was man's work.

It dawned on me, slowly, that John was returning from his childhood home with more than odds and ends. The shop seemed to be filling, quite mysteriously, with ever-growing piles of Browne mementos, furniture, and more and more books, stacked willy-nilly all over the place. One day, I came across a box that appeared to be old paperwork from his dad's office—an item that had zilch sentimental value. Really, it was no way to manage your family heirlooms. When John came into the shop to change into work boots, I said to him, "You know, we should get your family things organized."

John shrugged. "I'll get around to it."

Days later, I repeated my offer to help; however, John gently, but firmly turned me down. He'd seen me in action, doing my periodic decluttering of my office. When I came to clutter, I was a veritable Zorro, slashing my metaphorical blade to eliminate the enemy: outdated papers, unloved books, and items taking up space they didn't deserve. After one of my decluttering sessions, our recycling would be full, with plenty of donations for Goodwill and the public library. Given my attitude, I had to wonder if John felt I couldn't quite be trusted with his family gear.

I reminded myself that John was dealing with a big loss—only nine months since Wanda had died was *not* the time to pressure him about letting go. Besides, he and Sid had finally finished their work on the family home, and had accepted a purchase offer. The house where John had grown up, where his kids had run in and out of, and where his father had died, now belonged to another family.

Another shift was taking place. After Wanda's death, John's sister Becky had continued to lose mobility. Although Sid lived nearby, and frequently visited her, she was having more difficulties looking after herself. In one of those strange quirks of fate, Sid's stepdaughter Star, a sweetheart of a teenager, shared Becky's birthday, and she and Becky were like soulmates. Star began spending a couple of hours a day with Becky, to help with housework and meals. It seemed like an ideal arrangement. Yet with Becky's uncertain health, I could see why John was hanging on tight to any and every reminder of his family.

Besides, winter was coming. Why take on a daunting job like decluttering the cold shop, when we could spend the chilly days blissfully warm near the woodstove? As Christmastime approached, John and I counted our blessings. He still felt the ache of grief from his mother's passing, but over the last year he'd had a chance to grow closer to Sid. His sister Becky had a loving helper, *and* a new kitty to keep her company. All six of our grandchildren were thriving, and my daughter Meghann had gotten promoted at work. John's son Collin's new business was taking off in a big way.

Then came the phone message no parent ever wants to hear.

PART II

Dark Times

'Tis the gift to come down where we ought to be...
—From "Simple Gifts"

30 ❀ A Shock Beyond Words

New Year's Eve. I'd put a chicken in the oven (store-bought) to roast for a celebratory dinner. After John and I came inside from a walk and fetching firewood, he settled on the couch with a book and I went straight to the phone to make the first of our Happy New Year phone calls to the kids.

Finding a stutter on the line, I dialed in to our voice mail—and suddenly gripped the handset.

A woman was calling for John Browne. I listened in disbelief. *Nurse...hospital in Phoenix...your son...car accident.* "Oh no..." I gasped, tears spurting to my eyes.

I heard the word "surgery" but rest was a blur as I tried to copy down the hospital number the nurse provided. I managed to save the message, then turned to my husband.

John was looking at me, his face tense with alarm. "Oh, John." My voice broke as I held out the handset. "Honey, it's about Collin."

As I told him the rest, he seemed to age ten years. He took the phone with a shaking hand and retrieved the message. I watched his face go gray as he listened, then he immediately called the hospital.

A Son in Danger

When Sue played the message on New Year's Eve and I saw her knees buckle a little, a sick feeling hit me in the gut—and I knew something was seriously wrong. Sue, her voice choked with tears, told me that Collin had been in a head-on collision and he was in a Phoenix hospital. I swiftly dialed into our voice mail and felt a shock wave go through me—a stranger's voice said they needed a family member's permission to perform surgery.

Calling the hospital, I listened to the nurse's report, feeling like I had been socked in the heart. Images of Collin at four raced through my mind. At that age, my only son was the cutest, most cuddly little fellow and now he was lying in a hospital bed with his right leg fractured both above and below the knee, both bones in his left forearm broken and his left elbow shattered.

Then came the sad duty of calling Collin's mother and my daughter Sasha to tell them what had happened. Sasha is truly a force of nature, and living only a short drive from LAX airport, she was off to Phoenix early the next morning. Her mother got on a flight soon after that, but Sasha pretty much took charge of the situation from the get-go.

When my daughter arrived at the hospital, she was able to contact one of the officers who had been at the scene. She got ahold of the police department's accident scene photos and emailed them to me. The vehicle that had struck Collin's small pickup was a beefy, black SUV. Its front end had been punched in, but Collin's truck cab was so mangled that the first responders had to cut him free. It was a miracle my son survived, suffering only structural breakage but no head trauma or internal organ damage. I remembered how blessed I'd felt when Collin finished his four years in the U.S. Marines, especially after serving in Somalia, covering the U.S. Forces withdrawal in 1994. How ironic he'd faced all those dangers overseas only to nearly lose his life on a city arterial a few miles from home.

I arrived in Phoenix soon after Collin's initial surgeries and met up with Sasha and her mom in Collin's hospital room. A nurse was changing one of his dressings. As I leaned down to give my son a hug, seeing his mangled limb and the serrated look of his skin graft, I couldn't hold back my tears. Collin was receiving excellent care, but given the severity of his injuries, he would need several more procedures.

Collin was in the hospital for ten days, but by the end of his stay he was restless and exhausted, and eager to get home; one does not get much rest in a hospital. His mom got Collin's house ready for home care with a hospital bed, and Sasha set up a car rental with a suitable model: Collin would need a vehicle he'd be able to get into and out of with one immobilized leg. My next move was a no-brainer (made with a little nudge from Sasha): once home, Collin would need hands-on assistance. So I would stay in Phoenix with him and help him recover. For as long as it took.

Collin was transported home in a wheelchair-accessible van. Once he was settled in his home hospital bed, I met his eyes and my heart broke all over again. Seeing a combination of fear, uncertainty and relief on his face, I got a lump in my throat. I felt the universal parental heartache for an injured child, and even though my child was thirty-nine, it didn't matter to me. I hugged him again and told him we were going to get him back on his feet and as good-as-new as possible. Sasha and his mom had done yeoman's work to get him through his surgeries, but the long-haul recovery, getting Collin from horizontal to vertical, would be left to us boys.

31 🖝 Winter Alone

On my own at our little place, I was getting a taste of what widowhood might feel like.

Ever since John and I moved to our country place, we'd balanced out the workload. We shared the garden chores. I did the housework, dishes and cooking. He built and maintained the infrastructure, managed our firewood supply, and from late September through May, kept the fire going in the woodstove. Since he was tending the stove anywhere from five to ten hours a day, our division of labor was a more than fair trade. Without him, I was the one who had to keep the stove going. But I had a big problem.

I was running out of firewood.

John called from Phoenix nearly every night. Those early days, his voice was full of pain, telling me about X-ray and surgery results and seeing the devastating photos of Collin's totaled vehicle after the accident. "The truck was folded up like an accordion," he said, his voice trembling. "Collin was fully conscious while the EMTs cut him out of it. They're investigating a possible DUI."

As a former law enforcement officer, John tracked the accident down to the last detail. It kept him from feeling helpless.

"It turns out, the driver wasn't drunk, he was distracted," John told me with quiet fury a few days later. "They say the SUV was in the right lane, the driver rooting around on the floor of his car for something. The car veered into the left lane, then crossed the double yellow lines into oncoming traffic. Collin was just in the wrong place at the wrong time."

I felt helpless myself. Mourning Collin's injuries, and how his life had changed in an instant, I was still needed here, to keep our place going. Yet I grieved for John, and the pain he felt to see what his son was going through. Especially sitting by Collin's bedside a year after his mother had died.

And as the weeks passed, John would say over and over. "You never get over seeing your child lying there, with his broken body. You just never get over that."

It was January, and in the Foothills, the coldest month of the year.

I kept my worry about firewood to myself—caring for Collin so far away, John had his hands full. Still, my anxiety mounted. As I related in the first Little Farm book, I couldn't depend on our electric furnace to keep warm—in fact, I'd dissed it big time. This appliance was so inefficient that on a cold winter morning, say 30 degrees outside, and the thermostat read 55 degrees inside, you could run the furnace for an hour and the house temperature might inch up a degree or two.

So I had to get up to speed on wood processing, and fast— although with that awful wood-splitting reverb still fresh in my memory, I wasn't too optimistic about filling our empty woodshed.

Yet all was not lost: John had recently bought a new, heavy-duty splitting maul. The day before he left for Arizona, he gave me another quick wood-chopping lesson—this time without a wedge. This way, I could avoid the worst impact of metal on metal.

For my initial go at wood-chopping, I set a smallish, dry fir log on the stump, lifted the maul as high as I dared, and swung. *Thwack!* Two pieces of wood fell to the ground—it worked!

True, I felt the reverb, but splitting sans wedge wasn't nearly as uncomfortable as before. I did a couple more pieces, to give my arms a chance to get used to the impact, then quit for the day. The problem was, I didn't have the luxury of chopping a few chunks of firewood here and there. I had to make a quantity of firewood happen, and fast.

Of course I knew how to start and maintain a woodstove fire, but with John away, I had a real eye-opener: how much time and effort went into keeping the woodstove going all day. I also learned something else: to start the winter off with a few itty-bitty rows of firewood is asking for misery. Unaccustomed to the constant distraction during my writing time, I had to remember to check the stove window every twenty minutes, a half hour at the most, to see if I needed to toss in more wood. Often forgetting, I'd look up to find the fire down to tiny coals, and not hot enough to restart. In those cases, I'd often let the fire go out completely, and plan to start another one after I came in from my chores.

The problem with the shorter burn time was that I simply couldn't keep the house warm enough. I was *cold*. All. The. Time. Adding my post-holiday blues to the chill, for the first time in my life I found myself feeling depressed.

To cheer myself up, I kept the Christmas tree lit every night. The colored lights did boost my spirits, until the fir needles grew so

desiccated the sight began to depress me even further. I missed
John of course. But the other thing was, John and I had been
through a lot of Northeasters, when we'd awaken in the morning
and find the house temp was down to 50 degrees. John would build
a hot fire, and it would take most of the day to get the house
comfortable. Although we'd let the stove go out at night, curled up
together under a few quilts, we would be warm. But with John
gone, even though I was spared any severe windstorms, I felt
chilled to my very bones day and night.

By the third week of January, my split firewood was gone. I
wasn't strong enough to split the knot-filled maple the loggers had
cut; I had to resort to scrounging around in the woodpile for any
kind of small logs and chunks I could find. The split-able pieces I
chopped and brought into the house, the big ones stayed put for
John's return.

I became a wood miser. Each time I fed the stove I weighed the
need to keep the fire going against my craving to warm my chilled,
aching hands. After a while, my writing began to suffer. Instead of
thinking about my story—which every novelist has to do to keep
the words flowing—I was obsessing about my dwindling wood
supply and how cold I was.

You may wonder, why didn't I go into town and hang out at my
mom's house? Be warm for an afternoon, or stay a few days? Well,
I had the chickens to care for. Besides, my '94 Ford Escort was
marginal at best for winter travel. The possibility of getting trapped
on our lane in some snow, and hiking home in the dark was enough
to keep me home. Besides, if I left the house for any length of time,
the place would only be that much colder and harder to heat when I
got home.

With my chill-induced low mood, resentment toward John
began to creep into my thoughts. All our years in the Foothills, our
division of labor had always worked out—and he was supposed to
be in charge of our firewood supply. Having kept up my side of the
deal, I couldn't help being upset with him for leaving me in these
straits.

I once read a memoir about a young female journalist from New York City who interviewed a handsome upstate farmer for a magazine article. She ended up marrying him, giving up her high heels and silk blouses to help him run his sustainable farm. Her workload was unrelenting: taking charge of a hand-milking dairy operation, plowing with draft horses, and raising organic crops, plus she had the responsibility of cooking for the two of them and a crew of farm employees and interns.

She somehow managed it all, albeit in a fog of exhaustion. Yet her greatest difficulty was being surrounded by *dirt*. Dirt on her clothes, in her house, on her skin, in her eyes. Then she and her husband had a baby and she worked even harder. Her book was fascinating reading, up until the moment our NYC-girl-turned-farmer couldn't take it any more—her marriage went on the skids and she left the farm.

That book really made me think about our situation here. With the homesteading life, if you decide you don't feel like doing this or that chore, well, guess what? There are consequences. You don't bring in firewood, you get cold. If you'd rather lounge around with a book than pick and process berries, you won't have any fruit for the coming winter. If your power goes out and you don't feel like going out into a snowstorm to start the generator, your pipes can freeze or all the food in the fridge will spoil. The other thing is, if you're pursuing this life with a partner, you depend upon one another too much to allow disagreements to get the better of you.

I could see how this young woman gave up—she had the dreams and passions and expectations of youth. She hadn't discovered the acceptance that midlife can bring—and the ability to be content with what you have. And yet…maybe she did—because she ended up returning to the farm, to that back-to-basics, honest life of living close to the land.

The truth about my long, cold January: John didn't deserve my resentment. Okay, so he hadn't attended to our wood supply. But then, he'd been away, putting all the energy he could muster into other family responsibilities—his mother's house. Besides, it would have been unconscionable for John to permit his brother to fix and clean up the family home by himself. And even more so to allow his incapacitated son, two thousand miles away, to fend for himself. It was up to me to let go of things that neither John, nor I, or anyone else could have prevented. And these lonely winter weeks did teach me a few things. Besides appreciating John's fire-tending expertise, I was able to add firewood acquisition to my Homesteader Gal's skillset.

If you're interested in heating your home with wood, here are my top tips for Newbie Firewood Wranglers:

• GET TO KNOW YOUR WOOD.

After years of schlepping firewood with John and feeding the woodstove, I could identify most kinds of wood—maple, alder, birch, fir, etc. But for splitting, you need to look at the grain of each individual piece, and figure how each kind of wood splits a little differently. There's a reason maple is called a hardwood, as opposed to fir being a softwood—if you're splitting maple, you really need to put some *oomph* into it. (Needless to say, I only attempted small pieces of maple.)

• MAKE SURE YOUR WOOD IS SEASONED.

If there are cracks, or "checks" on the ends of the log, you're good to go. If you swing your maul and it bounces right off the log, you can pretty well conclude that puppy is too green for a newbie splitter. My advice is to stick the log back on the woodpile, and let it season for a couple more months before you try it again.

• WATCH FOR KNOTS.

If you try splitting a log, especially maple, with a knot in it, you just created more work for yourself. Because your maul will probably get stuck in the log. I learned this firsthand one day, when my maul got lodged in a chunk of wood tighter than the Sword in the Stone. I had to hack at the log with a hatchet to free the maul. But if a log is really, really dry, you aim your maul in between the knots, and luck is with you, you'll wind up with a nice split piece.

• POUND THE STUMP, NOT THE LOG.

I discovered another chopping technique that's easier on your wrists. You swing your maul to wedge it firmly into the log, then tighten your stomach muscles to help lift the maul (with the log) a couple of feet, then smack that log down on your splitting stump as hard as you can. If all goes well, you've started a small crack in the log, and you do it again. Hopefully, four or five more hits and you'll split the log. A side benefit to this technique: it helps build your core!

Sometimes, though, five tries isn't enough. I'm pretty stubborn, and have gone as high as maybe fifteen strikes without success. At that point, I take a breather. Also, I give up on the log.

• KEEP YOUR EYES ON THE LOG.

It's like in baseball, or golf—you've got to keep your eye on the "ball"—your chunk of wood. Or you might swing your maul, miss the log, and hit your leg instead. Then you have far bigger problems than no wood in the house. Besides, some of us come to the job with a high wood-splitting handicap. John will tell you, I can't throw worth a darn, and my aim is pathetic. However, employing intense focus, I've actually split some jagged logs—windfall that broke apart in various places—by aiming my maul into one of the crevices. But I still can't throw.

• NO MULTI-TASKING ALLOWED!

When I'm splitting, I can't be daydreaming about my heroine's escapades in the novel I'm working on, or what to eat for dinner. It bears repeating: you don't want to miss the log and hit yourself with that big old maul. Which brings us back to: keep your eyes on the log.

This winter's experience also taught me the ultimate firewood lesson: the split-as-you-go plan was a no-go. If you don't have at least a cord or two of stove-ready wood—or at least a cord of ready-to-chop wood—you have no business calling yourself a homesteader.

32 🍠 A Dark Cloud

🌲

The Long Road Back

After Collin returned to his home, I assumed a new role: my son's home-care helper. I found myself taking on tasks I'd never expected. Sure, preparing food for my bedridden son was a given, but I never thought I'd be giving him daily injections of blood thinners. It was reassuring, though, that a visiting home nurse would check in regularly, and put clean dressings on his surgical sites.

Collin's two cats, Sonny and Grumman, would supply Collin with spiritual support, especially Sonny, who is very affectionate. As my son grew stronger he took on more personal care tasks and even began to do some cooking. Once he was given the OK to begin in-home physical therapy, Collin dedicated himself to regaining his mobility, and his mood picked up. It turned out that his PT had also served in the Marines, so they bonded a bit.

The co-owner of a fast-growing landscaping company, Collin was not idle on the work front either. The long days at the hospital, he was anxious about his business, and all the tasks going undone. As soon as he was home, he began making phone calls from the hospital bed. Once he graduated to sitting up for longer periods of time, he was able to wheel himself into his home office and do paperwork for few hours a day. His doctors and I were impressed at how fast Collin was recovering; still, my son wanted to heal even faster, and before long he'd graduated to a walker.

At Week Six, Collin began to drive short distances around the neighborhood. At first he felt spooked, but after a few days of practice runs we went out into traffic. Collin started feeling like he really *could* get his normal life back.

At that point, I could tell Collin was set to resume his regular life. Jubilant, that my son really was on the road to recovery, I made plans to return home in another week. Right after my decision, I got another call from my brother—with news about our sister Becky.

After I talked to Sid, it was difficult to keep up my spirits in those last few days at Collin's house. Leaving my son was bittersweet; we'd had lots of quality father-son time that few dads get with their grown sons. Yet I didn't know how I'd handle this new dark cloud on the horizon, without the comfort of my own parents.

Or how I could ever be at peace with the way these last months had transformed the landscape of my life.

Each time John called me, he sounded more optimistic about his son's full recovery. Collin's medical treatment and rehab was clearly working. But one night, more than a month after leaving, my husband sounded very low.

"I heard from Sid," he said.

I tensed. John's brother was looking after their sister, and for him to call John in Phoenix... "Is everything all right?"

"No, it's not," he said.

"Not Collin..."

"It's Becky," John said. "Sid says her cancer has grown more aggressive. She may only have a few more months."

"Oh, Honey..." I felt a wave of grief—Becky had been a loving sister to me as well.

"She's just tired of fighting this thing," John said heavily.

Even with metastatic cancer, John's sister Becky had hung on so many years, calmly dealing with her illness, we magically thought she'd be with us until a ripe old age. Now, only a short year after Wanda's death, to hear that Becky's condition was no longer treatable, that she was giving up, was hard to even think about. "What do you want to do?" I asked.

"I can't leave Collin yet," John said. "But let's make plans to see her as soon as I'm back."

Visiting Becky was pretty dicey this time of year—to reach her side of the state, you had to get through the mountain passes. In February, the high-elevation interstate was still choked with snow, and prone to unpredictable, blinding snowstorms. Sudden highway closures were common; whether they were due to snow falling faster than the plows could clear, or semi-trucks jackknifed across three lanes of traffic, closed was closed. Waiting out the worst of the winter weather seemed prudent.

The news about Becky definitely cast a pall over Collin's progress. By the time his doctors gave Collin the go-ahead to drive alone—which meant he was ready to live independently again—John had been away six weeks, the longest we'd ever been apart in nineteen years of marriage. When I met my husband in the airport on Valentine's Day, he pulled me close. "It's so good to be home," he said. About three times. "But I'd do this again in a heartbeat."

We would never forget how close his son came to his heart never beating again.

I'd always thought of life here at Berryridge Farm as having two stages—the years before we got the hens, and how our routines had changed once we had animals to care for. Yet with the upheavals of our dear ones, the flow of our lives had splintered into an entirely different phase. The year Wanda had died and Collin nearly did, and after.

And now, our lives in the aftermath, and facing the loss of our sister, was the new normal.

33 🐦 Another Goodbye

Once home from Arizona, John resumed his usual habits, catching up on lodge meetings and paperwork, and getting our firewood supply back in shape. Besides the bad weather in the mountain passes, our area was still being hit by snowstorms and Northeasters, and the almost inevitable power outages. John and I needed to stay close to home a while longer.

Three weeks after he'd returned from Phoenix, he was splitting wood and I was winding up my writing for the day when the phone rang.

It was John's brother. "Becky's taken a turn for the worse," Sid said, his voice thick with sorrow.

"Oh, Sid, I'm so, so sorry." My heart went out to him—he'd always been very close to his sister.

Sid went on, "She wants to be done." I knew what he meant. Living in constant pain. Losing one function after another. Becky had been so brave all these years, fighting the good fight. But perhaps now, her bravery would be in letting go. "She's in Hospice," he added. "The staff thinks she only has a few weeks."

I could hardly take it in, that he and John would be losing their only sister so soon after Wanda's passing. "I'll have John call you right back."

I threw on a jacket and headed outside, finding John fetching a tool from the shop. His eyes were bright from the fresh air and exercise. "Sid just called," I said. "About Becky."

His expression changed instantly. "What…did he say?"

"I'm so sorry, love. It looks like she doesn't have long."

John's whole body sagged. I enfolded him in my arms as he shuddered, trying not to weep. In a moment, though, he had regained control. "I'll call Sid," he said. "We need to go see Becky, right away."

John and his brother had a long talk that night. During this last stage of Becky's life, she and Sid had had a lot of conversations about their spiritual lives, about death. She had made a conscious decision, like her mother had the year before. Becky was ready to go.

John's daughter Sasha, always dependable in a crisis, flew up from LA. She rented a car so the three of us could meet at the facility where Becky was staying. I could tell Sasha's presence was making this somehow bearable for her dad. Sid and his family were waiting for us at the care center. When John, Sasha and I entered Becky's room, Sid took us aside.

"Things have changed really fast," he murmured. "She probably only has a few days."

Across the room, Becky was barely conscious, twitching in pain. A nurse stopped in and briefly greeted us. "She's having a bad day," she said in a low voice.

I saw the staff had administered a pain patch, but it clearly wasn't enough.

Yet the following day Becky was conscious, fully present. I don't know if she realized it was St. Patrick's Day, her mother's birthday, but she was talking. Although her eyesight was failing, she seemed to recognize each one of us. All the family took turns sitting at the side of her bed as she peered at the photos Sasha had brought, smiling at the memories.

Later, as John, Sasha and I left the center for the evening, my husband sighed, his face drawn. "Becky has prepared herself for this," he said. "Better than we have."

The following day, however, was another bad one. Becky had lapsed back into semi-consciousness, a moan of pain escaping her every few minutes. John, Sasha and I tracked down her nurse, and when the woman bustled in, her face changed. "We'll up the pain meds," she said quietly.

At Becky's bedside, the nurse's clinical demeanor changed. Her voice crooning, she murmured loving words like a mother soothing her little child, her hands gentle upon Becky's pain-wracked body.

John's sister died two days later.

Losing John's mother had been so hard, but she'd had a long, full life. Becky's death felt all the more poignant to me, knowing she had struggled through illness for much of her sixty-two years. Too, I regretted that my sister-in-law, who had such a generous and loving heart, never found a life partner. What seemed the most unfair of all, though: she adored kids, but never had children of her own.

Like her mother, Becky had no memorial service, no "celebration of life," or any gathering of friends and family for a final goodbye. As I did with Wanda, I felt our sister's loss as sort of surreal, without that sense of closure you get from a more formal ceremony. Despite my regret, I was comforted by a gift Sid handed to us as we said goodbye at the facility: *Proof of Heaven*, a memoir by Dr. Eben Alexander, a neurologist. After reading this doctor's miraculous personal story, I felt no doubt that Becky truly was in a better place.

After we arrived home, I took John to the middle of our yard, where we'd had our original burn pile years ago—our lone Berryridge bonfire the day our well went dry. Now, the straggly pots of mint I'd half buried in the charcoal-filled plot showed few signs of life. "I'm tearing all this out," I told him resolutely. "To plant a remembrance garden. So we'll always have something to remember your mom and Becky by."

John took my hand. "I'm sure they would have loved it."

Still, my plan was a bit problematic. Ornamentals got short shrift in our yard. The second flower garden I'd installed a few years back was now a mass of overgrown weeds, crisscrossed with trailing blackberries. And if any of my flowers got a quick drink during the driest weeks of the summer, they were lucky. I would do better this time, I told myself, a new flower garden materializing in my mind's eye. It would be a haven for pollinators, with bee balm and coneflowers, mints and red, spiky crocosmia.

John and I had gotten to be quite the experts at making grandiose plans we didn't have time to carry out. Our biggest goal was to bushwhack a big section of woods next to the fence to make a quasi-pasture for the hens. So far, all we'd gotten around to was felling a few trees.

But for Becky, I vowed, with my flower garden, I'd ensure we'd cherish her memory for always.

Planting flowers in a wet and dreary March wasn't going to happen, so I got busy on the book I'd been polishing on and off for several years. One month later, I released my second Irish novel,

Mother Love. I felt I'd arrived as a writer, having published three books and three works of short fiction. Now, I was ready take a short break from writing—to not only start my memory garden, but to be super-organized for the approaching growing season: install more of the vole-proof raised boxes we'd been planning, get all the beds weeded, and buy the tomato starts. Most of all, plant everything right on time.

Life, however, had something else in store for us.

34 ☞ Plague

Fans of Laura Ingalls Wilder's Little House series will remember a seminal event from Laura's childhood that she described in her third book, *On the Banks of Plum Creek*: a plague of grasshoppers descended on her tiny town in Minnesota, devouring the wheat crop of every farmer in the area, including her Pa's.

When I was nine years old, growing up in Central Minnesota, I read *Plum Creek* over and over, like I did all the other Little House books. But there was one passage I could only bear to read once: about the grasshoppers. All but writhing in revulsion, my eyes glued to the page, I could *see* the strange glittery cloud Laura described, *hear* the plop-plop-plop as grasshoppers dropped from the sky, and worst of all, I could *feel* the squish-squash of the insects beneath my bare feet.

For young Laura, there was no getting out of stepping on them, *shoeless* yet, because 1) all farm kids went barefoot in warm weather to save wearing out their shoes, and 2) the cloud had released thousands, probably millions of grasshoppers, a mass that covered every inch of ground for miles around. My imagination working overtime with the horror of it all, I went to the Keeper of All Knowledge—my dad, a North Dakota boy. I asked him if Laura's experience was even possible. "Have you ever heard of that?" I asked him. "Clouds of grasshoppers?"

Dad pondered it for a moment. "When I was a boy, there was a grasshopper plague in a neighboring county," he finally said matter-of-factly. He'd lived through tornadoes—I suppose a few too many grasshoppers wouldn't faze him.

"But could it happen here?" I asked anxiously. Our town, St. Cloud, was maybe an hour's drive from where Laura's family had lived.

He shook his head. "Those things don't happen anymore." In hindsight, I realize he'd been referring to modern agriculture practices—that the state ag agency would've sprayed those grasshoppers into oblivion. As a kid, though, all I knew was sweet relief.

I could never have foreseen that a modern plague of insects was all too possible.

Hardly more than a month after saying goodbye to Becky, we were saying hello to a new sight in the neighborhood. The alder trees lining our mile-long lane were rife with tent caterpillar nests, all of which were too high in the trees to knock out. The caterpillars were tiny, but the nests, the "tents," were gross—dark gray webbing entwined on every branch, the leaves around the tent tattered or missing entirely. On my walks I'd look up at the tents anxiously, but really, what could you do about them? Besides, the acres upon acres beyond the road easement didn't belong to us. John and I could hardly go haul a ladder down the lane and start whacking at our absent neighbor's trees.

Naturally, I Googled tent caterpillars. "It looks like they leave the tents in the daytime to eat," I told John. "The caterpillars feed on the leaves around their tents, then go back to them at night."

"That doesn't sound so bad," John commented.

"Yeah," I agreed, but inside, I was dubious. There were just *so many caterpillars*.

Then came the day John and I learned that tent caterpillars didn't stay in the alders. And that there were plenty of other trees they liked.

By early May, we were seeing tents in our yard. Our cleared area didn't contain any alder trees, but our nine wooded acres had plenty, and the other six properties along our lane were jam-packed with them too. On our land, John began patiently cutting out the tents in the trees closest to our clearing, and when the nests showed up in our apple trees, same drill: cut off the branch containing the tent, carry it gingerly to a bucket, and when the bucket was full we'd have a little caterpillar burning party.

One of the first tents we cut, I carried in great ceremony over to the hens. "I've got a treat for you-oo," I sang. The girls loved insects, slugs, and creepy-crawlies of every kind, and eagerly gathered round. (Just like they always do when you walk in—I'm convinced that's why so many people keep hens. They're great for the ego.) Anyway, I wafted my cat-laden branch under their beaks. "Look at this!"

The girls not only didn't peck at the "treat." They seemed to pretend not to *see* it. "What's the matter?" I asked them. "You love bugs!"

I wiggled my branch in front of the hens one more time, and they actually backed away. Clearly, John and I couldn't count on our hens to help eat the excess. Which in a way, was a good thing to find out early on. Because soon there were far too many caterpillars to even *try* to get rid of.

June first. I put on some dressy clothes, fixed my hair, and applied mascara. I needed an updated head shot for my community college teaching gigs, and since John was our in-house photog, he got his camera. The two of us headed outside to get the most picturesque background for my photo.

I ducked into the shade of an Indian plum to see if the light was suitable (I wasn't sure broad daylight did this Boomer face of mine any favors), then saw a caterpillar drop to the ground. I looked up, and saw a line of caterpillars inching along a branch, and more moving down the trunk of the plum.

"Gross!" Backing away quickly, I said, "Look at all those! Let's move into the light after all."

After taking a dozen or so pics, John and I drove fifteen miles to the nearest Foothills restaurant for our twice-yearly dinner out. It would be our last carefree evening for a *long* time.

When we woke up the next morning, tent caterpillars were all over the yard. Since alders grew right up to our fenceline, the insects didn't have far to go to attack. They were feeding not only on our apple trees, but the plums, the Asian pears, and the filbert trees. Within hours, the cats hit the blueberry plants, swarming over every last one of them, then they started in on our strawberry patches. Crawling on the ground, up on the fenceline, and the creepiest of all, slithering up the exterior of the house.

Revolted, I could hardly believe my eyes. I'd always thought our worst enemies, the Villains of Berryridge Farm, were voles. Now I saw the truth. With a screened raised bed, you could keep voles from your crops. But these tent caterpillars were the real devil's spawn, destroying everything in their path. And like facing any other kind of adversary, you had only one choice for fighting this invader: with hand-to-hand combat.

(Warning: If you are easily grossed out, I advise you to skip the following.)

The caterpillars soon defoliated the alder trees outside our fence. Unless stopped, the cats would do the same to the food-producing trees we'd nurtured all these years. They could damage the fruit spurs, setting back the trees' growth a year or two. Or maybe permanently.

Not only the trees were in danger. The blueberry shrubs were my special pets. They'd started to bear the previous season, providing a few precious cupfuls of berries. If defoliated, this year they likely wouldn't produce any crop at all—or the plants could die outright. I couldn't bear even the possibility. Anxiety and revulsion churning in my stomach, I made a decision. It was the caterpillars, or Berryridge Farm.

John and I put on our oldest garden duds and gloves, and the war was on. Following his example, I began my attack in our blueberry patch, picking the cats off my favorite Chandler blueberry plant. Once I'd nabbed every last one, I moved on to our other seventeen blueberry shrubs. After defending my blueberries, I stepped over to the nearest Honeycrisp tree. Plucking one of the loathsome creatures, as before, I squished it between my gloved fingers and dropped it to the ground. Grabbing every cat I could see, I moved to the next apple tree. It was an out-of-body experience. *Is this really me? Killing caterpillars by the hundreds? By hand?*

Speaking of hands, it wasn't long before my gloves' rubber coating was drenched with bilious-green caterpillar guts, the moisture seeping through the rubber. Tent caterpillars aren't all that small, you know. True, you'll see teeny-tiny ones a quarter inch long, but within a week or two they'll mature into fat, three-and-a-half inch specimens. Those big boys were the most disgusting of all—you had to squish *hard*. Along with my soaked gloves, I was starting to get the sensation of squishing even when I wasn't doing it. I needed a new strategy.

I found an ancient rusted paring knife of John's, then got out a five-gallon bucket and filled it with water. Using the knife to pry cats off our plants, I started tossing the cats into the water. Problem: They were such hardy critters they could actually *swim*. Or at least wiggle in the water, then climb up the sides of the bucket before they got even close to drowning. Conclusion: I needed something more lethal than bathwater. I squeezed a generous dash of Joy dishwashing liquid into the bucket—a vast improvement. The smaller ones would quit wiggling within a few seconds; the big ones took longer. But the detergent was working.

Dumping the creatures in the bucket, I tried not to look at the dying caterpillars. But of course I couldn't help it—like you can't help staring at a car accident on the freeway. Despite myself, I'd watch the cats thrashing around in the soapy water, wishing they'd just get it over with. Before too long, my bucket got awfully heavy. I dialed down to plastic yogurt containers full of soapy water, and when they were full, I'd throw the whole quart of dying cats into the main catch-all bucket.

Having picked cats off our smaller plants, I fetched John's plastic-topped tool bucket to use for a stepladder, and started in on our most mature apple trees. I would grab every cat I could reach on the lower branches, then clamber onto the bucket and reach for the higher ones. The highest boughs we had to let go. And it showed: the top third of each tree was already bare of leaves.

Those buckets of soapy water got full really fast too—the liquid turning to a sickly green sludge.

I was killing one cat about every second. That's sixty per minute, say, 3600 per hour. With John working at the same rate, the toll added up to 7200 each hour. We were killing cats from five to eight hours a day. Doing the math, the casualties totaled up to tens of thousands every day.

After I'd completed my rounds on the plants in the yard, I plucked caterpillars off the side of the house, as far up as I could stretch. The death count was so immense John dug a hole next to the shop in which to dump the aforementioned sludge (soap, water, and cat guts). In the heat of summer, you can imagine how this smelled.

After three days of intensive warfare, I went into the woods with my kitchen scraps to my everyday compost pile. Passing the coop, I saw cats crawling all over the walls and roof. Another place I had to hit, I thought, resigned, and kept walking. It was then I got my ultimate eye opener.

The ugly gray webbing the tents were made of had another purpose. Caterpillars were rappelling down from the trees, on the tiny filaments from the webs. Then, walking toward one of our bigger alders, I spied an even more macabre sight. "John!" I yelled. "Come here!"

35 🍂 A Killing Zone

Caterpillars coated the trunk of the alder tree like a fur coat, from ground level to at least thirty feet up. In the branches, the tree was laden with more cats than you could ever count. John looked bleakly at the squirming mass. It was straight out of a horror movie. Then we saw other trees with the same "fur."

"I've got to take the trees down," he said. It was obvious: he was wasted doing the hand-to-hand fighting. I could do that, while he logged the trees. I helped with the tallest, most infested alders while he wielded his handsaw. As John felled a particularly laden tree, I stepped away, revolted as he ran his gloved hands up and down the trunk, doing a bulk squishing on the fur coats.

Despite my revulsion, I watched John in admiration. I always gave my husband credit for being pretty much immune to getting grossed out. "You doing okay?" I asked.

"I have to say, *this*," John said as he wiped his gloves, "this is *really* disgusting."

After we felled several more trees, I returned to our orchard for another round. Every so often John and I would meet up to brush the caterpillars off each other's backs. Mostly for my benefit—John didn't mind, but just *thinking* of cats on my person made me shudder. What you didn't know wouldn't hurt you, of course (how many cats you had crawling on your back where you couldn't see) but once you felt one on your neck—well, that was a different story.

I knew John was getting sickened with the whole thing—I was too. Seeing caterpillars everywhere you turned. Doing nothing but killing, while neglecting our place. Vegetable seeds went unsown. Beds unweeded. Plants unwatered. I no longer heard the birdsong, or the bees humming as they went about their work. No longer felt the soft summer breeze against my skin. I no longer paused to take in the glory of the mountain looming in front of us.

Living in a death zone, my world had narrowed to pick and dunk, pick and dunk. John and I had come this far, though. All we could do was keep going. Not give up.

Tents showed up on three of the birch coppices next to the house—the tree that shaded the hottest part of the yard, that I'd communed with in quiet joy. The tents were up too high to reach by ladder, so there was nothing for it. John took down the three coppices and we cut out the tents, then dragged the limbs close to the woodsheds for processing. The "tree" that was left looked deformed.

About a week into our caterpillar battle, our closest neighbor

Toni came by. By now, we knew this whole part of the county was having a severe infestation. Toni had a big garden too, only a much larger cleared acreage—hence fewer alders near her yard. Still, she looked as worn as we felt. "How are you coping with the caterpillars?" she asked.

"Just trying to keep them from killing our fruit trees," John said.

"I've been looking at a spray organic farmers use," she said. "Bt—have you heard of it?"

"It sounds vaguely familiar," I said, "but I don't know anything about it."

"Apparently you can spray your trees and it only kills the caterpillars," said Toni. "My son said he could do the spraying."

I thought of how much insecticide it would take just doing the trees along the lane, much less the amount we'd need for her property and our orchard stock. "Let us know what you decide," I said. "Thanks so much."

As she left, I bit my lip. "I can't imagine spraying," I said to him. "No matter how safe it supposedly is."

"I can't either," said John. "And it's got to be really expensive."

"I'll bet the county extension office can tell us about it." After my next bathroom break, I got on the phone.

Luckily an extension agent was available, and I told him about our extreme infestation. "Yeah—things are really bad this year," he said.

"I've been hearing about Bt," I told him. "Is it really safe? And how effective is it?"

"Organic farmers are allowed to use it," he said. "When the caterpillars eat the sprayed leaves, it works like there are razor blades in their stomachs. Their insides get cut to ribbons."

Sounds like a fitting punishment for these devils, I thought savagely. "Do you recommend it?"

He didn't answer right away. "Bt does work, but the spray is sensitive to ultraviolet light," he said. "It'll break down in about three days."

"Oh," was all I could say. In three days, a whole new wave of cats would crawl in from the woods. I thanked the agent and hung up, then went outside and told John what I learned.

"Spray doesn't seem worth all the money," he said. "Not if it's worthless after a few days."

"If the Bt did hurt our bees I'd never forgive myself," I said. "Anyway, there's no way we could spray all that." I waved my arm toward the woods. Not the nine acres of our woods, or the dozens of additional acres in our neighborhood alone.

In any event, our neighbor ended up not spraying—perhaps she'd reached the same conclusion we had.

So there we were, back to square one. Killing non-stop. The Foothills had a cool spell the third week of June, and I saw far fewer caterpillars in the yard. Yet as soon as the weather warmed, the cats returned with a vengeance. I'd watch the caterpillars crawl along the top of the fence, hatred in my heart.

The alders along the fenceline were covered with them—all the cats had to do was drop right onto our orchard trees and start eating.

One evening, John and I were finishing up another eight hour shift of killing. "We need a buffer," he said, gesturing to the alder trees pressing up against the back fenceline. "Create an open space all around the yard."

I watched another cat drop from a tree onto the top of the fence, then grabbed it. "Let's do it, then," I told him. "As soon as this is over."

After all these weeks, I was used to the revolting chore—although our cat warfare wouldn't have been my personal choice for curing me of squeamishness. And I, who hated even the idea of harming another living creature (okay, I do kill slugs, without remorse—ants too), was inuring myself to murdering critters by the hour. Would this never end?

The first of July arrived—and it seemed like all of a sudden, the number of caterpillars in the yard was way down. Within days, I saw only a few stray cats. It looked like the plague really *was* over.

Despite these encouraging signs, I couldn't shut down my state of high alert—watching for cats, peering in the apple trees for nests, hunching my shoulders when I left the yard to dump compost, ready to duck from a rogue cat drop from above. John and

I toured our food-growing areas, assessing our tattered apple trees. "They're still okay," John said, gazing up at the Akane "And the leaves will grow back."

Apparently, all our cat picking had kept the fruit trees reasonably healthy. The wild trees, though, were a different story—the alders were half-defoliated, leaving the woods looking oddly autumnal for early summer.

So the cats were gone. Instead, we were seeing cocoons everywhere. Under the eaves of our house, curled into leaves, even in strange places like the corners of the recycling bins. Surrounded by cocoons, though, was a piece of cake compared to our caterpillar horror movie. John and I were worn to the bone, and kind of depressed. I felt I'd lost one precious month of my life, the loveliest month of the year. Still, I was filled sweet relief that John and I had gotten through this terrible time. And saved our garden.

Speaking of, we had our vegetables to plant, the watering to catch up on. Our normal lives to resume. Although I had to wonder: after all the killing, feeling utterly revolted simply walking into our yard, would I ever feel the same way about Berryridge Farm again?

36 ☞ Stalked by Death

A week after the caterpillars petered out, I'd just finished breakfast when all four hens started squawking like crazy. Through the last insane weeks of caterpillar battles, John and I had ignored the hens. Sure, they got fed and watered, but I wasn't paying attention to whatever else they were up to. They often went off on one of these cackling choruses, so why worry. Still, to make up for neglecting them, I popped outside while John was checking email.

As I passed the woodsheds, it sounded like the birds were actually rattling their fencing. What were they up to—some kind of girl fight? I pulled a few greens from the side of the path, to toss over the fence, maybe help the hens mellow out a bit, and hurried to the safety zone. There, on the other side of the chicken pen, hardly fifteen feet away, was a large wild cat.

I stopped in my tracks. Was it the same bobcat that had killed our neighbor Toni's hens, in broad daylight? This animal's reputation for shyness must've been a rural legend. Because it locked eyes with me, and didn't even move when I yelled at it. After a long moment, the cat pounced against the fence one more time, as if to say, "Ha! You don't scare me!" and melted into the woods. Then I saw the feathers.

They were all over the inside of the pen. Three hens, Marilyn, Daisy, and Dottie, emerged from their favorite hidey hole next to woodshed #Three, out into the main chicken area. But where was Chloe? I ran back to the house. "John—I saw a bobcat right at the pen!"

He rushed into his work clothes, and "weaponed up" with a Bowie knife and a loaded .380 pistol, in case the bobcat got aggressive. We sprinted back to the chicken compound.

"Chloe," we coaxed, peering around the usual hen hangouts, but there was no sign of her. I got on my muckboots and finally went inside the safety zone. In the far corner, next to the fence, a hen lay crumpled and motionless. Chloe.

I looked at John. "Oh, Honey, the bobcat got her."

John didn't speak for a moment. "How could the bobcat have killed Chloe?" he said, and his voice cracked. "From outside of the fence?"

Neither of us had an answer to that. Sick at heart, John and I walked the fenceline, but didn't see any gaps. "I wonder if the cat had been waiting for a hen to come near the edge of the pen," I said, feeling ill, "and it snuck his paw through the steer wire." Hens were curious creatures. Drawn to the movement, had Chloe ventured to the fenceline, where the cat had mauled her?

"Whatever happened," John said, heaving a sigh, "at least this predator won't get to eat her."

I saw the sadness in John's face as he went to fetch a shovel. My chest felt heavy and tight, but I forced myself to take my daily bike ride. We'd been lucky, I told myself. Our neighbor had lost at least six hens. Living in the middle of the woods, you had to expect predators, and this was the first big cat attack in the three years we'd had the hens.

My little pep talk didn't make me feel better. Our place hadn't felt the same since the caterpillar plague, and now, after the hawk had gotten one hen, and illness got Maisy, we were down to fifty percent of our original flock.

I returned from my ride to meet John by the woodsheds. He was smiling. "I want to show you something."

I rounded the corner and what do you know. There was Chloe, standing, if just barely, on our splitting stump. Head drooping, eyes mostly closed, she was taking tiny sips of water from a little tin camp cup John had unearthed from the shop. He carefully parted the feathers on the back of her neck to show me her injury—a bloody patch of skin, but it wasn't actively bleeding. "It looks like only a surface wound," John said, "and maybe she's just in shock. She might bounce back."

"Should I call a vet?" I asked him. We had sort of a "survival of the fittest" outlook—our hens weren't pets, but farm animals. Our budget had no wiggle room for chicken veterinary care.

"It couldn't hurt," said John. "If she got an antibiotic or something, maybe she could pull through."

I called around to a couple of vets, and found one who dealt with chickens. "A bobcat attacked on of our hens," I said in a rush to the receptionist. "Is there any chance the doctor could prescribe an antibiotic?"

"You'd have to bring her in," the receptionist said regretfully. "I'm sorry."

Chloe seemed so fragile, I could imagine the trauma of a car ride would send her over the edge for sure.

Through the afternoon and evening, John didn't leave her side. "C'mon, have another sip of water," he'd coax every few minutes. He'd always had a soft spot for this particular hen. And since we didn't want to put her into the coop with the other three hens who might peck at her injury—the girls often picked at the bald spots of their molting sisters—John fashioned a little temporary coop for the night. In one corner of the orchard, under the fir tree that was the hens' favorite outdoor shelter, he tenderly settled Chloe in, with food and water next to her. "How about that—she's still hanging on," John said as we went inside for the night.

"Chloe's our toughest girl," I said. Ever the Pollyanna, I added. "I'm sure she'll be better tomorrow."

We never saw it coming.

First thing in the morning, I went out to John's little shelter to check on Chloe. When I reached the fir, my stomach turned in nausea. All I found was a pile of feathers, and a small mound of entrails studded with flies. I ran to get John. He surveyed what was left our hen, his face grim. Neither of us said anything, but I knew he was thinking the same thing I was.

We'd either overestimated the safety of the temporary shelter, or underestimated the determination and ingenuity of the bobcat. Did the animal snake a paw through the steer wire and kill Chloe, or climb the fence? Still, what did it matter? Dead was dead.

"We can't let the hens out of their pen anymore," John finally said. He glanced into our orchard. Two years ago, that was where the hawk had gotten our chicken. "I'd better cover their exercise area with steer wire," he went on. "They'll be completely protected."

I gazed over at the other three hens, pecking inside their safety zone. They were getting older—they probably had another year or two of laying, but now that we were down to three hens... "I guess we won't be sharing eggs anymore."

John shook his head. "I'll get the shovel," he said heavily.

I never asked where he'd buried the first hen, killed by the hawk, nor Maisy, who one day had simply turned up dead. And I didn't ask now, where he planned to bury Chloe. I didn't want to know.

John never got a chance to put up the steer wire.

Two days later, I went outside, pulling on my muckboots to greet our three hens...and found another death scene.

The big cat had returned—and had actually gotten inside the covered safety zone. I stared at the grisly sight before me, hardly believing my eyes. There was Marilyn and Dottie in pieces just outside the coop. Daisy lay nearby, her body intact but her head bitten off. Sickened, I dragged my eyes away and peered inside the coop.

There were feathers everywhere. The bobcat had gotten in through the small hen-sized door too. Had they been asleep when it first attacked, and they'd run outside, only to make it easier for the cat to kill them? Our little flock, whom we'd nurtured for three years and was the heart of Berryridge Farm, was gone.

And it was all our fault.

John and I had never gotten around to tacking chicken wire in the slender gap beneath the safety zone's new roofline. As I stared around at the carnage, it seemed clear what had happened: the bobcat had climbed up the fence, slid through the opening, and went for the kill. Bile rising in my throat, I left to tell John, trying not to cry.

John didn't speak for a long time. "I'll...I'll be out after a while," he finally said. *To bury them*, he didn't need to add. Seeing the remorse in his face, I knew he needed a little more time to face the task.

I went back in the coop, and shoveled piles of dirt on top of the remains. John stayed inside all day. And we didn't talk to each other that night. It was just too awful.

But the bobcat wasn't done with us yet. The next day, I walked to the safety zone—and found another gruesome sight. The big cat had obviously climbed up the fence again, slid through the roofline opening, and uncovered the hen's remains. It must have eaten its fill of the dead birds. Then, in a sort of blood lust, torn them up even further.

I'd seen bobcats enough that this murderous instinct seemed unbelievable—how a relatively small animal could be so destructive, so bloodthirsty. Had this one been a particularly aggressive, resourceful bobcat? Had the cat been hovering nearby for months, and waiting patiently to strike? Whatever was driving the bobcat didn't matter—the utter relentlessness of Mother Nature was like a blow.

That day, John quietly buried what was left of our hens. And once again, I didn't ask where. I never wanted to pass the spot, and hate it. I never wanted to know the place where the pieces of our girls lay, under the earth instead of on top of it because we hadn't taken care of them. Without saying anything to John, I took on the last job, a task I didn't want to put off. Decommissioning our chicken run and coop.

As best I could, I cleaned up the feathers. There were hundreds of them, strewn everywhere—I couldn't get them all. Then I collected every bit of manure from the coop. I scooped the straw from the nest boxes, leaving them bare, then removed the feeder and waterer from the run. Scrubbing the metal until it shone, I set the equipment in the sun to dry, then wrapped both in plastic bags. I set them in the storage side of the coop. And finally, I closed the door to the safety zone. We would not open the door again.

All that remained were scattered goldy-brown feathers.

37 🐓 Eggs Over (Un)Easy

In the days that followed, John was quiet, his face drawn as he went about his work. As I tried to catch up on all the postponed gardening, my own heartache made every chore an effort.

Like I said, I'd never been much of an animal person—and would never have guessed I could grow fond of chickens. Yet I found myself missing our girls terribly. My heart lurched every time I passed the coop, though I kept my eyes averted. I missed their companionable hen clucking and chatter, clamoring for some scratch, or to come and hang out with them. I even missed the rattle and squeak of the feeder that had annoyed me before. I'd always loved the silence of our Foothills life, but now the quiet seemed unnatural. Even eerie.

The empty chicken coop felt haunted.

"We can get more chickens," John said a couple of weeks later, in a half-hearted kind of way.

"Sure we can," I said, as ambivalent as he sounded. "But it's almost August..."

"Yeah," he said glumly. "Too late to find pullets. And nobody would have chicks for sale."

Not that we'd ever considered raising chicks. After the cat attack, it was obvious that bringing in such defenseless creatures as baby chickens would be as good as calling, *Here, (big) kitty, kitty—come and get your chow.*

"Maybe next spring," I said. Thinking of the mediocre taste of the grocery store eggs we'd just brought home from the store, I had a sudden inspiration. "How about I'll look around, and see if we can buy any local farm eggs."

I found an organic poultry farm that had a Community Supported Agriculture program (CSA) about twenty-five miles away. While I did some long-postponed weeding, John drove the Ranger down the same highway we'd traveled to buy our flock. He returned with two cartons of eggs—beautiful, brown ones, albeit much smaller than our girls had produced. At $6.50 a dozen.

"The egg farmer was really nice," he said, "and she even showed me around her operation." He sounded enthusiastic for the first time since the hens had been killed. "They'll even do a delivery."

"Oh, perfect!" I said. Who knew getting fresh eggs would be that simple!

It wasn't. "Actually," John added, "they can only deliver down to the village. On Fridays."

For John and me, the cost of fresh organic food in time, energy, gasoline and money had long ago become sort of...skewed. If I were to do the math with how much we'd invested in having a small flock of chickens, and how many eggs we'd gotten in return...well, I really didn't want to know. Only today, John had traveled fifty miles for a few eggs; now we were considering driving another sixteen miles to the village every week to have farm eggs on our table. Still, John and I had gotten so spoiled on the taste of fresh eggs from our free-ranging girls that I didn't blink. Well, not too much.

One thing was clear, though. Right now, neither of us had the heart to even *think* about having chickens again.

Having fresh farm eggs again lifted my spirits, but it didn't last. For the first time since we'd moved to the Foothills, I wanted to get away. Our beloved Berryridge Farm, the place that had always given me such joy, now depressed me. In my mind's eye, I could still see the sad little corpses of our hens, the feathers strewn around the chicken run. I wanted to escape from the guilt John and I both felt—that we'd let our girls down by not protecting them.

Grieving, I daydreamed of going on a spa retreat—with nothing to do but be a lady of leisure, getting mud wraps and massages. Or how about a trip to Hawaii, to lie on a sunny beach. Of course we couldn't afford a spa or a trip. And there was no way I could abandon our garden in the middle of summer, with our full plate of watering and weeding tasks. I simply didn't want to be *here*, with the endless chores and the fight with nature that seemed like we always lost.

Then a couple of weeks after the hens were killed, a new situation arose. That made leaving impossible.

38 ✍ Revenge of the Moths

Remember all those tent caterpillar cocoons we'd found around our place? That we'd breathed such a sigh of relief to see? You might also remember those science lessons about metamorphosis—the life cycle of certain insects: eggs hatch into larvae, the caterpillar stage, which then develops into the pupa, growing inside a cocoon. Sometimes, out of a caterpillar cocoon comes a beautiful butterfly. But sometimes not. Sometimes, what emerges from a cocoon is a *moth*.

Suddenly, we had moths *everywhere*. The air was filled with them. You'd be minding your own business, weeding a bed, while moths flew around your head, flapping in your face. At night, they banged against the screen door of the slider, their fat gray middles reminding me too much of the caterpillars they'd been only weeks before. I was already so *done* with cats—I absolutely would not *tolerate* these annoying insects. "John," I said four days into our moth invasion, "we've got to do something! I can't stand it anymore."

"How about one of those mosquito zappers?" he proposed. "They seem worth a try."

"That's a great idea," I said fervently. "At this point I'll try anything."

You've probably heard of these gadgets, or even seen them in action. The "zapper" is an electric device that emits ultraviolet light. In the dark, the light attract insects, and as soon as they make a landing, *Zzzzaapp!* They're hit with a tiny lightning bolt. And any insect dumb enough to fall for it is instantly a goner.

Not wasting any time, John left for town that very afternoon. A few hours and $79.95 later, he was home with a Flowtron Insect Killer. By the evening, John had fashioned a hook on the back fence near our orchard trees, hung the zapper, and plugged it into his long extension cord. As darkness fell, the device was surrounded by dozens of flapping moths, the yard filled with the crackling sound of *Zzzzaapp!* Several each second. The device was doing its job.

I missed the lovely quiet of our place, the soft summer nights where all you'd hear was the hoot of an owl, or the occasional *yip, yip, yowl!* of the neighborhood coyotes. This noise was irritating beyond words. Still, each *zap* meant one less tent caterpillar moth.

The next morning, John and I went out to see how well zapper had worked. Well, it had been effective, all right—there were moth corpses inside the device and scattered all over the ground. There were also tons of other dead insects: mosquitos and flies. Sadly, butterflies too, large and small, and bees. Then John peered around a little more carefully, looked over at our Jonagold apple tree, and muttered one of his rare expletives.

"What?" I said, and joined him. It was then I realized...no. Actually, I was hit completely upside the head and back down. Here was proof of the one and only purpose of a moth. Its ultimate life mission.

To lay eggs.

John and I gazed in horror at our little tree. Tent caterpillar egg sacs were wrapped around nearly every twig. The moths we'd seen flapping wildly around the zapper? They'd still managed to lay their eggs before succumbing to the lure of the purple light. And they didn't stop on that one tree. The adjacent fruit trees were covered with sacs too. In the area surrounding the zapper, the moths had even laid eggs all over the steer wire of the fence.

Before you can say, "Death to Tent Caterpillars!" John was moving the zapper hook to the other side of the yard. I fetched the rusty paring knife I'd used to kill the cats and started removing the egg sacs from the trees. We'd discovered a few on our fruit trees the previous weeks, but we'd been too busy cutting out caterpillar tents. Also, the egg sacs—a small shiny, dark gray mass—can be hard to see on a tree, unless you're looking for them. Wrapped around a twig, the sacs easily blend in with the color of the tree's bark.

Extricating a sac is a fairly tricky operation. Especially since their texture is somewhat brittle, reminiscent of a tiny piece of charcoal. You have to insert the knife just so between the twig and the egg sac, so you don't nick the soft wood, then pry off the firm sac. I knew enough by now not to leave a sac on the ground! If an egg sac attached to a fruit tree can survive a winter of Northeasters, it sure wouldn't have any problem hunkering down on the grass to hatch in the spring.

That night, I listened to the zapper in its new location with more foreboding. The moths were laying eggs, then getting killed. Yet the collateral damage—exterminating Berryridge Farm pollinators—made me feel sick. I'd learned Mason bees look a lot like houseflies. At this moment, the zapper was probably taking out all kinds of beneficial critters. The destruction reminded me of that deep-sea commercial fishing you hear about—sure, the nets might be full of tuna, but there will be an immense bycatch of dead dolphins and other sea creatures.

The next morning, John and I found a similar scene—tons of dead moths, and more egg sacs on the fence. I pointed at another dead butterfly on the ground. "Honey, it's just not worth it."

John only nodded. He took down the zapper and stuffed it back into the box, adding it to the stacks of other boxes, bags and unused garden items in the shop. The twice-used device had been another expensive experiment—one that had taught me something else.

There were always consequences when you messed around with nature's balance.

39 ☜ Mistaken Identity

I couldn't seem to bounce back.

After all the blows since that terrible phone call on New Year's Eve—Collin's accident, Becky's death, the caterpillar plague, then the hens getting killed—I felt permanently on edge, waiting for the next horrible thing to happen. I went through the days listlessly, on autopilot—not quite ready to give up on our place, but feeling lost. What I didn't want to think about was this: without Berryridge Farm, who was I?

John must have felt as low and distracted as I did. One evening, he was working the chop saw, cutting up the alder trunks we'd logged during the plague, when I heard him swear. I dropped the carrot I was peeling and rushed outside. He was hurrying toward the house, his face white, and his arm outstretched. He'd lowered the saw right onto his hand, leaving a deep, inch-long gash.

This was our first medical emergency since John's heart scare our first year in the Foothills. Then, as now, it was a Saturday night. The small clinic fifteen miles away would be closed, while the closest hospital was an hour's drive from our place. We called John's family doctor, and *Thank God*, the office had a physician on call. After she and John conferred about the slice on his hand, they decided that driving all that way, only to wait who knows how long in a Saturday-night emergency room, wasn't necessarily the best option. Instead, if John kept the wound clean and carefully bandaged, it should heal without a problem.

John's cut did mend. Still, when I realized I'd lost my pleasure in our place, I knew getting away wasn't an option. Not if I wanted my sense of self, my very identity to return.

Little Megs, our wise, sparkly granddaughter, was now a tween. School would be starting in a week—she and I had just enough time to take a trip to Astoria, Oregon to see my daughter Meghann and her sons: tall, sturdy Seamus, and his younger brother, smart as a whip Rowan.

The last evening of our visit, my daughter, the kids and I piled into Meghann's small SUV and drove five miles to the nearest ocean beach. In the setting sun, I watched the silhouette of my granddaughter frolicking in the surf, took in the golden-pink light bathing my grandsons' rapt faces as they gamboled in the sand, and I felt an incandescent joy I hadn't felt in long time.

Two months later, in late fall, John and I flew to Los Angeles to see his daughter Sasha and her family. I had never visited before. Over the years, I'd convinced myself that I was afraid of flying—my previous foray with John to California had been our misbegotten (and very expensive) Amtrak journey to attend Sasha's wedding. On that trip, three days of delays and breakdowns, the train had arrived at our destination sixteen hours late. We'd had to miss the rehearsal dinner; another two hours and we would have missed the ceremony. The last few years, to see the LA grandkids, John had traveled by himself while I'd stayed home to look after the chickens.

But now, after our recent losses, my fear seemed irrational. I had to admit the statistics on air travel safety were pretty convincing—and simply could *not* lose out on getting to know three of our grandchildren any longer. Once we arrived at Sasha's, I knew I'd made the right decision. Seeing the kids' bright little faces, having them call me Grandma Sue for the first time, walking on the California beach in the warm sunshine, when Berryridge Farm would be dark and cold, I felt my heart lift even more.

On the last leg home from LA, bouncing 10,000 feet up in a turbo-jet Bombardier aircraft, I fervently hoped life would simply stay put for a while. I was so ready for a "steady as she goes" kind of routine. And John and I deserved a break, didn't we?

Maybe we didn't. We returned home to the grinding of chainsaws and excavators working one of the slopes to our southwest. The noise was unrelenting. I thought our immediate area in the Foothills would be safe from logging, but I was wrong.

Feeling bleak, on my bike rides, I tried not to look at the denuded hillside. A week before Christmas, the racket ceased, the landscape forever changed. This past summer, John and I had been forced to take down numerous trees. But alders, as I'd said, come cheap. Seeing the grandeur of the fir-covered hill laid bare was painful.

I admit that like the rest of us, I appreciate books and newspapers. I *really* like toilet paper. And I totally coveted a wood house instead of the plastic one I had. It doesn't make sense, I know, but these trees, this clear-cut—it felt like a personal loss.

The logging operation must have displaced some wildlife.

A few days after the last of the log-filled trucks wound down the hill, I spotted a big cat from our living room window. It was staring longingly through the fence, like it would have liked to nab a rabbit, but had no intention of exerting itself too much.

My gaze was drawn to its short body and bobbed tail—then I met the cat's eyes. "Oh my God," I breathed.

The animal's face was narrow and streaked with black markings, like the one I'd seen a couple of years ago right outside our bedroom. Just like that cat, this one didn't look threatening at all. If the cartoon character Tweedy Bird had seen this critter, he probably would have said, "I t'ink I see a puddy-tat."

In my mind's eye, I saw again the animal I'd found at our coop four months ago. Hardly fifteen feet away, the cat had a long, lanky body, and a wide, tawny-colored face, with piercing eyes that stared right back at you. The cat's expression, though, was what I would never forget. Fierce and insolent. And the brazen way it had banged against the fence was unforgettable.

In my fear and panic, I'd assumed the animal was a bobcat. After all, it had been a bobcat that had killed our neighbor's chickens. And I'd never seen any other kind of cat near our yard. Now, I realized how wrong I'd been. It was a *cougar* that had killed our hens. A cougar that had had the nerve, the *guts* to climb our fence, and squeeze through the hens' tiny door, and go on a wholesale killing spree. Not a bobcatty thing to do at all.

I still get cold shivers when I think about how I reacted. Like my Foothills friend said, it's cougars, not bears, you should be afraid of—and if you encounter one, you're supposed to keep facing the big cat as you quietly and slowly retreat. Thinking the hens' attacker was a bobcat, I'd yelled at it, flapping my arms, then turned my back and raced to the house.

All I can say is, if there's a next time, I hope I remember what *not* to do. Even more, I hope that any cougars around here return to their former habits of laying low.

As Christmas approached, the somber events of the past year weighed heavily on John and me. One gloomy December day, thinking of my sister-in-law Becky, whom we'd lost in March, I pored over the fairy book she'd given us, then glanced at her gift of the fairy king wall decoration. It seemed the right time to cheer ourselves up by watching *Fairy Tale: A True Story*, a film based on a World War I-era fairy sighting in rural Yorkshire, England. A pair of young girls had reported seeing an entire fairy village, and had even taken photos. The story had appeared in the English press, and *Sherlock Holmes* author Sir Arthur Conan Doyle and even Harry Houdini were part of the storyline—the former, a fairy Believer and the latter, a Skeptic.

The movie reminded me of another one John and I had watched years ago, called *Fairy Faith*. This film was actually a documentary about real children experiencing sightings of fairies in the woods. Yet as these kids grew up, most of them stopped seeing the fairies, or forget they ever had. The idea of children's fantasies being real fascinated me—and I wondered, *maybe I can write about that someday.*

Whether I would ever get around to writing about fairies or not, a little fantasy and whimsy was exactly what we needed to celebrate the New Year. Having been raised in Minnesota, I kept the words of Garrison Keillor, a fellow Minnesotan, in mind: Being joyful, he said, is a large task for Midwesterners, "where our idea of a compliment is, 'It could have been worse.'"

As John and I celebrated New Year's Day, I didn't realize how true that could be.

40 🐾 A New Threat

John and I finally bit the bullet.

For over three years, we'd gotten super-spoiled on fresh farm eggs, between having own laying hens, then being supplied by the egg CSA. However, when our poultry farmer's chickens quit laying for the winter, the jig was up. We had to switch back to store eggs.

After New Year's, I began a new Irish novel, about a Dublin wife and mother who dreams of having a farm. My project brightened the long, cold winter weeks. By the time March arrived, I figured the time was right to call up the poultry farm about this year's egg CSA. John and I could already taste those pastured, organic, orange-yolked eggs. And with warmer weather not too far off, I was anticipating asking our chicken gal if she or any local folks she knew would have some pullets for sale. But as soon as John went into the orchards for early spring pruning, we had no thought of farm eggs, or chickens. Or anything else.

I was bringing a box of firewood toward the house when John came from the north orchard, a twig in his hand. "You're not going to believe this."

I looked at the small branch he held, then dropped my box on the steps, my blood running cold. "Oh, no." The foot-long twig had a half dozen distinctive shiny gray "growths" wrapped around it. Which of course could only be…

Tent caterpillar egg sacs.

"The apple trees are covered with them," John said. "I'm pruning off what I can. The rest, though…" His voice trailed away.

"We'll have to remove them by hand," I said. "We can do that." I tried to sound encouraging, but inside, I felt a familiar sickening sensation. "I'll just get this box inside."

I found a tarp and spread it under our most vigorous apple tree, the Akane. It hadn't bore much fruit last year—a blessing in disguise, given the caterpillar infestation. As John stood on our old wooden stepladder, tossing down four-foot lengths of new growth onto the tarp, I tried not to look at the sacs on them. Although we never burned brush—we tossed it into the woods on the advice from Garrett, our contractor from way back—we'd burn these prunings, no problem.

While John pruned, I started in on prying the sacs off the tree branches within reach, carefully placing them into a single-serving plastic yogurt container. Like I said before, if you tossed the sacs on the ground, they'd probably hatch anyway. Pretty soon, I'd filled my carton with egg sacs and had to fetch a quart container. There were that many sacs.

John climbed down to move the ladder, and looked past the fence at the dense woods. "As soon as we're done pruning, we've got to start that buffer."

During the worst of the caterpillar plague last summer, we decided that cutting down trees to create an alder-free buffer zone around our yard was absolutely essential. At the time, it hadn't seemed like a big job. Big jobs, in theory, never really do. Now, I gazed bleakly at the trees and brush surrounding our one-acre clearing, and realized what an immense task this buffer project would be. But we had to start somewhere. And right away.

That is, as soon as we finished pruning and removing egg sacs from our twenty-plus fruit trees. They were so laden with egg sacs, I tried not dwell on what could be in store for us on the other side of the fence.

I was planning a delayed book launch party for my latest published novel, *Mother Love*. Since the story was set in Ireland, the event I had in mind would be a St. Patrick's Day party. I envisioned a big splash—hopefully one as festive as the book launch I'd done years before for *Little Farm in the Foothills*. I contacted the area media, asked my sister, a talented baker, to supply some treats, created a poster for the bookstore to display, and even lined up an Irish fiddler. I was really anxious about the event—despite all my teaching and public speaking, I wasn't a party-giving kind of gal, and wondered if I'd get even a handful of attendees. Still, it was helpful to have something else to think about.

Because just outside our windows, a nasty situation was brewing.

John and I started this second war on caterpillars by tackling the woods closest to our most mature orchard. The alders were thirty to forty feet high now, and the birch coppices that had been a tangle of saplings when we moved here were now multi-trunked trees, each about six or more inches in diameter. Our acreage was also covered with younger birch and alders anywhere from six to eight feet high, and in many places, there would be several saplings growing per square foot.

Creating our buffer wasn't simply cutting down trees. You had to whack through brushy, hard-wooded Indian plum and vine maples, upright and trailing wild blackberries, whose uber-sharp thorns posed a hazard everywhere you turned. Add the easy-to-trip-over sword ferns with three-foot fronds covering the ground and you really had your work cut out for you. Even after clearing around the base of the coppice, you couldn't safely work a chainsaw in the mess.

John preferred hand saws anyway. Taking down a birch coppice, he'd start on the most accessible trunk. This kind of birch has soft, fibrous wood that catches easily on saw teeth. I would press on the trunk in the direction John wanted to fall it, so he could wield his saw more efficiently. As the first trunk came down, I rushed to check the tree top.

I wanted to throw up. "I thought tent caterpillars only fed on alder trees," I said stupidly.

The birch's smaller branches were covered with egg sacs. I mean, *covered*. John glanced at the sacs, and reached into his pocket. "Apparently not," John said in his calm way.

I dragged the birch out of the way so John could start on the next coppice trunk. "What do we do?"

This coppice had—I counted—fourteen trunks. If each tree had this many sacs...and there were so many, many birches right at the fenceline...Well, it didn't bear thinking about.

"Do?" John pulled out his clippers. "We cut 'em."

And so began our new woods routine. We'd get a tree on the ground and clip off the twigs and branches with egg sacs on them. John and I would do our falling and clipping until it was nearly dark, then John would burn the piles of clippings. You couldn't dispose of these sac-laden prunings in the woods, like we had with all of our other brush. Besides, birches are a breed unto themselves—a little bit mutant, you might say. As I mentioned, you can cut down a birch, only weeks later, the tree will still *sprout leaves*. So a logged tree could still be a food source for the growing caterpillars.

John and I were tree lovers. My husband even confessed that as a kid, he'd *hugged* trees. I contemplated the blessings of even these "junk" trees as I'd called them—their shade, habitat for birds, even the music of rustling leaves was part of why we valued them. Now, instead of forest bathing in our woods, John and I had become tree mass murderers.

As we worked out way down the fenceline, I saw egg sacs not only on the birch and alder trees, but the vine maples, and more shrubs I couldn't identify. Pretty much every deciduous species had them, except the big leaf maples. It was only March. The hatched caterpillars would start migrating from their nests around the end of May—we had only two months or so to avert a disaster.

Some days, John and I would feel we were making progress on our tree-clearing, but in reality, it was only a dent. Still, there was nothing to do but keep going: fall the trees, cut off the branches, burn them. Lather, rinse repeat. Day after day.

41 ✍ Shock and Awe

First, the good news: My St. Patrick's Day book party was a success.

All my friends and family had shown up, even a few acquaintances I hadn't expected. We had a lively discussion about being Irish-American, and the lilting strains of Irish fiddle music made the atmosphere especially festive. Along with my sister's lemon bars and brownies, I'd brought my homemade "Spotted Dog." It's a rich Irish quick bread, traditionally served when you want something more special than ordinary soda bread, and I'd splurged on made-in-Ireland Kerrygold butter to spread on top.

The morning of the event, I awakened with a sore throat. While I enjoyed the celebration, by the end of it I was drooping with fatigue. The stress from the weeks of preparation, added to the worries about the caterpillars had taken a toll.

The bug put me out of commission the next few days, then, as soon as I was back on my feet, it was time for our spring visit to the California grandkids. Enjoying LA's April sunshine (at our house, it was raining) and the warm ocean breezes (the Foothills' winds were chilly and brisk), I couldn't help worrying. There was so much to do at home.

And we didn't know what we'd find when we returned.

Once back at Berryridge Farm, John and I got the bad news. The caterpillars had hatched.

Do you remember that scene from the Alfred Hitchcock film, *The Birds*, when Tippi Hendren creeps down that road lined with hundreds of crows? Birds alongside her, birds hovering above her, their beady eyes watching her every move. There's only the occasional cackle, a twitching of wings, yet her face is pinched with terror, and you can just *feel* her panic, her utter horror.

Walking down our lane our first day home, I couldn't help thinking of poor Tippi as I saw hundreds, if not thousands, of tents lining the road. Tents alive with caterpillars. In late April, the leaves were beginning to unfurl on the alders and birches. I'd always welcomed the rich, green sheen of the woods this time of year, yet this day, the sight made my heart sink. The leaves meant the cats would have a ready food source. The insects were tiny at this point, about the size of a fingernail clipping. But you couldn't miss them, crawling by the hundreds down from the top branches.

John and I returned to our tree falling, but this time, we weren't clipping egg sacs. We were lopping off bigger branches, cutting them into pieces to dunk into buckets of soapy water. With every cat-covered branch, John joked, "Here's another bunch, ready for the spa." I laughed. Well, the first few times he said it I laughed. Until I saw masses of them on the trunks, with the fur coats like last year's plague.

On some level, our tree-falling and cat-killing was pretty ludicrous—each day we were taking down a coppice or two, twenty or thirty trunks in all, and killing thousands of cats. Yet our woods alone contained thousands of trees, containing what had to be millions upon millions of caterpillars. We were either the Don Quixotes of the Foothills, pursuing our noble quest to save our place. Or we were completely nuts, wasting our time on an impossible task, and killing trees for absolutely no reason.

I opted to see us as the former. And our frenzy of tree-cutting, branch-dunking, or full-on mass-cat glove squishing continued apace. Then, despite our buffer, despite the trees we'd killed, in late May, the cats descended on Berryridge Farm.

Again.

While John and I battled caterpillars, other people were actually living their lives. The day the cats showed up in the yard, I got some wonderful news: My daughter and her new fiancé were going to have a baby!

I was happy for them, happy for *us*. A baby! Here we'd thought all our four children were done having kids. Still, I couldn't fully take in the joy of a new grandchild. My thoughts and my days were filled with nothing but killing.

After less than a year, John and I were back to the previous June's routine. We would pick caterpillars together, until he'd go into the woods and take down more trees, and I'd go it alone. No matter what we did, though, it wasn't enough. You could pick an apple or plum tree clean, and in ten minutes, *every leaf* would have three cats on it. Same goes for the caneberries: boysenberries, loganberries and my favorites, the marionberries. The supports John had built for the canes made cat incursions easy. No crawling around the deadly marionberry thorns, No sir! We cats have easy access, up these nice smooth wood posts!

As for the blueberry plants, you'd go around the patch harvesting cats, and by the time you finished cleaning off the last bush, the first one was covered again.

The caterpillars were in the strawberries now, during the fruiting season. The pleasure of picking strawberries turned into a loathsome task—brushing away caterpillars with my bare hands to get the berries. I could feel my face taking on a constant wince of revulsion.

The house siding was dotted with cats too—they seemed to follow an instinct to climb straight up. For a better food source? For a better cocoon site? Who cared? When I finished my rounds on our food-producing plants, I started picking cats off the house. Which is completely, totally ridiculous, right? But all I could think of was, *Every caterpillar on the house I kill is one less I pick off our trees.*

Watching caterpillars crawl up the foundation just as I grabbed their compatriots a few feet higher was beyond discouraging. I stared at the invaders for a minute, then got a brainwave. With a whisk broom, I walked around the house foundation, brushing cats off the concrete until my dustpan was full. I'd dump them in our usual bucket of soapy water, then start back in. Once I'd circled the house, it was time to get back to the orchards.

The one break I took each day was to ride my bike. But my time away wasn't relaxing at all. The infestation was horrible up and down the main road too. I had to be vigilant, watching for the areas with nests above the pavement. Often, I had to swerve, to avoid caterpillars dropping on my head from the treetops.

Within a few days, one—no, make that two, realizations hit me. The cats were eating not only the leaves of the apple trees and blueberry bushes. They were *eating the fruit.* I headed straight into the woods where my stalwart husband was sawing at another coppice. "John," I said, "I swear to God, this is way worse than last year."

He wiped the beads of sweat off his face. "I wouldn't have thought it was possible. But I think you're right."

"I'm seeing three times as many cats. Or even more than that! I don't know how much longer I can take this!"

"I don't either," he said. "All we can do is just keep going." He began attacking another cat-laden branch. "We don't have any other choice."

As I turned to go back to the yard, I stared, arrested, at a young hemlock. The top was stripped of needles. The cats were eating a *fir* tree.

It was like nature had gone completely mad.

42 🙊 This Is *War*

Every day, more cats kept coming. Masses of them. You could look on the ground and see them swarming. You could check a cluster of blueberries and see the browned scars of the blossom end, where the cats were nibbling. It was the insult to my beloved blueberries that got to me. This year, for the first time, the fruit was heavy on the shrubs. And I got mad.

I started to take this plague personally. I felt like Scarlett O'Hara, raising her fist to the sky. Only I wasn't nauseated from a gnarly root vegetable, I was sick to death of caterpillars. As I killed them, hour after hour, I was yelling in my mind, *You will not defeat me!*

Still, there was an appalling new element to this year's infestation. Last year, we'd mostly seen one type of caterpillar. The markings were darned clever, I have to admit—variegated in brown and gray-green, with dots of pale orange. The cats easily blended in with the vegetation they were attacking. Now, John and I began to see some with gray and blue markings, and soon more and more of them. I did more research and discovered the orange ones were Western tent caterpillars, and the blue were forest cats. Not that their names mattered one iota, because both species grew larger by the day.

Although we looked far and wide, as far as John and I could tell, these critters had absolutely no predators. No creatures in these woodlands, from raptors to songbirds to rodents ate these horrible things. This year, the forest cats were in ascendance. They were not only bigger, they were—and I'm not putting you on—*wilier*.

You could reach for one on an apple leaf and they would slip off to the ground—nearly impossible to pick out in the grass and weeds. Or you'd try grabbing one off the side of the house, and the cursed thing would throw itself down onto the gravel alongside our foundation. This year's feistier bunch were undetectable among the gray-blue rocks.

John and I ran into our neighbors Jake and Barb, who had a young orchard they were desperate to protect. When I asked them how their trees were faring, Barb looked almost hopeful. "We found this tape at the farmer's co-op," she said. "You circle the base of the tree, sticky side out, and the cats get stuck on it."

"Wow, that's a great idea!" I said, and we hurried home. I got busy winding duct tape around the trunk of our fruit trees. Once our plants were protected, I could *finally* get caught up with the rest of our garden.

But the tape had almost no impact. For every cat that got stuck, there were ten more crawling right past it. And the blueberries were being hit the hardest.

We'd already let some things go—the raspberries had been stripped of leaves, and I'd been too busy to water them. The whole patch was a goner. Our big Japanese plum by now was completely bare of leaves too, the knots of fungus standing out against the defoliated branches. I'd stare at it from the dining room window, and think, *It's turned into a ghost tree.*

But, I thought fiercely, I would be double…um, ding-donged if I would let that happen to my blueberries! I rigged up a crude sort of "fence" around the drip line of each blueberry plant, and using sticks for "posts," I wound the tape all around the sticks to make a barrier.

My wee fences were not the success I'd hoped for. The cats would crawl right up to the tape, and some would stick. But many, many others, especially the bigger ones, seemed impervious to the "stickum." More of them would find a teeny-tiny gap beneath the tape. So I still had caterpillars making a beeline for my shrubs.

I do realize that by now, I'd developed like this very OCD approach to caterpillars. I'd put my current novel on hold to laser-focus on fighting them. Despite the millions of cats surrounding our yard, I was still trying to hold back the tide. The proverbial Dutch boy with his finger in the hole of a cracking dike.

If it was up to John, at a certain point he would have done his Browne philosophical thing—shrugging his shoulders, he'd conclude, *We can only do so much, and if we lose some trees, or berries, that's life.*

But he was too loyal to stand by while I broke my heart, trying to keep the devastation to a minimum. And he also knew there was a certain, inescapable force at work—the compulsive streak that I share with every member of my family (my FOO, you may recall from *Little Farm in the Foothills*). And my streak at the moment had completely dropped the germophobe thing—worrying about germs seemed silly now. A waste of energy. Not when I could kill more and more caterpillars and save our place!

I sought out John, once again in the woods taking down trees, to kvetch about my tape problem. Trying not to look at the thousands of cats swarming on the branches he was cutting, I said, "It's like the tape's not even there!"

John stopped sawing. "After a few hours outside, the sticky surface probably dries out."

"I can't change out the tape every hour!" I was already doing it every day.

He looked thoughtful for a moment. "What if you put something on the tape to deter them? Something chemical?"

"Like what?" I asked, feeling despairing. Here I was, taking valuable time away from cat picking, and I wouldn't use chemicals anyway. "Wait..." I thought for a moment. "I've got an idea." Without telling him what it was, I hurried to the shop.

I found a small container of vegetable oil John kept around for lubricating tools. Then I shucked off my workclothes to go into the house. John kept a supply of hotel sundries from our infrequent stays away from home. Sensitive to the strong perfumes, I didn't use them, and John preferred the local goat's milk soap he bought in the village. Still, he kept the cheap, stinky soap around because...well, he kept a lot of stuff around.

I cut a half bar of soap into bits, dumped it in a yogurt container and mixed it with a small quantity of vegetable oil, then hurried to show John. "What do you think?"

"It just might work," he said. "You can apply it with one of the paintbrushes in the shop."

He actually broke out a brush he'd been saving to stain his new building. I advanced into the yard with my evil-smelling potion, and prepared to do battle.

I began my rounds with the fruit trees, and coated the tape circling each trunk liberally with the perfumy oil. Then I did the same with my little "fences" around the blueberries. I'm sure the oil and soap didn't do the fruit trees any good, nor the soil near the berries, but I couldn't worry about that now.

My tactic actually worked.

I watched caterpillars climb up the base of a tree, and as soon as they hit the tape, turn away. It wasn't foolproof, though. Plenty of cats would get past the stuff. And like the stickum on the tape, my potion lost effectiveness after a few hours. So I "painted" the tape twice a day.

The potion didn't kill the cats. But it was slowing down the tide of destruction.

43 ☞ A Method to this Madness

At the height of the plague, with my blessing John left Berryridge Farm for a couple of days to attend an out-of-town conference. The second night of his absence, I was putting away my filthy caterpillar-killing weapons. One was the rusty, sticky-with-cat-guts paring knife of John's, a knife I hadn't even washed after last year's plague.

Weary after a long day, I nicked my hand with it.

I stared at the cut, in the V of my right thumb and forefinger. My pulse started to race. I hadn't had a tetanus shot since my twenties—and the hospital was a long drive away. As my heart began pounding, I felt like I would puke, almost dizzy with fright and anxiety. I was going to get tetanus, my jaws would lock up, John would come home and find me dead...

Stop! I told myself. *Think!* I tried to take deep breaths, feeling too sick to drive, then spied the hand sanitizer we kept in the shop. I squeezed a big dollop of gel on my cut and gasped—it felt like I'd stabbed myself in the hand. With a dagger, not a paring knife. Still, the pain must've meant the alcohol in the sanitizer was cleaning the cut.

I hardly slept that night, and the next day, I examined the wound every few minutes to see if it was turning red or swelling. But no. Just like John's far more severe hand cut a year ago, this would heal just fine.

After my tetanus scare, I took a short break from caterpillar murdering. While John continued his attack outside, I went online. My motto: Know your enemy.

The state Ag Extension site held a wealth of knowledge. The experts still clung to the fantasy that tent caterpillars pretty much feed on alder trees, but I learned about the *why* of the plague. All these caterpillars are simply part of Mother Nature's method.

In the forests of our region, as I mentioned before, the first trees that grow after a clear-cut are alders. They provide shade and protection from weather extremes for the tiny fir saplings. Yet alders, within a few short years, actually shade out the small firs, stunting their growth.

Yup, I thought. I've seen that. Both the firs and alders on our land, after the clear-cut, had reseeded at the same time. Yet by now, the firs had reached a height of eight feet while the alders were around thirty. The role of a caterpillar infestation is to defoliate the alders (and in our case, the birches as well), allowing more light for the firs.

Additionally, as part of the plan, the cats provide fertilizer to the developing forest—think of all that poo. Another reason for an infestation's astronomical numbers is because, as John and I had already concluded, tent caterpillars have few predators, save for hornets and yellow jackets. We'd seen some spiders attacking the little cats, but there weren't enough spiders or hornets in the *world* to eat all these caterpillars.

Still, a glimmer of hope appeared on the horizon. I discovered that the trees under attack begin to exude a compound—a sort of antibiotic or repellent—that will make the cats sick. Hallelujah! I was ready to run outside and tell John, when I started reading the next section.

My heart plummeted. Apparently these tent caterpillar events occur about every ten years. That was bad enough: John and I would have this horrible experience awaiting us a decade from now? But it got worse: the length of the infestations occur in *three year cycles*. Oh. Dear. God. Did this mean we'd have yet another plague next summer?

Horrified, I closed the Extension site and clicked on a few media stories. One article was about some woman who'd been so freaked out by the caterpillars in her yard that she left her home *and* her husband to stay at a hotel out of the area until the infestation subsided. That was funny enough to give me the strength to go find John and tell him what I'd discovered.

He was encouraged to learn about the trees' repellent, and that there are actually benefits of a tent caterpillar plague. But as for the natural cycle...

"Three years?" John said incredulously.

"Yes," I said gloomily. "If last year was terrible, and this year was three times as bad..." I didn't want to say it aloud.

"Next year could be the worst of all," John finished.

I stared out at the trees, beyond the small patch of ground John had recently cleared. If the last caterpillar cycle in the Foothills had been around ten years ago, the trees around here would have been too tiny to attract the pests. But now, the original 73-acre parcel we and our neighbors lived on was nothing but alders and birches as far as the eye could see. No doubt the whole area was providing a target-rich environment—i.e., all the elements of a perfect storm of caterpillars.

John and I went about our work the next couple of days without talking much—the thought of next summer hung over us like a giant black storm cloud. Then one late afternoon, John called me over.

"Look at this," he said, pointing to a clutch of cats on a birch trunk.

I didn't want to—I'd seen enough cats these last weeks to haunt my dreams—but I gave the caterpillars the briefest of once-overs.

"Do you see it?" he asked.

"See what?"

"The caterpillars—they're like, shriveling."

Suddenly, I did see it! "Oh my God." Instead of the thriving, robust cats we'd been fighting, this bunch looked weakened, and yes, shriveled.

"And these guys don't really move much," John added. "They're not leaping away when you grab 'em, like they did before."

"Maybe that natural tree repellent really *is* working!" I said hopefully. At any rate, these shrunken specimens wouldn't add quite as much bulk to our caterpillar cemetery back in the woods. A square of ground that by now, despite my throwing a bucket of dirt over the decomposing remains, was a stinking, slimy mess.

In the coming days, John and I saw more and more shrively cats. As the numbers dropped off, and cocoons began to appear in the yard, something else was happening. John and I began to collect all the cocoons we came across. Upon further examination, instead of a healthy-looking pupa inside, we were finding dried-up, dead material—something that obviously *used* to be a caterpillar.

With even more hope in my heart, I said to John, "Maybe this *is* the third year."

"Maybe," he echoed.

I knew he was feeling the same thing I was. If this year wasn't the last year of the plague, neither of us knew how we could stand to go through this gruesome experience three summers in a row.

44 🐛 Plague Aftermath

Shortly after our cocoon discovery, John and I had the neighbors over for a block party potluck. We gathered under the plum tree that the cats had completely defoliated, but the tree had actually started pushing out buds again. Our small group talked of nothing but caterpillars: Roberta's apple trees had had every last leaf eaten; Jake and Barb's blueberry crop had been decimated; another neighbor had watched waves of caterpillars crawl over her grass and completely destroy her raspberry crop.

"I had to sweep our patio several times a day," reported Kay. Our newest neighbors, she and her husband Henry had recently built a gorgeous custom house down the hill, as their vacation home. (If this is your second home, I'd wondered privately, how big and grand is your first?) "I just couldn't stand it anymore," Kay went on, "so we're going to spray."

I didn't ask if they would be spraying Bt or old-fashioned pesticide. I didn't want to know. If they chose the route of chemical warfare, nothing I could say would change their minds.

At least they lived a half-mile away. Hopefully our own resident bees and birds wouldn't be affected.

Ever since early spring, when John and I had commenced our caterpillar battle royale, the garden had been sorely neglected.

The grass and weeds that made up our "lawn" were already sprouting seed heads, long overdue for a date with John's weed-eater. And we had so much to catch up on: weeding and planting and harvesting. The nursery starts we'd bought in late spring were still in their pots and root-bound, barely alive. Some I got into the ground, some I ended up tossing. What mattered was that we'd kept our trees and permanent plantings healthy enough for this year's crops.

Healthy doesn't necessary mean beautiful, though. I picked quarts of blueberries scarred by the cats noshing on them. Unable to bring myself to eat them fresh—I still hadn't recovered from the repugnant task of picking cats off my berries—the damaged ones went into berry sauce. The apple harvest was a few weeks away—and like the berries, any chewed-on apples could be cooked.

One long-delayed chore was also the hardest. It had been over a year since the chickens were killed. Neither John nor I had been inside the safety zone or even the chicken pen since he'd retrieved their torn-up corpses two days after the attack. By now, the weeds in the compound were taller than I was.

Thinking of how all those weed seeds would sprout around the yard, I was spurred into action. John tackled the exercise yard while I took on the hen "hidey-hole" he'd created alongside the woodsheds. It was sad, finding many more feathers. And tearing weeds out of the still-decomposing lumps of chicken manure wasn't the most fun job I'd done lately. Still, after you've hand-picked thousands of caterpillars, your gross-out threshold is so much higher.

Reaching down to clip yet another thimbleberry root in the tunnel, I drew away, revolted. On the ground lay a decomposing opossum skeleton.

"Oh, yuck!" I said to John. "I'll bet it's been here for months." The tail was still intact.

"Once it got in, it probably couldn't figure out how to get out," said John.

After I carted my pile of weeds and bits of possum off to the woods, I fetched a saw. The big leaf coppiced maple stump in the compound had suckers that were twelve feet tall by now, and I was determined to get this puppy under control. The hand saw was no match for rock-hard maple, though. John watched me for a moment, then disappeared, shortly returning with his Saws-All.

After John's quick demo, and a few minutes of hands-on guidance, I realized this was a power tool I could love. The vibrations made the saw hard to handle, but I stuck with it. By the end of the day we had a tidy chicken run. But with our safety zone untouched, and choked with weeds, our place was far from ready for a another flock.

"Maybe we can save that mess for another day," I said to John.

He only nodded. He, like I, still wasn't ready to go in there. Into our hen's graveyard.

Once the hen compound muck-out was finished, I felt like we'd come out of the other side of...*something*. A major shift in our lives—one that meant my husband and I were...well, *safe* now. Maybe at this point, like the song says, John and I were somewhere over the rainbow. Ready to start a new phase at Berryridge Farm.

Yet despite our relief that the caterpillar plague was over, and occupied with a full plate of chores, John and I still felt the niggling anxiety about next spring. Would we see yet another infestation?

PART III

Reaching for the Light

And when we find ourselves in the place just right...
—From "Simple Gifts"

45 ☎ Taking a Risk

It was John who came up with a cure for our post-caterpillar funk.

Musical Healing

Like Sue, regrouping from our second caterpillar plague, I was sort of searching for a new chapter to my life. When I had some free time, I'd check YouTube for musical talent, a habit I'd gotten into in Phoenix, while taking care of my son. One day, I discovered a video featuring a family band of twelve kids, all accomplished singers, musicians, and dancers—The Willis Clan. They performed a mix of Irish tunes with bluegrass and country, and every kid old enough to play an instrument—from tweens to early twenties—could play several. Fiddle, guitar, bass, mandolin, keyboards, accordion, percussion, not to mention Irish bodhran drum and uilleann pipes, you name it, they played it. The breadth of their talent was really off the charts: the oldest six of the Clan also placed or even won national Irish step dance and swing competitions! I was so impressed I had to purchase their two albums and download several more of their YouTube videos.

Checking out The Willis Clan website, I discovered the band was selling tee-shirts with their logo. Wanting to further support these kids, I ordered a shirt. Looking around the site a little more, I learned The Willis Clan had a big fan base in Ireland—and it was at that moment I got a wild, improbable idea. After all the wear and tear on our bodies and spirits these last two years, Sue and I needed an adventure in the worst way—but would she ever be game to go for this one?

One summer evening, after we came in from the garden, John turned on his computer. A few minutes later he called out, "Sue! I've got something to show you!"

Hearing a smile in his voice, a rarity in the last few months, I hurried to his office. I knew John been looking into The Willis Clan, his new musical find. The other day, he'd shown me one of their videos, and I was quite taken by these fresh-faced Irish-American kids and their Irish-bluegrassy sound. As I came in, John opened an email. "I just heard back from the kids' mom—she thanked me for my tee-shirt order."

"Wow," I said. "That's a personal touch you don't see much these days."

John beamed. "Read this."

I wanted to let you know, she'd written, *that we'll be doing a fan tour in Ireland next June.* On the screen was a link to the tour details.

"A fan tour?" I asked.

"Yeah," said John. "A band will go on a concert tour and invite their fans to travel along. You get to ride the bus with them, and go to all their shows. The Willis Clan is doing one."

"Um…that's nice." I wasn't sure what John was getting at.

"Hang on—didn't you see? Their fan tour is going to be in *Ireland*," John said, and clicked on another link. "Look! They're going to the *west* of Ireland! That's where your books are set, right?"

I looked at the computer screen, featuring breathtaking photos of the Emerald Isle, and another group shot of the twelve beautiful kids. You'd think the combination of youth, lively music and the chance to see John's and my ancestral home would make this trip a no-brainer. But this was me we were talking about, the Queen of the Homebodies. "Um…yes," I said slowly. "County Galway."

"Well?" He looked at me expectantly.

"You mean, you actually want to go? On the *tour*?"

"Why not?" John looked more animated than I'd seen him for

a long time. "You could do research for your books!"

John is typically very cagey about expressing his preferences. He'd done this all our married life—always sort of scoping out how I felt about this or that, before jumping in with what he wanted to do. For him to come right out, and *almost* say, *Yes, I want to do this tour!* was quite a departure. Besides, my husband (who hadn't traveled abroad since a trip to Japan in his thirties) wanting to go to Europe was a bit of a freaker, as the Irish would say.

"But...how much does it cost?" Since I was no traveler, I didn't even have a passport. As far as going anywhere...sure, I'd gotten past my fear of flying, visiting LA. But traveling across the Atlantic? Being away from my home routines all that time? And most importantly, being separated from Berryridge Farm?

John clicked on the price link. "Look—it's not that much."

"It's over three thousand dollars!" I protested. "For *each* of us!" *And since when do we have the budget for jet-setting to Europe?*

"I could pay for it." John had some savings.

"No," I said immediately. "I'd never let you do that." I'd been saving a chunk of my book royalties—I had the money.

"If you did book research, you could declare the trip as a business expense," John added. "But we'll have to decide soon—the deadline for the deposit is coming up."

It was true, I *had* dreamed of going to Ireland. *Someday.* I wasn't at all ready, though, to turn an idle daydream into reality. "I'll...have to think about it."

That evening, we took a long walk together. His eyes bright, John talked about the tour: the historical sites we'd see, the band's live concerts we'd get to attend. And how about this serendipity: the itinerary included visiting the Browne clan's ancestral home in County Mayo!

"You won't believe this," John told me. "We'd also go to the village where 'The Quiet Man' was filmed!"

My all-time favorite Irish movie, I thought wistfully. "But... there's the new grandbaby." My daughter's due date was this coming February, six months away. "What if the kids need us?"

"The baby will be four months old by the time we'd leave," John pointed out. "And if there's some emergency, we'll deal with that if it comes up."

"What about the garden?" I asked. "The strawberries?" June was the most intense, all-hands-on-deck month at Berryridge Farm. It was not only strawberry season, but prime planting, weeding and tending time. How could I miss that?

"We'll be gone less than two weeks," John said. "The garden will still be here when we get back." He was silent for a moment. "I realize this trip means we can't get chickens next spring."

Chickens. I hadn't thought of that. "So, we'll have to put that off another year."

"Yeah," he said. "We'll still get hens, just later than we planned."

John could be really relaxed about the future. If we had a lousy apple harvest, or a crop failure, he'd say easily, *there's always next year*. It may be the Irish in me or something, but I could be really superstitious. I got anxious about counting on things going the way you planned them. As in, what if something terrible happens, and our lives are completely different next year?

What if our county's volcano blows? Or that zombie apocalypse we keep hearing about finally occurs, and we're not *here* next year?

Once again, I was looking for trouble. I knew John was right, we could always get hens another time, only I couldn't help myself. "You've forgotten about the caterpillars. Remember the three-year cycle? What if they're back next summer? And worse than ever?"

"That's a big 'if,'" said John. "And if we did lose some crops, it wouldn't be the end of the world."

I knew he wasn't being cavalier about our place. Simply stating a fact. Still, I couldn't help thinking, what if we did leave home next June, and when we returned, found our place stripped bare?

Then John said gently, "We can't live our whole lives, worrying about what might happen. Sometimes you just have to take a chance. Just go for it."

I nodded. "I still have to think about this."

John had never pressured me to do anything. I often had to coax him to make a simple request. This Ireland trip was different. I could see he *really*, truly wanted to go.

If I refused, asked him to forget it, I knew it could risk our relationship. Was I so nervous about leaving home, so unwilling to try something so new that I'd turn down an experience like traveling to Ireland?

And in doing so, was I ready to say, *Okay, John...go ahead, and I'll stay home?*

Two weeks later, John and I were at the county courthouse. John was renewing his passport, while I was applying for my first one ever.

It was the thought of John taking the trip without me that persuaded me to sign on. I paid my share of the trip deposit, thinking, *It's only three hundred dollars. Something could happen to keep us from going. I can live with losing a few hundred bucks.*

Our travel plans became more real when I was writing our checks to the county clerk. Application fees, service charges. It's not wasted money, I told myself. If we don't make it to Ireland, we had friends in Canada—once I had my passport, we could actually visit them!

Anyway, I was thinking as we left the courthouse, *a lot could happen in the next ten months.*

46 🐦 Process of Elimination

Actually, something did happen a week later—and it wasn't good.

One early morning, I was gazing out the kitchen window at the garden, as I do each day. Scuttling around the strawberry beds, only to disappear behind the stack of pots near the shop, was a critter that John and I had never seen anywhere *near* our place.

"Oh *no*," I wailed. A *rat*.

Why was I shocked? After all, I'd been keeping our bucket of kitchen scraps next to the shop man door, only a few feet away from my rat sighting. I'd also seen a few animal droppings on the floor of the shop. Wait—to be honest, I'd seen a *lot* of them. And in my heart of hearts, I knew these black bits were too big to be mouse poo. So I sort of *pretended* not to see them. Or when I did, I sort of *pretended* they couldn't possibly be the mouse alternative. Rats were something I simply wasn't ready to deal with, only a few weeks after our second caterpillar plague.

The other reason I should have seen this coming: the shop was a *wreck*. We hadn't swept the place out since before John's mom passed away. Now, the building was filled to the rafters. Besides John's tools, building and handyman supplies, the shop was packed with the aforementioned scads of family mementoes and furniture John had brought from his mom's house.

The shop also held stacks of items purchased for projects we'd never found time to start: a supply of solar lights to set along our pathways, installing the drip irrigation system for one of our blueberry patches, and assembling a kit for a vegetable storage rack. The shop also held other objects whose time had come and gone— like the fifty pounds of pasture grass seed, stored in a plastic garbage bin, that we'd purchased to create a ranging area for our chickens. Also in the bin was a sack of organic chicken feed we still had a year after the hens had been killed. With this mound of paraphernalia, even a simple chore like sweeping seemed overwhelming.

Now that I'd spied a real, live rat, however, only a few feet from the house, I knew my denial days were over. With a fire in my eye, I told John what I'd seen.

"I'm not surprised," he said with his usual Browne serenity. "Wherever people go, rats generally follow."

I was in no mood to be philosophical. "How can you be so calm about having rats so close by?" I was still shaking in disgust.

He shrugged. "They're just part of life." He was quiet for a moment. "While we had chickens, they probably kept a lot of critters out of our yard."

I thought of the possum remains I'd found. With our Ireland trip next summer, John and I had no chance of getting hens for almost two years. If we managed it at all. "We have *got* to clean out the shop."

John agreed with me. (He usually does, bless his cotton socks.) "We'll get around to it," he said. "In the meantime, I'll put up a hook so we can hang the compost bucket—no more keeping it on the ground."

"That would be great," I said, relieved. Why hadn't I thought of that a long time ago? "But cleaning the shop?"

"I know, we've got to do it. First, though, I have to..." John reeled off a long list of tasks that had a higher priority: Weed-eat the yard. Split firewood. Install the roof on his new shed before the fall rains hit. "Before I tackle all that, I need to make a trip to town to buy that generator."

John and I had been talking about getting a second generator for *years*. Having a power source for the house and shop, not only the pumphouse, would be one less worry during protracted outages. Still, yet another piece of equipment would crowd the shop even more.

Before I could point that out, I saw a determined glint in his eye. "Right after I get that compost bucket up," he said, "we're going to take out those fruit trees we decided on."

I had to admit, all of these tasks were important. It also struck me that maybe John wasn't ready to deal with his family's memorabilia. All those keepsakes had to be a stark reminder of the mother and sister he'd recently lost, and the family home that was gone.

I wasn't ready, though, to take on the shop by myself. The fruit tree removal that John and I always did together was an unsavory enough job.

We had several trees in the yard that were barely hanging on. It made no sense to prune trees every spring that weren't bearing, plus water them during the dry season when I was already anxious about our water supply. And now that John and I might be looking at a third caterpillar plague, it would be a complete waste of energy to pick cats off trees that simply weren't earning their keep.

Previously, John and I had girded our loins to take out the two blighty apricots, the two European pears, and the half-dead heirloom apple tree. It was time to finish off the other wastrels. Down came the small plum tree afflicted with black knot fungus. The Ashmeads Kernal heirloom apple had shown few signs of life for the last few years, and the only fruit this tree had ever produced was so scabby and deformed even un-picky John wouldn't eat it. So it had to go too.

He decided one of our three Asian pears, crowding out its neighbor, had no place in the yard either. "The fruit just doesn't taste good," he said. "It almost tastes…bad." Interestingly enough, not even the tent caterpillars had eaten the fruit.

With this renovation of sorts, our orchards felt more open. Maybe with better circulation and room to grow, our remaining trees would be more productive.

I busied myself with all the weeding and harvesting of late summer—watering went a bit faster with three fewer trees to tend. The fungus-laden monster plum in the middle of the yard still had to be dealt with. But after this last winnowing project, plus five months straight of taking down the woods to battle caterpillars, John and I were so very sick of killing trees.

Facing the fact that we were not going to have chickens in the foreseeable future, one Saturday afternoon we loaded our sack of hardly-touched layer feed into the Ranger and headed to the village mom-and-pop store. We were acquainted with one of the clerks, and knew she had a small flock. As a single mom with two little kids, her budget had to be pretty tight.

As luck would have it, the young woman, who had cropped hair and a definite "earth-muffin" (John's expression) vibe, was working checkout that day. "We've got some extra feed around, but we won't have chickens for a while," John told her. "Would you take it off our hands?"

Her smile widened. "Oh, thank you so much!"

"We're happy the feed will get used," I said. "It's organic too."

"I share my eggs with a lot of people, but they've never contributed any feed," she said with a resigned look. She fetched her keys so we could load the sack into her car.

Once home, John and I moved the plastic bin we'd stored the feed in to one of the woodsheds—the grass seed still inside, waiting for a pasture. True to his word about the compost scrap bucket, John installed that hook on one of the beams in his cutting shed and got the bucket out of reach. I didn't see another rat. But as the weeks passed, what I did see was an increasing amount of rat droppings on the shop floor.

47 🐌 A Forest and a Fairy Tale

As late summer turned to fall, I put aside my concerns about forsaking Berryridge Farm for Ireland. I had bigger things to worry about. My pregnant daughter was having frequent Braxton-Hicks contractions in her second trimester—upping the risk for a premature baby. Visits and phone calls and prayers alleviated some of my anxiety; still, it was a nerve-wracking time.

Closer to home, one early morning I had yet another development to wring my hands over: a new racket started up in the neighborhood.

Chainsaws.

This logging operation was much closer than the last one—a short distance down our private lane, on the far side of our neighbors' Jake and Barb's place. The crew would start at daylight, and for hours, the buzzing was relentless. By mid-afternoon, the saws would finally be silent, about the time I'd go for my bike ride. It was heartbreaking to see more open space each day, where a mature forest used to be. The loggers were fast. Within a couple of weeks, the entire tract was clear-cut.

Then the excavators moved in to load the logs onto trucks, grinding away by the hour, the roar of equipment ringing in my ears long after they'd quit for the day. "It could be worse," I said to John, when the din had me feeling crazed. "This clear-cut could be happening in the summer, when we're outside all day."

When the site had been quiet for a few days, John and I hiked the short distance to the edge of the clear-cut. Just inside the tract's boundary lay a hemlock, its trunk nearly four feet wide, its needles turning rust-red.

Although I'd studied forestry in college, writing a major term paper on the effects of logging on an ecosystem, I'd never actually been in a fresh clear-cut. And before me was acres of one—at least fifty, I guessed.

Like I said before, I wasn't against cutting trees. Selective logging could be good for a woodland, providing more space, sunshine and nutrients for the remaining trees. Keeping the ecosystem healthy, I felt you could preserve the spirit of the forest, and hopefully most of the creatures in it. Not so with clearcutting. Now, as I gazed at the devastation around me, a snarl of dead trees and brush, I could feel the essence of the forest, its very soul, was gone. Nothing but emptiness.

You can dismiss all these mystical musings as the ramblings of a tree-hugger, and I suppose it is. But I wanted, in some way, to bring the soul back to this place.

Talking with the neighbors, John and I discovered that since the logging started, they, like we, had seen more wildlife out in the open: Owls, bear, and one neighbor had two cougar sightings within days of each other. The day before, I'd laid eyes on the first skunk I'd ever seen in the Foothills.

Carefully backing away before the skunk could see me, I realized what happens when you take down a forest—all the creatures in it have to find new homes. The memory of the fairy movie John and I had watched the previous Christmas piqued my imagination: what if there are more kinds of forest "wildlife" than we could ever know? And with that, a thought crystalized: What if a band of woodland fairies live in a forest, and the trees get cut down?

My daughter Meghann's contractions were getting so frequent her friends and her sister Carrie made a spur-of-the-moment decision: they would move up the baby shower to mid-December. Meghann and her fiancé Matt were making plans for a quiet, no-family courthouse wedding, but the prospective bride was game for a pre-baby celebration.

A couple of weeks before Christmas, Carrie, granddaughter Megs and I headed down to Astoria for the party. Carrie's a total extrovert, the kind of girl who can balance marriage, a high-level career, raise a wonderful, well-adjusted teenager, and keep up with a huge circle of friends and extended family. Naturally she could plan the baby shower, purchase and pack a carload of party favors, then make a whirlwind weekend trip with one hand behind her back. (I generally just stand back in awe.)

Held at one of Astoria's boutique hotels, the party was great fun. Lots of happy faces and kids gamboling around. One of Meghann's devoted girlfriends had gifted her with a "diaper cake." It's constructed to resemble a tall, layered wedding cake, only it's made with Huggies!

On the way home, as I reflected on the precious moments I'd had with my grandchildren, my nebulous ideas about fairies in the woods began coming together. I was currently working on my novel about the Irish city girl who dreamed of a farm, and was reluctant to set it aside. Previously, whenever bits and pieces of a story would come to me, I would generally jot them down, and wait for the right moment to work them into a book. But as Christmas drew closer, this fairy notion took hold of my imagination like no other had before. I set my novel aside and threw myself into my kids' story with abandon.

The approaching holiday turned into The Christmas That Wasn't. John and I like to make a big deal out of the season, with rituals that we look forward to all year. Before I started my new book, we managed to get a tree up, but as this story grabbed me, I went on an unprecedented writing binge, banging on the keyboard for hours each day. Holiday cards went unwritten and baking went undone. The book was finished in six days, and after John proofread it, I gave my fairy tale its final polish.

To my own amazement, on Christmas Eve, I finished *The Mystery of the Christmas Fairies*, and posted it online. This second story featuring my young heroine Morgan was about memory and family. Experiencing hair-raising adventures in a magical forest, she had found the strength and confidence to avert a devastating fate, aided by her three young, spunky cousins. Not coincidentally, this courageous trio bore an uncanny resemblance to our LA grandchildren!

My haste proved to be my undoing. Christmas Day, I discovered a major error in the book file. Due to a software glitch, most of the story was missing! Mortified, I pulled the book offline, and fixed it immediately. But this experience did bring one point home. I take it back: Two points.

Good things come to those who wait. And when you're used to the Slow Life, you are so much better off *not* rushing.

48 ☞ The Blob and The Baby

They called it "The Blob."

Soon after the holidays, meteorologists identified an extensive mass of unusually warm water in the Pacific Ocean. It was the cause, the experts said, of the Pacific Northwest's unseasonable winter temperatures.

In the Foothills, most clear weather in January is accompanied by a frigid Northeaster. This winter, we had sunny days that reached over 60 degrees. Both our generators were gathering dust; John had no reason to fire up the new one he'd bought a few months ago. Although I was enjoying my garden chores on such pleasant days, I couldn't help feeling uneasy, seeing new leaves emerge from the strawberry crowns. All this warmth and growth simply wasn't *natural*.

John and I had recently mailed in the rest of our money for our Ireland tour package. I'd written the check with definite trepidation, but like it or not, there was no going back. The warm weather was foreboding for another reason: without any super-cold spells that might impact the caterpillar's life cycle, I was imagining the potential for yet another explosion.

On the other hand, not having any snow or ice to worry about definitely came in handy one January evening when we got *the* phone call. It was Carrie. "Meghann's pains are every ten minutes," she said. "Megs and I are leaving for Astoria right now."

"Oh—right!" I'd been on edge for weeks—every time the phone rang my heart would start pounding. Now, I began shaking from nerves. "John and I will get out of here as soon as we can."

Given Meghann's unrelenting pre-labor contractions the last months, we all expected the baby to be early, and I had done some preliminary packing. Still, I just didn't *feel* ready! After throwing the rest of my kit together (John can completely pack for a trip in about ten minutes—something that takes me several hours), we hit the road.

We'd never set off for Astoria this late before—six-and-a-half hour journey. Luckily, John's experience in law enforcement had made him a stellar night driver. Meanwhile, my stomach was churning all the way down I-5, as I fretted that we wouldn't arrive in time. Meghann had last given birth eight years ago, to our grandson Rowan—was there such a thing as being out of practice?

And most worrisome, coming more than three weeks early, would the baby be all right?

We pulled into our Astoria lodgings around 2:30 am, and groggily checked in. Carrie was still awake, though our granddaughter Megs was stretched out on the bed, fast asleep. "You're not going to believe this, but the pains stopped," she said ruefully as she hugged me. Rowan had pulled the same trick—we'd raced down the highway for the birth, only to cool our heels for days while our little guy took his sweet time showing up.

"At least we didn't miss anything," I said. After saying goodnight, John and I headed for our room.

After I'd written the ginormous check for our Ireland tour, it pained me a bit to be staying in an expensive hotel, hanging out while our grandbaby was in no rush. After two days, Carrie, with great reluctance, decided she couldn't miss any more work. Nor could Megs have any more school absences on her report card. Naturally, a couple of hours after they arrived in Seattle, Meghann was in heavy labor.

Carrie jumped back in her car to head south again. John entertained our grandsons at our hotel while I stayed in the birthing room with our new son-in-law Matt. The baby didn't make us wait long. I was able to witness the miracle of a new life coming into the world. Flora, a perfect little fairy, arrived a bit after three in the afternoon. Her aunt Carrie had missed the birth by a half an hour.

Three days later, when it was time to go, I was in tears. This was the third time I'd had to leave my daughter with a newborn. This time, however, our very capable son-in-law Matt, a doting dad and former Marine, had the situation covered. And for all my grandmotherly anxiety, the baby thrived. The winter flew by with not one, but two visits from Flora and her proud parents. It seemed clear that I could go off to Ireland in June and this little family would do fine.

I didn't feel nearly as sanguine about leaving Berryridge Farm.

49 🐀 Ratatouille

The rat droppings in the shop had become too plentiful to ignore.

We'd always had mice in the shop. We accepted them, we lived with them, and John caught enough mice in his traps that we felt we had a semblance of a handle on the rodent population.

Not that I was okay with mice. I was a *really* tidy person before we moved out to the Boonies. In the years since, I learned a new trick: not the habit of tidying up, but being able to walk past a mess without my tidy gene having a spasm. I *got* that mice were part of country life. But this new rodent incursion turned my spasms into a full-on *fit*.

To me, rats were a whole 'nother story. As the winter weeks passed, I discovered another reason to freak out: you'd go into the shop, and actually hear the scampering of little feet over my head. The nerve of them!

A couple of years before, John had built a "catwalk" of sorts in the shop for storage, a rough, plywood platform under the ceiling. For easy access, we kept an aluminum ladder leaned up against it. The ladder had obviously given easy access to the catwalk for our friends the Ratatouilles too. To make sure they'd keep their distance, every time I entered the shop I'd bang the ladder, and the noise would get them running.

Before now, I'd comforted myself with the thought that the rats were only going inside the shop now and them to hang out, go potty in a warm spot, then head back outside where the food was. (All those delicious bits in the compost pile!) But I had to stop pretending—the vermin were getting downright brazen about invading our place.

In between working on my Irish novel, I found time to read *The Life-Changing Magic of Tidying Up*. In this self-help book, author Marie Kondo takes decluttering to an entirely new level. Her theme: because your possessions have a life of their own, getting rid of unwanted items releases energy you can put to better use. Okay, I could be on board with that. So magical or not, I was determined to organize the shop and clear it of rats in one fell swoop.

There is one, huge stumbling block to making decluttering magic happen on your homestead: country life, food gardening, and generally living closer to the land requires a ginormous amount of…stuff.

If you, like John and me, are running a small country place without benefit of a tractor, rototiller, or any other large, labor-saving equipment, you need a *lot* of hand tools. And when your husband is the purchaser/purveyor of your tool supply, you will find that he never met a tool of any kind he didn't like. Given that John and I were engaged in all kinds of homesteady activities—cutting and splitting wood, digging garden beds, clearing ground and cutting brush—my husband was of the firm opinion that we could find a need (or even invent one) for this or that tool: a new hatchet or splitting maul, cultivator, shovel or small garden implement. Whatever it took to at least *try* to keep up with our workload.

Yet profligate tool acquisition was no idle excuse for unnecessary shopping! Oftentimes, John and I worked our tools so hard we rendered them completely unusable—so off to the farm co-op he'd go to replace them.

There's so much more to the homestead life than tools, though. If you're not having enough trouble keeping your place tidy, there's the maintenance. For repairs and tweaks, you always find yourself needing a bit of wire, a length of rope or twine, a chunk of pipe, a piece of lumber, an unidentifiable thingummy, oh, how I could go on. So in addition to all your chores, you need to keep building more and more sheds to hold your stuff.

You may ask, how in the world did you get yourself into this mess? Well, the reason you have so much stuff is directly related to the # 1 Rule of Homesteading: you never, ever toss something out because you might *need* it…*Someday*.

Which goes along with the #2 Rule of Homesteading: you never, ever toss out a busted tool or broken piece of equipment because you might find the time to *fix* it…*Someday*.

If you're also married to an ardent hobbyist (say, a sportsperson, a woodworker, or keeper of the family archives) who's too busy to do these fun and useful activities but has many, many plans to tackle them when he or she has the time, you discover that on a homestead, *Someday* is a hotly anticipated date.

Yet, with our rat infestation, *Someday* had to happen soon. One late winter day, I hit critical mass. It coincided with a day I was brimming with the energy and motivation to take on this badly-needed job. I told John, "I'm cleaning up the shop."

"*Okaaay*," he said slowly. I think he realized the jig was up. You know, that jig of knowing that something you've been postponing forever is something you can no longer put off.

"It hasn't been swept since the septic backup," I said, to drive home my point. "You can help or not, but I won't be responsible for what happens to your things."

Of course that threat was one I'd never carry out, but I was desperate.

John nodded. If he was joining in only to protect his possessions, that was fine by me. I knew he didn't mind the rat poo as much as I did. However, I'd finally faced the fact that having so much of it around wasn't simply offending me in an aesthetic way. The droppings were also a health hazard, and you could get all kinds of illnesses just inhaling the dust around them. Now, after all this time, I resolved to make magic happen. Or at the very least, get the shop floor swept. Happily, my critical mass coincided with a rare afternoon of dry winter weather.

Dressed in my oldest work duds, sweatshirt hood pulled tight around my face, I folded an old muslin dishcloth in half to make a triangle, and tied it over my nose and mouth. It was a real fashion statement, for sure. John suited up as well, using a store-bought face mask. I martialed together as many black plastic garbage bags as I could find, and thus armed, we started moving bags, boxes and loose items out of the shop.

You never realize how much stuff you have until you actually lay hands on it. The area outside our man door quickly became impassable—time to start piling our possessions out into the driveway. Then I commenced The Big Sweep Out of Berryridge Farm.

Like Marie Kondo's tidying up book suggested, I tackled one area at a time. Haul the items from one spot, sweep the area, and before moving anything back into place, figure out what you can toss. Then you do the same for the space next to where you'd just cleaned, and so on. With all this shifting of paraphernalia, what John and I found was something neither of us had prepared for.

Nests were all over the shop. In every little hidey-hole, every corner, every nook and cranny. "Rat's nest" was the expression my parents used with my siblings and me when one of our bedrooms got really messy, as in, "Clean up this rat's nest!" I realized now, they couldn't have possibly seen a *real* rat's nest.

The nests were the strangest amalgam of every kind of material imaginable, stolen from all over the shop. Chunks of insulation, blue threads from a fraying tarp, bits of plastic, pieces of string (two rolls of cotton twine had mysteriously "disappeared" the previous summer—now we knew where they'd ended up). Most interestingly, and sadly, were the pieces of paper. Most of the paper in the nests had originated from the boxes of treasured books from John's childhood. Whole books shredded, including the covers. The destruction was unbelievable.

What was also surprising—and not in a good way—was the material they'd chew. Garbage bags, okay—they weren't all that thick, even if the plastic couldn't have tasted good. But heavy-duty Rubbermaid storage bins? Yep, even they had holes in them. Why the rats had gotten into them I had no idea, since the bins held piles old Christmas lights, neither chow nor nest ingredients. Apparently, rats are indiscriminate about what they like getting their teeth around.

Through that long day of moving and sweeping and organizing, I realized decluttering involves making a massive number of decisions. Keep an item or let it go? Toss the item in the trash, or if usable, give it away? De-cluttering alongside a partner who hates, I mean *hates* to get rid of his possessions wasn't easy. But three hours after dark, John and I had seven giant bags of trash lined up in the driveway, and a car full of giveaways. John's tools and stored lumber was newly organized, other items stacked neatly. Best of all, the floor was cleared of rat droppings.

Wait—the real best of all was that our marriage survived! Operation Ratatouille Elimination had been a major Berryridge Farm success.

50 🐀 Spring Cleaning 2.0

Mucking out the shop, I decided, had used up our tidying-up energy for the next five years.

Besides, this time of year, John and I didn't generally get anything major accomplished. At dusk, coming indoors with a long evening ahead, John and I would watch a video or two of The Willis Clan, the band we'd be touring Ireland with.

One day, when he was looking a little distracted, I figured he was daydreaming about our fan trip this June. But he surprised me. Two weeks after the shop-cleaning project, he announced, "That plum tree is coming out."

He was talking about our monster Japanese plum, the one smack dab in the middle of our garden. John had made this statement so many times before—especially last summer, when the caterpillars had devoured every single leaf—that I thought him saying it once again was only his familiar refrain: "We really should do _____" (fill in the blank). Still, when John pulled on his workclothes, armed himself with three saws and his big red loppers, and actually headed for the tree, I knew he was serious this time. That Godzilla was going.

While the plum provided the only shade in the yard and fruited like a champ, its downsides outweighed the upsides. This tree was unsightly—the black knot fungus John had cut away two seasons in a row had roared back. The fruit wasn't particularly sweet either, and each branch and twig was covered with extremely sharp thorns. The real problem with the tree, however, was that *it wouldn't stop growing*. It was about five times the size of every other fruit tree we'd planted the same year. Worst of all was its untrammeled expansion below the soil.

Suckers from the roots were showing up all over the yard. You'd try to pull them up, only to discover you couldn't budge them, and would have to dig down to clip the sucker from the feeder root. Suckers in your strawberries are one thing, but shoots emerging right next to your septic drain field are another. As John and I imagined the cost and inconvenience of roots infiltrating the field, rendering it ineffective, and having to install a new one...well, that, my friends, was where the rubber met the road.

Lopping off the main and secondary branches took John and me a couple of hours. After John cut down the trunk, he took on the stump and root mass—and we discovered our work had only begun: The largest roots stretched dozens of feet past the drip line of the tree. I stuck my spading fork in the ground to lever up the roots as John yanked on them. We cut roots and more roots and always found more. But by the time the sun was going down, John said, "I think we've gotten most of them."

"I just want to get this last one," I said, grunting as I pressed hard on the fork handle. John sighed, but obligingly pulled on the root I'd exposed. The final task was gathering up all the tree parts, then sanitize the loppers that we'd used around all that black knot.

Without the big plum tree, the yard definitely looked stark. But if the worst happened, and the caterpillars returned, they'd have one less tree attracting them into the yard.

In my Pollyanna way, I so wanted to think we'd never see a third plague.

I kept a death grip on that belief. Until one early spring day, when I walked down the driveway. Peering at the birch treetops, my heart dropped like lead in my chest. I spied what I hoped I never would: caterpillar egg sacs.

Not waiting for John, I grabbed one of his light saws and took down the smallest trunk of the coppice. I hadn't been mistaken—there were numerous sacs on the tree. I could no longer wait to call in the troops: "John!"

He suited up right away, and the two of us took an entire afternoon to take down the rest of the coppiced tree. John and I cut off the twigs that had sacs, then tackled another sickly-looking alder on the other side of the driveway. Yet I could tell John's heart wasn't in it. Not like last year, when he'd been a tree-cutting, cat-killing machine. He pointed to another coppice nearby, saying without enthusiasm, "Do you want to do that one too?"

Ready to say, "Yes, let's do 'em all!" I managed to hold my tongue.

I had to admit the truth: John and I were slowing down. I would be sixty this year, and John was seven years older. We were still running this place without any big equipment, trying to keep the brush and woods at bay by hand.

I took one look at my husband's face and said, "Well..." then gazed around the near woods. Two years in a row, we'd spent countless days, weeks and months taking down birch and alder trees, cutting out sacs or tents, and picking cats in hand-to-hand cat combat—time John and I would never get back. We still had so many trees. And at this moment, I was as sick of destroying trees as he was. Besides, I didn't know if either he or I had the "fire in the belly" to take on more months of clearing.

Okay, our Ireland trip was paid for—a done deal. Cats or no cats, I would be away for two weeks. If we *did* get an infestation, I wouldn't be around to do anything about it.

"No, we can let it go," I told him. At that moment, John's *que sera, sera* attitude had finally rubbed off on me. *What will be, will be.* "I think we're done."

51 ❧ Drought

As winter flowed into spring, "The Blob" was still at work in the Pacific Northwest. January through March had been so warm that copious rain, instead of snow, had fallen in the Cascade Mountains. In our state, people depend on a deep mountain snowpack, which, once it melts, will keep rivers and streams filled over the summer, and aquifers fed. But the backcountry of the Cascades looked bare. In our county, the glaciers on the majestic volcanic peak forty miles away were shrinking to an alarming degree. Here in the Foothills, instead of our usual drenching April rain and frequent 40-degree temperatures, days, even weeks passed without precipitation.

I published *The Hopeful Romantic*, my Irish novel about the city wife and mother who longs for a country place. With that project off my plate I had a lot more free time to fret about our bizarre weather. In early May, it was so dry I was watering the blueberry shrubs, a task that ordinarily isn't necessary until July.

While the blueberry plants looked a little worse for wear after two years of being attacked by caterpillars, the strawberry beds were in bad shape. During the winter, the crowns had apparently gotten a jump start, pushing new growth long before spring. But over the course of a few weeks, my best-bearing plants had curled up their toes. When John asked about the dying crowns at our go-to Foothills nursery, their gardening experts said lots of local growers had experienced the same thing. They thought the problem might be a virus—perhaps the kind that ordinarily gets frozen out over the winter, only we'd had no major freeze.

I wondered too, if the crowns had pushed out their buds too soon, and this growth had been too new and tender to withstand a few frosts. Whatever the cause of the dying plants, prospects for a decent crop didn't look promising.

On my bike ride one Sunday afternoon, about five miles from Berryridge Farm, I encountered a sign next to the road. *Eggs for Sale.*

The sign was attached to an expertly-constructed fence encircling a recently developed property. I'd been keeping my eye on this place for several months. After I'd seen a middle-aged couple regularly working around the acreage, I called them "The Boomer Homesteaders Down the Road."

These folks had created the kind of country paradise John and I could only dream of. After a "Sold" sign first appeared near a five acre field, within a few short months a structure materialized in the center of the parcel: a gorgeous brick, stick-built home with a *porch* (oh, if only I could have a porch, my life would be complete!). The owners quickly established a groomed lawn, and soon, as if by magic, appeared a small red barn, an orchard of a dozen trees, and rows of mature blueberry shrubs. Plus a mid-size tractor. *And*, creating a fresh stab of envy in my heart that the house, barn and tractor hadn't, a small flock of hens scratching next to the barn.

We'd been buying store eggs for the last year and a half, but John and I still craved farm eggs. And now, these neighbors were going into the egg business! I turned my bike onto the wooded lane leading to their property, ready to introduce myself and buy some farm eggs ASAP. Mounting the steps to their immaculate porch, I rang the doorbell. No answer. I peered around the place and called,

"Hello?" Nobody replied. Okay, the Boomers were clearly not home. I did see their name on the house, though, which gave me hope.

When I got home, I looked them up in the phone book. No one with that name was listed at that address. I vowed to try again, as soon as I could. But I never again found time to visit the house. The Boomer Homesteaders seemed to be away in the afternoons when I was biking, and busy with spring chores, I let farm eggs sort of drop off my list of priorities.

Water rose to the top of it. We—not only Berryridge Farm, but all over the Pacific Northwest—had what you call a "situation."

By May, the Foothills were experiencing significant heat waves. Normally, a mid-spring hot spell might entail 70 degrees, but temperatures were often in the 80s. Soils all over the state were losing moisture fast. The experts were calling the heat and lack of rain a drought, one like the region never had before. Farmers and growers in the eastern, drier part of the state were already losing crops due to lack of water. The forests were dry too, with forest fires breaking out shockingly early in the year.

Our apple trees were nearly bare of fruit—even our reliable, abundantly-bearing Akane had maybe ten apples on it. Had the winter been too warm? Or had the spring rains been insufficient? One day, I gazed at our orchard trees and garden beds that would need so much water over the growing season, my feeling of helplessness and fears for the future returning. Visiting John at his new shed, I asked him, "What if our well goes dry? Like it did our first year?"

He didn't look concerned. "Our well's forty feet deeper than it was then," he pointed out. "I'm sure things will be fine."

Well, what if they're not, I wanted to say. *What if we need to drill still deeper, and there's no water down there?*

I was doing it again, worrying about something that hadn't happened. Yet by the time June arrived, our usual "Junuary" weather (June + January) of ample rain and 60 degrees was nowhere to be found. Instead, it was day after day of clear skies and heat. This warmth and sunshine would be beneficial to our crops, but I was so anxious about our water supply I was getting kind of compulsive about it. Okay, full disclosure: I was obsessed with saving water—washing my hands beneath a mere trickle, minimizing toilet flushes, and taking shorter showers.

Outside, though, water conservation wasn't happening. With our newly-sprouted garden seeds, I had rows and rows of thirsty seedlings, and with all this freakish sun and heat they'd need a lot of water. With all my fretting, however, there was one problem I *wasn't* seeing: caterpillars. Still, my apprehension mounted. We were leaving for Ireland in a couple of weeks. What would we find when we returned?

The woods around Berryridge Farm exploded with greenery.

The caterpillars' defoliation the last two growing seasons had allowed more light to penetrate to our woodlands' underbrush. Overnight, it seemed, the thimbleberry was six feet tall, covering nearly every square foot of ground on the other side of our fence. Dwarfing the wild berries, brackenfern was growing like Jack's magical beanstalk in Mother Goose, with many ferns eight feet high. Tough-rooted native Indian plum sprouted all over the place. Under the onslaught, our paths and cleared areas outside our garden pretty much disappeared, the brush growing faster than we could cut it down. Slogging my way out to my compost pile was challenging, my bucket and shovel getting tangled in the mess of weeds.

John and his trusty Weed-Eater were no match for these plants on Nature's steroids. One hot afternoon, a few days before our Ireland departure, I was weeding in the shade next to the house. John had just plopped into a nearby lawn chair after a long session of weed-whacking. "One of these days," he said, "we're going to have to break down and get some kind of tractor."

We had talked about tractors before. Like, many times. A few months back, one had almost dropped into our laps. Our neighbor, the veritable hermit who'd so kindly plowed our road years ago when we were snowbound, was selling his place. He talked to John and offered his tractor for $10,000.

It was a good deal—our neighbor's John Deere had only a few hundred hours on it. (Large equipment use is measured in hours the engine has run, not miles like a car.) The tractor wasn't one of those huge farm models that take up an entire lane of road pavement, but plenty big for mowing a hayfield, or plowing up some acreage. When John and I discussed the tractor, he admitted, "It's way bigger than we need. And where would we keep it?"

The decision had made itself. Another neighbor couple, Henry and Kay, were doing some major landscaping around their McMansion. Henry had recently bought a Kubota riding lawn mower, but after a few days, he discovered it was way too small for what he needed to do. While John was out walking one day, Henry nabbed him and offered us the mower. For nothing. Nada.

Naturally, John thanked him, profusely. Hurrying home, he told me about Henry's proposal. "The mower's brand new."

"Wow," I said. "But I'm hearing a *but* in your voice."

Besides the fact John and I felt *really* strange accepting such a valuable piece of equipment for free, our yard was laid out in such a way that there wasn't room for a riding lawn mower. "Henry's machine just isn't big enough," John had pointed out. "Not for all the projects we want to do."

Now, kneeling near John, I yanked on a dandelion going to seed. Our dilemma reminded me of our shovels. We had a Daddy Bear shovel, a Mama Bear, and Baby Bear. In terms of tractors, the Daddy Bear and Baby Bear sizes on offer simply weren't a fit. We needed a Mama Bear machine.

"What about maintenance?" I asked John. "Having to keep up a piece of equipment we won't use that much seems like a waste of money." I hesitated. "And there's our trip..." We'd pretty much cleaned out our savings for our Ireland visit.

"You're right," said John. "I guess it'll be awhile before we can spring for the kind of tractor I have in mind."

John and I were back at square one. And fighting the weeds severely under-weaponed.

Every time we go on one of our rare sojourns away from home, I vow to be *super* organized: finish up last-minute packing and chores in the afternoon, get dinner at a reasonable hour, and head to bed early. Admittedly, I generally miss the mark, but the night before I was leaving on the biggest, most arduous journey of my life, I was pathetically off-schedule.

As the evening waned, I postponed dinner to inspect the strawberry beds, and felt a few sprinkles begin to fall. This year's crop was tiny, compared to all the berry-fests of previous Junes. Despite the slim pickin's, it was hard for me to let go of our harvest—the few berries that would ripen while we were away would get eaten by the critters, not us.

John had a meeting in town, and wasn't around to gently scold me about finishing up the yard work. So there I was, still outside despite the shower, giving the berries and vegetable beds a drink in the near-dark. It was after 10:30 pm when I stumbled inside.

I realized that being so disorganized, I was resisting our Ireland visit. Even at the eleventh hour, I was indulging in my deep-down, secret hope that something would keep us home. Yet I really did want to take this trip. Too bad I couldn't get myself into some kind of wormhole, and see the place I'd been dreaming of for years, while simultaneously staying home! However, I'd already started a fourth novel, featuring the heroine of my last story, *The Hopeful Romantic,* and her new life on a little Irish farm. I reminded myself that visiting a *real* farm in Ireland—our tour itinerary included spending an afternoon at a large sheep operation—would be the inspiration to make this new book really sing.

At that moment, shucking off my workclothes in the dim light, I took a page from John's playbook: I told myself we'd be gone less than two weeks, and everything would be okay. If the worst happened, whatever that was—heat waves, seedlings burned to a crisp, even caterpillars—we could deal with it. Like we'd managed to do with every other challenging situation we'd encountered.

Still, I hardly slept that night.

52 ❧ A New Land

Less than forty-eight hours later we landed in Dublin, in a misty, chilly Irish dawn. Bedtime back in the Pacific Northwest. My eyes gritty from the sleepless night on the plane, I gazed in wonderment at the horse pasture on one side of the runway, and the green hills a stone's throw from the tarmac—a scene so different from the hundreds of acres of heavy industry that surrounded most big airports in the U.S. Yet John and I had no time to contemplate the landscape. We groggily trundled into the tour bus with our fellow Willis Clan tour attendees, and began our long-awaited adventure.

I was exhausted and overstimulated, and we'd only just arrived. But my fried brain proved to be an advantage. Every thought or concern about our little place back in the Foothills completely flew out of my mind.

My first and most startling discovery about Ireland was how much it looked like home—only with grassy, sheep-covered hillsides instead of deep green firs. To my surprise, I found wild blackberries growing along the sidewalks, like you find all over the Northwest, and across the green vistas of rolling fields, there were large stands of evergreens too. Joe, our tour guide, was a sociable Irishman who was short in stature but long on personality. He sort of resembled a life-sized leprechaun. Joe began his tourist-y patter with a question. "Hey guys," he called from behind the wheel. "D'you know what George Bernard Shaw said about Ireland?"

"No," chorused we bus riders.

"It's the largest open air asylum in the world," Joe deadpanned.

We all laughed heartily. Clearly, Irish people took a perverse pride in their eccentric reputation. But as Joe continued talking about Irish history and culture, he mentioned that he'd grown up on a farm. I'd have yet another source for my book research! I turned to John. "You know, Honey, I think this trip was meant to be!"

My second big discovery: Ireland is basically an agricultural country. In a nation of four million people, there are more dairy cows in Ireland than people living in Dublin! Pork raising is *big*, and sheep outnumber humans by a ratio of four-to-one. I soon observed that outside its largest city, Ireland looks like one gigantic sheep pasture, only broken up by homes and small towns.

The country has a northerly latitude, around 55 degrees, the same as the Canadian province of Newfoundland. But similarly to the Pacific Northwest, where the Pacific ocean keeps the climate mild on the west side of the Cascades, warm Atlantic currents keep Ireland's weather cool and rainy, yet rarely cold. The climate's a lot like the Foothills in April, only year-round.

In mid-June, when we arrived, it appeared that farmers had recently finished haying—every farmyard was full of the big round plastic-wrapped bales you see in the U.S. Only in Ireland, the plastic is black instead of white. "The black plastic keeps crows from pecking holes in the bale," said Joe. "Once you get a hole in 'em, the whole bale will spoil."

Fascinated, I scribbled this information in my notebook, thinking of my farm-themed novel. But after being up all night (nodding off on an international flight for a few minutes does *not* count as sleep!), I was getting hungry. In a jet-lagged, nauseated kind of way. More to the point, I needed some caffeine. Luckily, the tour's first official stop was at hand: Racket Hall Country House in County Offaly.

I stumbled into the medieval-looking dining room, complete with a gigantic stone fireplace, desperate for a cup of hot, sweet tea. Of course there was tea—I mean, this was Ireland!—but I could never have dreamed up the plentitude of chow laid out before me: the Full Irish Breakfast.

I'd first heard of the Irish fry long ago: the meal includes eggs and meat, with some mushrooms and tomatoes tossed into the frying pan. But Ireland's traditional breakfast is so much more than that. Whether you're a carnivore, an omnivore, or vegetarian, there's something for everyone. And all I can say is, you've got to see it to believe it.

For the Racket House's FIB, I found scrambled and fried eggs, rashers (it's Irish bacon that actually looks like ham, but is much saltier, according to John), pork sausage, grilled mushrooms and halved tomatoes, and white and black pudding, the generous portions served up by a smiley, hair-netted Irish gal. But to clarify the term "pudding": Lest you anticipate spooning up some nice vanilla and chocolate dessert with your eggs and meat, you need to know that these puddings aren't a sweet.

I'd read about the white and black Irish delicacy, so I had a general idea what I was dealing with. For the uninitiated—count me in, because I never did take a bite of either—both puddings consist of a mix of um…animal products, bread crumbs, flour and spices stuffed into casings…i.e., pig's intestines. For "white" pudding, the meat is pork belly, plus pig organs. For "black," there's no meat at all—you use pig's blood. If you want to check out a recipe, Irish chef Darina Allen's *The Forgotten Skills of Cooking* has directions for making both puddings from scratch. Darina's serving suggestion: cut your pudding into slices and pan fry in butter or bacon fat, and eat with bread and more butter.

If you're a somewhat persnickety eater (guilty), you may find this dish bizarre. Simply *thinking* about eating it may render you a bit queasy. But if it makes you feel better, Darina's recipe calls for a free-range, freshly slaughtered organic pig. Not feeling better? Me neither. Anyway, the Racket House array included far more than the items coming off the grill. The place also had a table with a toaster and three kinds of bread: what the Irish call brown bread, molasses bread you could cut in whatever size you wanted, and sliced white bread, with loads of butter for spreading.

A big pot of porridge sat on yet another table—steel-cut oats cooked into mush—and an assortment of cold cereal with cartons of non-fat milk. Also available were bowls of prunes, non-fat fruit yogurt, three kinds of juice, and coffee and tea. The meal was buffet-style—all you can eat. Needless to say, I felt a bit pukey from jet-lag, so I had to limit myself to a cup of tepid tea, a few bites of scrambled eggs, and a piece of brown bread. This wholegrain soda bread, another Irish specialty, turned out to be super-yummy, and also helped settle my stomach.

Then it was time to get back to the bus—we were off to Killarney, the Tourist Capital of Ireland!

Like the Foothills in June, Ireland was awash in wildflowers. Wild fuchsia was in bloom, a splash of rich red in the hedgerows, along with pink and white foxglove; thistle and heather created a light purple sheen on the hillsides. And like you'd find in the woodlands around Berryridge Farm, birch trees, mountain ash, holly and even brackenfern were everywhere.

As our tour bus cruised at a stately pace toward County Kerry— Irish motorway speeds are quite modest, and country roads are so narrow and twisty-turn-y that you can't go must faster than twenty miles per hour—I realized my first impression of "one gigantic sheep pasture" was slightly inaccurate. Ireland is actually one big pasture dotted by ancient stone ruins of every kind: Towers, churches, castles and abbeys; monk's "beehive" dwellings, cottages and ring forts. Everywhere you look is a reminder of antiquity, and a past that is still entirely present.

Along with our fellow Willis Clan tour participants, John and I spent the afternoon meandering around Killarney National Park. With its lush woods, full of brackenfern and rhododendron, the place resembled the Foothills so closely that for a while, I felt I'd never left home. The sensation was quickly shattered once I entered the town of Killarney, right next to the park, bustling with tourists. The sidewalks were so swarmed with people you often had to step into the street to proceed.

Accustomed to the silence and solitude back at home, I soon realized the noise and crowds required a different mindset. Happily, when John and I attended our first Willis Clan concert that night, their show of rollicking Irish tunes and soulful ballads, along with lots of country-pop songs, was relaxing, yet invigorating. The band is truly a family affair—even the four youngest kids come onstage to join their siblings for a rousing Irish step-dancing finale. At the end of the show, as John and I staggered to our hotel room around 11 pm, I noticed another extraordinary thing about Ireland: at that hour, it was still *light* outside.

If you were an Irish gardener, just think of everything you could accomplish, working into the long summer nights.

The next day brought a true Irish treasure: Tomas, another one of our tour guides. Tomas was tall and self-contained, in contrast to Leprechaun Joe's conviviality. But he was a veritable fount of knowledge, and it turns out, he'd been raised on a farm too! Tomas picked up on the Irish history and culture where Joe had left off yesterday.

"See the turf, just there," he commented as we passed fields of black peat "bricks." He told us people are out on the bogs in early summer to cut the peat into small rectangles, then they stack the bricks (in what looks like a pretty ingenious pattern) so it will dry out over the next few months. Or maybe dry out as best it can during the cool, showery Irish summers. Thinking of the nice wood fire John and I would've had at home in this kind of weather, I asked Tomas, "People still burn peat?" I thought using turf for heat was a long-discontinued tradition.

"Oh, sure," he said. "Mostly in rural areas, though."

Tomas explained that a given peat bog isn't owned by an individual, but belongs to the community. Each family is assigned a plot. "You don't take your neighbor's peat," he said, smiling, "or else you'd have to move away."

Fascinating, I thought. Sort of a "we're all in this together" way of thinking. In the U.S., we're very independently minded—not necessarily open to sharing our property. We Americans prefer to have our own stuff.

We also like being able to do exactly what we like. Including owning firearms. Tomas said that in Ireland, the police (Garda) don't carry firearms. In fact, the only citizens who may legally have guns are farmers! They're allowed own a .22 or a shotgun to control pests like martens (a kind of weasel) or other vermin that attack livestock.

While Irish rural areas are a green patchwork of low stone walls as far as the eye can see, you won't come across many barbed wire fences to keep those millions of sheep from straying. Sheep are quite free to climb up steep grades, or graze two feet from the road if they like. And the Irish don't brand their sheep. Instead, you'll find a flash of colorful paint on their hindquarters! That to me encapsulated the whimsy and community-focused outlook of the Irish people.

I looked in vain for the picturesque red wood barns we have in the U.S., which I've coveted ever since our move to the Foothills. In Ireland, most of the barns are gray or dark green metal, with corrugated roofs that are often rounded for hay storage. I quickly decided these barns were pretty homely "articles" as the Irish would say.

There's a reason for buildings to be mostly built of brick, stone, and metal: lack of wood.

Centuries ago, the English basically deforested Ireland—cutting down the country's vast oak forests to build naval ships. In the last few decades, the Irish have pursued a reforestation program—the fir stands I've mentioned—with seedlings from Washington and Oregon!

I also noticed the abundance of fully-laden clotheslines in back gardens. (In Ireland you call your yard a "garden.") Apparently, electricity is so expensive that people still hang out their laundry even when it's wet outside. "We should get a clothesline," I said to John, and added, "I mean, for sunny days." I considered trying to dry laundry during the Foothills' nine months of soggy weather, and made a quick decision: if you tried to make me get rid my clothes dryer, you'd have to pry it out of my cold, dead hands.

A Touring We Will Go

In between all the new and unforgettable sights and experiences in Ireland (and Sue's notetaking), she and I got acquainted with lots of the other fan tour folks. Many of our fellow travelers were mid-lifers around our age, but there were plenty of young people on the tour, including a step-dancing teen who'd gone on the dance competition circuit along with The Willis Clan, and a young woman farmer from Australia. What made the trip even more unique was that we fans weren't segregated from the band, who rode on the bus with the tour participants. Sue and I became even bigger fans of the Willis kids, discovering that they're extremely smart, talented, and articulate in conversations.

We had several lively interactions with the oldest Willis, Jessica, about books and songwriting. Jess answered my questions with enthusiasm and took an active interest in all the fans who approached her. I also had the pleasure of sharing breakfast with both Jack Willis, the band's percussionist, and Jeremiah, who goes by Jair. Jair is an exceptionally versatile musician, skilled at guitar and cello, the Irish whistle and the uilleann pipes, and who has also competed in or won national dance contests.

The vitality of The Willis Clan was infectious too—during a short break in the non-stop action, Sue confessed to me that if the kids weren't so sweet and down-to-earth, you could feel really intimidated by all their talent and movie star looks! As it turns out, all that positive Willis energy came in handy, to keep our spirits up during the more difficult moments of the tour.

53 🐦 Hunger and Plenty

At dinner one night, John joked that Ireland was "a meat-eater's paradise." All those millions of sheep and beef cattle on Irish hillsides ensured that meat was in ample supply the length and breadth of Ireland. Whatever your carnivore craving, you could partake of lamb, mutton or beef at every eatery: lamb chops with gravy, mutton in shepherd's pie, and gigantic hamburgers were always on the menu, and on our trip John sampled them all. Pork was always available too, and he made sure to have a few rashers and sausages for breakfast every morning. He also tried the Irish specialty "bangers and mash" (sausages and mashed potatoes) for dinner. With those daily three square meals, John and I were well fueled for the long hours of sightseeing.

As the days passed, despite my near-fog of exhaustion, I soaked in as much information about Ireland as I could, filling my notebook with every little impression and factoid I came across—whether I could ever use it in a book or not. There is one aspect of Irish history, though, that I didn't see ever putting into one of my Irish stories. Yet it's a critical chapter for Irish-Americans to know about. And for visitors to Ireland, there's no getting away from it: The Irish Famine of the 1840s.

Irish people also call the Famine "The Great Hunger." I thought I was well-versed about this tragic time in Ireland—how the potato blight led to evictions of the tenant farmers, disease and mass starvation. But being in Ireland, I discovered how deeply ran the scars of this tragedy. In a 19th-century country awash in food, a million people starved to death. Before the blight, for generations poverty-stricken tenant farmers and their families lived mostly on potatoes, while the livestock and grain crops produced on the landowners' holdings were exported to England. You may wonder: why potatoes?

On a small plot of land, a farmer could grow enough potatoes to feed a family of five or more. When the blight caused potato crops to rot in the ground the length and breadth of Ireland three years in a row, and the peasantry had nothing to eat, landowners continued to ship out virtually all the meat and cereals produced in the country. Because of the support of the English ruling class, modern scholarship has determined that this cold-blooded, heinous practice was essentially genocide.

Famine memorials and museums abound in Ireland, every one of them a poignant, heartbreaking reminder of man's inhumanity to man. At the foot of St. Patrick's mountain in County Mayo, you'll find "The Famine Ship," a bronze sculpture with ghostly, macabre skeletons flying like flags from the mast. It's a representation of the "coffin ships" that thousands of immigrants had been forced to travel on to leave Ireland. These ships were rife with disease and carried minimal food supplies. As a result, many Irish didn't make it to the new land they'd sought.

Deeper into the mountains of County Mayo stands a Celtic cross in a lonely valley. The cross honors the Famine Walk, where four hundred starving men, women and children walked more than twenty miles in a cold December rain for promised food. When they arrived at their destination, the landlord, instead of feeding all those hungry people, turned them away. On their return journey, every last one of the four hundred died. To this day, the scenic valley is deserted.

The day we visited, I looked around the landscape for a village or two, but there was nothing. I saw only a handful of dwellings, and a few sheep dotting the hillsides. Perhaps the place is haunted by the ghosts of those who died.

John and I saw "living" memorials too. In County Kerry, we viewed the ruins of a cottage from which Bridget O'Shea, a pregnant widow, and her six children were evicted. The roof was gone, but the stone walls of this tiny dwelling remained. The fate of the O'Shea family is unknown. Perhaps they went to the poorhouses, or starved.

"The workhouses were the last place you'd want to go," our tour guide Tomas told us. "People were too proud to beg or to take alms." Instead, he said, they'd steal food, risking deportation. "To this day," he added, "the weather report here mentions blight warnings."

Shortly before our trip, my mom told me about her grandmother, Anne McCormack, the daughter of immigrants. "Never let them take you to the poorhouse!" Grandmother Anne exclaimed to Mom, a

century after the Famine. Perhaps the Irish have passed down grief
and trauma through the generations, leaving a genetic imprint—
showing up in one's DNA, like my mother's green eyes, or my
freckles.

I discovered another reminder of The Great Hunger soon after
seeing the O'Shea ruins. On the shore of Galway Bay, about a mile
from the Galway City center, stands a small, isolated statue of a
little girl. Eileen McNamara, I think her name was. At six years old,
she starved to death.

Listening to the waves lapping the shore, I gazed at the statue
for a long time. Silently blessing little Eileen's memory, I returned
to the city, contemplating the rich bounty of our own country. I
couldn't help thinking of my own tiny plot of potatoes. All the
years my crop had turned blighty, been eaten by voles, or otherwise
rotted in the ground, I could just shrug. How many times had I said,
"Oh, dang it, I guess I'll have to buy potatoes at the store this year."

Not in my wildest imagination could I ever conceive of what it
must have been like to look at your blackened fields and realize
you'd have nothing to eat for the next year.

54 ✿ Farming, Irish Style

In the hills of western County Mayo lies Glen Keen Farm—which
means "gentle glen" in the Gaelic (Irish) language. To John and
me, the second to last day in Ireland brought a welcome respite
from the dark chapter in Irish history—a visit to one of the largest
farms in the region. At Glen Keen, you'll find a culinary school,
tearoom and bakery, a petting zoo, and of course, loads of sheep.
But the heart and soul of the farm is Holly, border collie
extraordinaire.

I'd seen plenty of Irish sheep being herded by four-wheelers, but
I learned that when you're running sheep on steep hillsides,
motorized vehicles simply don't cut it. That's where sheep dogs

like Holly come in—she's a girl who really loves her job. At Glen Keen Farm, her sheep-herding demonstration is the main attraction. When she isn't actively guiding sheep, she'll crouch, one eye on her master, the other on the herd, poised for the next command. As I understand it, on many sheep farms, the herding call, "Come away" or "Away" means the dog should herd the sheep counterclockwise, and "Come around" or simply, "Around" means herd clockwise. Jim, the farm's co-owner, explained that Holly can't distinguish between "away" and "around." So instead of calling "Around," Jim calls "Come by." Holly, though, not being your average border collie, can also understand French! As we watched the demo, Jim also used the calls, "à droit" (to the right) and "à gauche" (to the left) when the fancy struck him. And Holly understood perfectly.

Jim calls Holly his best friend—after all, they spend every day together. At his command, she'll explode into action. Holly can finesse forty sheep into a pen within a minute or two. Or she can pick one sheep out of a crowd and herd it into a separate pen just as quickly. Sometimes she can't contain herself, and she'll start herding even when she's supposed to wait. But at the command "Stay, Holly," she instantly stops whatever she was doing. Well, almost instantly. Watching her, I was thinking she stops herding only with the utmost reluctance. Or to humor her master. You pick.

As Jim gathered the tour visitors around the sheep pen, I wondered idly how sheep might do at Berryridge Farm. We wouldn't have to bother with weed-whacking; the animals could be our living grass mowers! That fantasy lasted only a few minutes. I immediately realized what prime targets sheep would be for the local cougars. Second, I saw the downside as Jim filled us in about the realities of sheep farming.

You raise males (castrated for meat) until they're nearly one year old. Ewes produce the wool. Each July, Jim said, you have to bring the sheep in from the hills for shearing. This process isn't optional: to keep your sheep healthy, you must shear them to control mites and maintain their general health. He also revealed a startling fact. "In Ireland, it costs more to shear your sheep than you make selling the wool." (There are some farm subsidies at work, through the Irish government and the European Union, but Jim didn't get into them.) My own takeaway was that if John and I were interested in raising sheep, it would have to be because we simply liked sheep.

Jim went on to explain that in Ireland, you don't need to own a huge amount of land to run hundreds of livestock. Glen Keen Farm owns more than 1,000 acres. But they have access to far more grazing land—4,000 additional acres. A farming district in Ireland often contains what's called a "commonage," an area with communal grazing rights. I imagined how well land-sharing would go over in the U.S., and quickly decided, *not very.*

While Jim had Holly "pose" for photo ops, I chatted with Declan, a lanky, dark-haired Irishman who'd recently become a part-owner. He told me the farm had switched from hand shears to electric only six years ago, and that this part of County Mayo was a Designated Conservation Area—meaning no machinery would be used. I realized how quiet the area was, without the drone of tractors. On our county's rural roads in summertime, gigantic raspberry-picking machines or grain combines the size of a small house are ubiquitous.

While Declan took a group of folks, including John, off to the bogs for a peat-cutting demo, the rest of us accompanied Jim on a hike—"hillwalking." We strode through thick native grasses and gorse, which sheep love, even though their wool often gets tangled up in the prickly shrub. The hills were also covered, I mean, *covered* with sheep droppings.

Earlier that day, we'd toured Cong, the small Mayo village where many scenes of "The Quiet Man" were filmed. Now, facing acres of sheep poo, I had to once again cultivate a new attitude. Ordinarily, given my germaphobe tendencies, I would have picked my way carefully through this pasture. Then I remembered Maureen O'Hara's spunky performance in the movie, especially the part where John Wayne drags her through a real-life sheep pasture. (It's a scene we now view as disgracefully abusive but then it was meant to be hilarious.) Maureen had probably gotten sheep manure all over her cute wool skirt and Tam-o'shanter, and you didn't see her complain. So onward I strode through the droppings with the rest of the seemingly oblivious/not-scared-of-germs visitors. Jim showed us a circle of stones over a millennia old, in an arrangement the Irish regard as a fairy fort. I appreciated this whimsy until we reached the crest of the hill, and found a large area of more stones in the grass. Only these stones were set in squares. Dozens of them. "There was a village here once," Jim told us. "Until as late as 1860, there were forty-two homes and a school." County Mayo, he said, had been one of the areas hardest hit by the Famine. Perhaps those who survived had been able to hang on for a few more years. I wondered if the residents had left to find work in the cities, or emigrated. Not that it mattered—they were gone. Whatever dwellings had once been here, had been knocked down—not even a few stone walls remained. I wondered, did ghosts linger in these hills too?

Holly and the sheep weren't the only animals on the farm. We visited the farm's petting zoo, which included a few hens in a small mobile coop, and one enormous pig. She had her own pen, and a few people braver than I petted her between her ears. Another pasture held two donkeys and a pair of Dexter cows. Dexters are a much smaller breed than most cattle you'll see in the U.S., and are known for being good for both milk and meat. Jim didn't mention what the farm used these cows for, only joked that he was scared of them.

After the outdoor activities, we had lunch in Glen Keen's tearoom—basil tomato soup (excellent), ham and egg salad sandwiches, mini-baguettes *and* buttered scones with jam on top. Desserts were also served, and if you were too full (I was) you could buy take-out house-made pastries—cream slices, cheesecake, pies, and petit-fours.

After the meal, we were treated to an Irish step-dancing show from a young lad and lass, and an older gent did a bit of a clog-shuffle. Still, I think the best Irish dance of all was watching Holly's fancy footwork on the hills of Glen Keen Farm.

55 🕊 Farewell to Ireland

O ur last day in Ireland was a blur, except for one of our final outings. For a mid-morning break, the tour stopped in the little farming town of Swinford, where the maternal side of the Willis Clan hails from. Although we tour participants had eaten a Full Irish Breakfast only a couple of hours before, the Swinford Hotel had a snack (the Hobbits would call it "elevenses") waiting for us: pots of hot tea, with platters of buttered scones and brown bread with jam on top. The proprietor and his wife bustled around the tables, smiling and offering more platefuls of goodies. I wasn't hungry, but given this warm welcome, I succumbed to one final round of Irish carb-loading.

This traditional hospitality came naturally in Swinford, an old-fashioned country town—no one had owned a car until the 1960s!

After our scone-fest, John and I had about ten minutes of free time before re-boarding our Dublin-bound bus. I walked up the street, John trailing behind with his camera, toward the odd sight of a tractor parked in front of a hardware store. Not that tractors were in short supply; Ireland, I'd observed, was full of your John Deeres and your McCormacks and your Massey-Fergasons. But this one, I saw as I drew close, was a Landini. A rich, deep blue, the machine was completely spotless. Painted on the door in curlicue letters was "3 Steps to Heaven."

I have to say, I wanted a red barn far more than I wanted a tractor—which I guess makes me a farmer-wannabe instead of a real one. Still, this machine was impressive. "A tractor like this would be way bigger than we'd ever need," I said to John.

"Yeah," he said, envy in his voice. "But think of everything we could get done."

Like clear a pasture for that new flock of chickens we'd dreamed about? My thoughts were interrupted by the shopkeeper coming outside to say hello. "This guy really loves his tractor," he said. John and I chuckled. "With good reason," said John. "It's a beaut." With a quick goodbye, we turned to go. I only wish we'd gotten a photo.

That evening, just hours before our departure, I was desperate for some fresh air after the crowds and traffic of Dublin. Luckily, our airport hotel turned out to be right next to another horse pasture. I hung next to the fence, watching the animals as a kaleidoscope of our time in Ireland swirled through my mind.

John and I had met loads of fun, interesting people. Besides our fellow travelers, there was the kind lady from Northern Ireland who'd taken our picture in Cong, next to the statue of John Wayne and Maureen O'Hara, the two chatty Irishwomen John and I had sat with at one of The Willis Clan concerts, and the generous shopkeeper who'd offered me a special price on chocolate bars "because you're on holiday."

I would never forget hanging out with the Willis kids and attending their shows, the hours of terrific music and dancing that had passed far too quickly. We'd seen so many wonders: ancient, mystical ruins, splendid cathedrals of Connemara marble and stained glass, grand manor houses and picturesque villages, museums of unimaginable treasures, and majestic scenery so beautiful it brought tears to your eyes. Ireland's history, traditions and culture had come alive wherever we went.

And yet...I couldn't wait to get home.

When we arrived at Sea-Tac the following evening, I bought a newspaper to catch up on the news, especially the weather. My heart sank when I saw the headlines. The Pacific Northwest was in the middle of another record-setting heat wave. The day before, Seattle had reached nearly 90 degrees, and the current forecast for the next few days was ninety-plus. All I could think was, had

Berryridge Farm's blueberry shrubs wilted without water? Had all our vegetable seedlings even survived?

Our journey ended about 1:30 am. John and I had been up for twenty-four hours. I stumbled out of the car—home to our beloved Berryridge Farm at last! In the dark, my bleary eyes went straight to the silhouette of the grand Foothill, standing sentinel before me, and I heard to the muted swish of the leaves, nearly motionless in the middle of the night. I was too exhausted to peer at our orchard trees for signs of caterpillars, or inspect the rows of vegetable sprouts to see if they'd survived. If our place been hit by caterpillars or our garden was full of dead vegetables, I couldn't do anything about it now.

I would have knelt to kiss the ground, but I was too tired.

56 🐾 Hobby or Real Job?

You've heard this before: If a tree falls in the forest, and there's no one around to hear it hit the ground, does it make a sound?

I offer a modern homesteader's corollary: If you pour your heart and soul into looking after a beloved plot of land and raising food without pay, is your work still only a hobby?

I realize I take our food-growing a *little* too seriously. Almost as seriously as if John and I actually *would* go hungry if our crops failed. Or if we were dependent on an income from our place.

The last day of June, I awakened around noon, in a fever of impatience to discover how Berryridge Farm had fared in our absence. I had only to look out the windows to see our fruit trees intact. "Do you see that, Honey?" I said to John. "No caterpillars!"

John grinned. He wasn't one to ever say, "I told you so," but as I pulled on my garden boots, I wouldn't have minded if he had. I nearly sprinted outside to check our beds. The feathery carrot seedlings…alive and well. The small beet greens and spinach, still growing. The tiny parsnip sprouts…still green. My heart leaped in my chest. We had left our place to its own devices and the vagaries of Mother Nature, but our little veggies had survived.

Not so our strawberries. All I found were a few small, seedy specimens. Any berry plumper and riper had been ravaged by our little friends the voles and chipmunks. The boysenberries and loganberries were shriveling on the canes—we'd missed their season too. Losing out on all three crops, I felt I'd let down Berryridge Farm.

The potato bed, in the warmest spot in the yard, was anything but thriving. Out of eight hills I'd planted, only three were pushing out plants. The missing potato hills—which I'd previously hoped were simply taking their time to come up—were clearly dead. I thought the warm spot would have produced an earlier crop—but I might as well have planted my seed potatoes in black pots. The unseasonable weather had simply been too hot for them. Or else I'd brought bad potato vibes from Ireland, but that was a long shot.

Our crop failures did have me doubting myself as a food grower. I could *try* to accept the ups and downs I had no control over, like weather, or pests. Yet this summer, our losses were due to being too casual about our place, not committed as deeply as we should be. So maybe I *was* no better than a hobbyist.

I didn't have time to dwell on my doubts—there was watering and weeding and more planting to catch up on. I was also working on another book: my third fantasy-adventure for kids, this story set in a haunted Victorian house in one of my favorite towns, Astoria, Oregon. With a publishing deadline one short month away, I couldn't put all my energies into tending our place.

Family members needed our attention too. Mom had surgery for a small malignancy. I went out of town to help my sister through some medical tests. My Astoria daughter—her hands full with the new baby—needed some hands-on grandma help. Any time I spent at home, keeping our crops watered and helping John with firewood would come first. Finishing my book would have to be whenever I could fit it in.

One early August day, I gazed across the yard, my eyes drawn to the deserted chicken run. The weeds were as tall as I was, and the whole area was ready for another major clearing. For what purpose, I didn't know, but the sight of that tangle of weeds and brush, no doubt shooting seeds into the rest of our garden, just plain *offended* me. When it came to that job, however, like the other projects we intended to do *sometime*...well, I had to give myself the most helpful advice I could.

Forget it.

One day, John returned from buying a few groceries at the village mom-and-pop store, and held up a carton of eggs triumphantly. "I scored some local pastured eggs!"

"That's wonderful!" I smiled back at him. We'd been buying the nicest eggs we could find at the grocery store, though the flavor and quality was nothing like farm-raised. Checking the package, I saw these eggs came from The Boomer Homesteaders Down the Road, the owners of the acreage I'd admired earlier in the spring. In the short time since I'd first seen their small flock, they'd officially gone into business—now John and I could give up store eggs, however "cage-free" they were, for good.

I opened the Homesteaders' carton to find lovely brown eggs. "Maybe...we won't need to keep chickens after all," I said slowly, in mixed relief and regret.

"That's okay," said John. "We seem to have our hands full these days."

Cracking the first egg of the carton, I found a rich orange yolk, and one taste told me the Boomers' product was nearly as delicious as our eggs had been. For now, any vague plans for hens at Berryridge Farm were off the table.

The heat wave upon our return from Ireland was only the first of many, during that long hot summer. Trying to finish my book, and busy helping my family, I didn't make much progress in the yard. It seemed clear that Berryridge Farm, for me, really *had* turned into a mere pastime.

Our orchards had produced only a handful of apples. Perhaps the trees had been traumatized by two caterpillar plagues, but whatever the reason, we'd be buying store apples until next summer's fruit came in. The blight, as usual, had hit my potatoes hard and early, both beds yielding only a few pounds of spindly spuds. I couldn't help thinking of the terrible potato blights in Ireland. At least we had the luxury of getting potatoes at our local co-op; still, next year, I vowed, I'd get it right. Or at least better.

The delicata squash, even in a warm spot, had pushed out only a few fruits before giving up. I'd been late harvesting the garlic, and by the time I got to it, the cloves had begun to separate in the ground; past experience told me the heads would spoil within a few months. The summer's heat made for a decent tomato harvest, although the blight crept in while we still had a couple hundred green ones still on the vine. All in all, given the limited food John and I had produced this season, we wouldn't have been able to feed ourselves for long.

Watering our garden consumed nearly all my time outdoors, so I had to turn my back on our chicken run jungle. There would be no chance to clear it this year.

I finished my book in the nick of time for my deadline. *The Secret Astoria Scavenger Hunt*, the tale of three tweens, two ghosts, and a mysterious quest, felt like one of my proudest writing accomplishments. Yet with all the demands at our place—hobby or not—I had no time to celebrate.

As the drought continued into late summer, I became even more obsessed with water saving. Turning on the tap, I'd get a jolt of anxiety. Like in the spring, though, I wasn't about to conserve garden water. Even after you harvest your strawberries, caneberries and blueberries, the plants still need regular watering—they're already developing buds for next year's crop.

A few showers brought some relief, but not enough to truly soak the ground, nor replenish the ground water. The seasonal streams in our area had long since dried up. By summer's end, the iconic volcanic peak in our county was partially bare on the top, a sight I'd never seen before in my forty years in the Pacific Northwest.

Wildfires were devastating the eastern side of the state—farms and ranches hit hard. Grazing lands burned to a crisp. Livestock killed. With nature's destruction so extreme this year, it finally occurred to me: what if, despite all the effort I poured into Berryridge Farm, this year's poor yields happened next year—and the years to come?

What if our region's hot, dry weather became the new normal?

57 ✍ Starting Fresh

One September day I opened the shop fridge and looked glumly at the meager number of apples, then closed the door with a snap. This season's skimpy harvest stuck in my craw. And I wanted to prove (at least to myself) that running Berryridge Farm really *wasn't* just an optional activity. Time for some hands-on education.

Later that week, our county's agriculture community was holding its annual farm tour. On a sunny Saturday, John and I piled into the Ranger and headed west, toward our county's farmlands. Our first stop was twenty-five miles away, at a commercial apple orchard. After the grower's group talk, he was available for questions. "We got a decent apple crop last year," I told him, "but this year, nothing. What's going on?"

He looked thoughtful for a moment. "If you don't manage your trees, they only bear biannually."

"Manage?" I asked.

"Thin your fruit," he elaborated. "If you let every fruit mature, the tree will take every other year off."

So we'd been Doing. It. Wrong. For the last few years, we had indeed gotten a crop only every other year. John had been pruning our apple trees, but we hadn't been able to bring ourselves to pull any baby fruits off the trees. On our way to the next farm, we vowed that this coming spring, we would thin our fruit, even if it was sparse.

John and I visited a couple of fledgling farms specializing in vegetables. Still in the scaling-up process, these small operations were only about three times the size of the cleared area at our place. Both farms had a sort of glorious messiness, a state of near-chaos that inspired me, only in reverse: to not allow Berryridge Farm to go too feral.

Our final stop that afternoon was a dairy farm that sold our favorite local cream and eggnog. Produced by Jersey cows, the milk and cream was bottled right at the farm—yep, their dairy products came in *bottles*, just like when I was a kid. The creamery was stone's throw from a grazing herd of heifers. John and I and a half dozen other folks had a chance to hang around the fence of the young cows' pasture. The heifers seemed very mellow, many approaching the fenceline curiously, gazing at us with gentle brown eyes.

I'd been up close to cows lots of times at the county fair, but many of the animals appeared to be miserable, stuck in a hot livestock shed teeming with flies. Here in the open air, these fifty-odd heifers seemed content. It's funny, but I felt a kind of connection to them, and filed away my experience to use in the novel I was writing.

In the story, my Irish heroine finally gets the country acreage she's been dreaming of (a place that is a lot like Berryridge Farm!). I knew enough about farms and farming—Irish or American—to realize how much I *didn't* know, but I forged ahead with the book anyway.

Shortly after the farm tour, the rains returned. As fall deepened, the jagged, bare peaks of our area's volcanic peak softened with snow. In December, the Foothills got the biggest snowfall we'd had in three years. The question was, would this precipitation be enough? Our region would need way-above normal precipitation for many months to refill the thirsty rivers, reservoirs, and aquifers. The tiny anxiety I felt when I turned on the tap began to ease. Maybe the water emergency of the previous months was over.

The winter seemed to pass in a blink. In between a couple of visits to Astoria, and falling more deeply under my little granddaughter Flora's love spell, I was busy creating a "visit Ireland" travelogue class. John was drawing up plans for one of his most ambitious building projects yet, a carport.

Around the neighborhood, two new go-getting Boomers appeared on our radar. Our near neighbors Jake and Barb had sold their property, and the new buyers turned out to be a nice-looking, energetic couple about our age. Here in the Foothills, Al and Gretchen's business-casual attire made them look a bit out of place, but their warm smiles and conversation were full of neighborly bonhomie. They had big plans for their future homestead, and were planning to live in Jake's small, hand-crafted apartment until they could build a house.

Further afield, our new egg suppliers, the Boomer Homesteaders Down the Road, were expanding their operation. Passing the place on my bike throughout the spring, I watched with admiration at their progress. The property owners had a large hoop house now, and what appeared to be a sizable raspberry patch. It was their growing chicken flock, however, that drew my gaze. One day, a mobile coop the size of small cabin appeared in their pasture, just outside their orchard, and dozens of hens pecked at the grass.

As soon as I got home, John wandered out of his office, as he often does after my rides. "See anything new out there?"

"Actually, yes," I told him. "The Boomer Homesteaders' are going into *serious* egg farming."

John stepped toward his coffee pot and poured himself a cup. "We're off the hook then," he said, with an indecipherable expression. "Having our own chickens, I mean."

"Looks like we don't need to." I peeled off my jacket. "So...if we're not going to get chickens," I ventured, "maybe we should think about repurposing the coop for storage."

Neither of us had so much as stepped foot in the coop since I cleaned up the feathers after the hens had been killed—over two and a half years ago. Retooling the coop meant, of course, we'd actually have to go *inside* it. "We could knock down the inside wall," I added. "Make it a big shed."

"Maybe," John said vaguely.

I could tell he didn't want to take that on. He was in the middle of building the carport, and we already had more garden projects than we could finish. With mixed emotions, I filled a glass of water. "Whatever happens," and I took a drink, "we're really set for eggs now."

58 🦃 Homegrown Letdown

For gardeners raising food, each growing season gives you a clean slate.

Sure, you're always at the mercy of the weather, of the critters, of the weeds. Of fungus or how well your seeds germinate. All of which involve golden opportunities for failure. But still, you carry on.

Nearly a year after our trip to Ireland, with the arrival of mid-spring, John and I got the exciting news that daughter Meghann was expecting another baby. Naturally, we were thrilled. At the same time, however, the prospect of more grandparenting trips to Astoria had me considering our food-growing in a new way—that is, putting my efforts where they would be the most advantageous.

With that goal in mind, I decided to dial down my potato growing. After so many hills kicked the bucket the previous year, I simply wasn't motivated to go for the big time, and planted only eight hills. They took their time coming up, no doubt due in part to the chilly, wet weather.

The Foothills had an unusually warm, sunny spell in mid-May, prime seed-sowing time. This summerlike weather didn't last long; the growing season was proving to be as cool as last year's had been hot. Apparently "The Blob" in the Pacific Ocean had moved on. The berries seemed to love the mild temperatures—John and I produced bumper crops of strawberries, caneberries, and so many blueberries we didn't need to hit our Foothills U-Pick for freezing.

I visited Astoria to help out with the kids and give my pregnant daughter a mini-mommy break, but unlike other summers, I didn't have to worry if John would be able to manage all the summer watering and harvesting chores alone.

As you summer squash-growers know, if you don't pick zucchini every day you'll end up with bushels of seedy, over-matured fruit. Not this year: out of seven zucchini plants, we got a total of three mature zukes. *Three!* It seems to me if you can't grow zucchini, you might as well hang it up as the most amateur gardener ever. The tomato situation was even worse. The plants grew all right—rich, green growth that needed massive support structures. John spent many an afternoon in his Zen tomato mode, carefully adding support poles, and tying up tomato branches. The cherry tomato varieties produced a decent yield, but the two Muskvich plants (bred in Russia, mind you, to tolerate cool weather), gave us *two* ripe tomatoes before the blight hit.

Given our poor harvests all around, I again wondered if I was merely *playing* at growing food. As the summer waned, I watched my potato bed anxiously. Something really wasn't right. In this showery weather, the foliage should have been turning that nasty brown-black—as they had every other year. Instead, the plants remained a suspicious, healthy green. What was going on?

In August, I finished drafting my Irish farm novel. Now that I'd cleared my writing plate, here was my opportunity to buckle down and catch up on outdoor work. The summer showers had freed up time I would normally have spent watering, so a-weeding I would go!

Part of the chore was simply maintenance, like hacking my way through the thimbleberry and brackenfern to get to my compost piles. Or crouching over the vegetable beds to pluck out shotweed, a cursed, useless plant if ever there was one. After shotweed goes to seed, when you so much as brush the darn thing, seeds shoot out in a three-foot radius! One day in late August, however, I was ready to take on a real challenge.

I assembled the tools of my trade. Spading fork, check. Hand fork, check. Dandelion digger with the long handle (although the actual digging part got bent somewhere along the line, it was still functional), check. Biggest loppers, check. I took a deep breath and for the first time in two years, entered the jungle of our deserted chicken exercise area.

After all this time, it was still painful to walk by the empty run, much less go inside. Sometimes I imagined I could still hear the hens clucking. Yet it had been over three years since we'd had our four happy girls running all over, keeping the weeds down the all-natural way.

Turning my mind from the memories, I set to work. Yanking three-foot high weeds. Clipping stubborn thimbleberry. Ruthlessly cutting out giant cut-leaf blackberry. Early in the evening, John wandered over from the carport site. "Looks really great," he said.

Taming this jungle felt like a real accomplishment. As I collected my tools, I couldn't help preening a little. "It does, doesn't it?"

He gazed around. "It makes me want chickens more than ever."

I nearly dropped the loppers. "I didn't know you still wanted chickens."

"Of course I do," he answered, looking surprised. "I wanted to get hens ever since we lost the girls."

I didn't know what to think. Part of me liked the time I'd freed up from chicken-wrangling, having much bigger chunks of the day for writing, and more chances to spend time with my family. In my heart, though, I still mourned the girls and all the life they'd brought to Berryridge Farm. And I missed that connection to animals, taking care of them so they can take care of you. "Maybe," I said, "we can think about getting chickens next spring."

Spring was a half a year away. Plenty of time to figure out if I really *was* up for hens.

59 🕿 Apple of My Eye

It was epic. It was *insane*. It was…apples.

For weeks, John and I had been gazing at our orchards, gobsmacked. We had taken the advice from the county grower we'd talked to and thinned the fruit in early summer, filling one five-gallon bucket after another with immature apples. Despite the "edit," now that it was September, mature fruit dripped from every tree, even the ones that in eight years had never produced an apple. Some, like the Jonagold, bore so heavily a main limb broke off. John made his Mr. Fix-it rounds to all the trees, rigging up supports, but still, many uber-laden branches sagged almost to the ground.

Everyone I knew with an apple tree was talking about this year's yield—Lori, my Foothills friend, told me her two little trees that never had fruited before were completely loaded. The folks at our Foothills nursery said the abundance was due to the previous spring's weather—May's brief spate of warmth and sunshine brought out an unusual number of pollinators, so that nearly every blossom on the trees had set fruit. Our Asian pear trees were bearing massive amounts of fruit too. You may be thinking, what's the problem? You can't have too much of a good thing. And yet… you actually can.

On the cusp of apple harvest time, I was inspired to finally start the long-delayed sequel to my *Little Farm in the Foothills* memoir. Despite the challenges John and I had faced in the years since I'd published that earlier book, I was still living my farm dream…and wouldn't have traded one day (except maybe during our two caterpillar plagues) for our former city existence. Writing about this hands-on life we'd created would, if nothing else, commit it to memory.

Not surprisingly, I had cross-pollinated some of my real-life experiences with the novel I'd recently drafted. Kerry, my Irish story's heroine (the one who now lived on a small farm), faced many of the trials and tribulations I included in the new memoir. And because fiction so many times draws from true life, Kerry had a small flock of chickens. While I found myself envying my character for her hens, this was no time to be daydreaming—we had apples to pick!

"Come here!" John hollered from the other side of the yard one September afternoon. "I just saw the strangest thing!"

John is not one to shout at me to come running. Or exaggerate. So what in the world could "the strangest thing" be? I hoicked a pile of wild spinach into my weed bucket and hustled over. "What is it?

"I never would have believed it if I hadn't seen it with my own eyes," John said, heading for our biggest Asian pear tree. "A rabbit," and he pointed to a pear on the ground, half its flesh exposed by bite marks, "was eating *that!*"

I stared at the pear—okay, a pear-eating bunny really *was* the strangest thing. Despite our best efforts to keep up with picking, during this crazy season the trees were dropping fruit all over the place. I'd seen half-eaten apples on the ground for weeks, and it had been a challenge to keep up with collecting and composting all the ruined fruit. And to be completely honest, I'd figured that whatever was eating it was…um, I hate to admit it, but…*rats.*

But…*rabbits?* I'd never seen our resident bunnies eat anything but fresh greens, and in winter, the occasional tender shrub. John's presence had scared the rabbit away, so I moseyed over to Queen's Cox apple tree nearby. I found an apple dangling nearly to the ground with bites taken out of it. Our bunny was not only stealing pears, but apples. It occurred to me that when a certain kind of food is in abundance, the wildlife will modify their eating habits to take advantage of the new food source. In this case, the rabbits had tuned their taste buds to fruit-burglary.

Only a few weeks ago, as the first fruit was ripening, John and I had already started to wonder; what the heck will we do with all these apples? We had three trees that were ready at the same time, including a small crabapple tree that must have had thousands of fruits. Problem: there were two of us, and truckloads to harvest. How many people in our circle would actually want some of our bounty?

We brought a basket of apples to three different potlucks, and several family gatherings, but those giveaways hardly made a dent. John brought a grocery bag-full to the local Food Bank, but their irregular hours made it a challenge to contribute. He made four ginormous batches of applesauce, I gave fruit to all my friends, and both of us were eating a couple of apples a day. But our fridge already had two giant boxes full, with hundreds of apples still to pick. What were we going to do?

A few days after discovering our fruit-eating bunny, I saw an article in our local paper about a cider brewery in town, and hurried to see John. "Look, Honey," I said. "We're saved!"

The article was about the brewery getting the local community involved in their new cider project. You could bring your apples— and pears—to the brewery, which would be made into hard cider. In return, you'd get a coupon for a free glass!

Well. You'd better believe John was on board too. Personally, I couldn't *wait* to jettison all our extra fruit. Less than a month since picking our first apple, on four different trips to the cidery we brought in about a dozen grocery bags full of apples, plus two large boxes. We also donated three more grocery-bags full of the gnarlier fruits to my sister for her horses. This season's harvest seemed so out-of-this-world I like to think there was a bit of Mother Nature's pixie dust at work as well, but that's just me.

Still, I wasn't sure I could face another crop like this one next year. All I could hope was that Mother Nature would take pity on Berryridge Farm and give us a break.

60 ☞ Mighty Mouse

For all my fears the previous year about shifting weather patterns to a hotter, drier climate, the Foothills had the rainiest October I could remember. The one day it didn't rain, we actually got our first light freeze, over a week before the average first frost date.

Still, I didn't harvest my potatoes until a few days later. With all that lush, green growth over the summer, the plants had clearly escaped the blight I'd seen every single year before. And the spuds were some of the largest I'd ever raised. But once I washed off the soil, I realized the downside of keeping the crop in the ground so long. They were the scabbiest taters I'd ever seen, rife with little worm tracks. Well, yet another lesson learned—just because you've protected your root crops from voles, doesn't mean you get to relax. Still, I did a lot less of my usual hand-wringing over their poor quality—maybe learning more about Ireland's Famine was teaching me to be more philosophical. At least about potatoes.

With all the rainfall, the ground around the orchards was positively spongy. One day, not long after the frost, John and I were inspecting our fruit trees. He put a little pressure on the scrawny trunk of the Queen's Cox tree—it had so little stability you could wiggle it easily. "Look at that," he said, pushing his foot down hard to make a depression in the grass. "There's got to be a huge network of tunnels down there."

I pressed the ground with my boot too. "It sure looks that way," I agreed. The mice and voles were clearly having a party. "So what do we do about it?"

"Remember our Honeycrisp tree that broke off years ago, and blew away?" John asked. "I'll bet voles eating the roots were the reason it couldn't stand up to that storm." He was quiet for a moment. "I'd like to till the ground, break up the tunnels," he said. "Kill those suckers for good."

We both knew our soil was too rocky for a Rototiller. "Even if we do it by hand," I asked, "won't that damage the tree roots?"

"I suppose," he said gloomily. "But these trees are never going to thrive with so many rodents around."

John's least favorite job at Berryridge Farm was one you couldn't slack on: Mice patrol. He would set out peanut buttered-traps in the shop, the sheds, and the house crawlspace, then dutifully remove the corpses and toss them into the woods. Of course, given the thousands of mice that like roamed our acreage, the death toll was a drop in the bucket.

People would ask us why we didn't get a cat. Well, outdoor cats would no doubt take out a lot of rodents. But they also stalk songbirds. Besides loving the hummingbirds, John and I were very fond of our other local feathered friends, the chickadees and sparrows, the goldfinches and towhees, even though those two particular *friends* pilfered our pea shoots and blueberries. We were even fond of the thieving robins. We'd lost enough birds in the yard—that had gotten entangled in our berry nets—that we didn't want an on-site predator.

So there we were, *stuck*, with voles eating more of our crops than we did, and mice having their run of the place. I'd learned not to completely freak out when I found their telltale black specks in the cupboard under our bathroom sink—though it still made me nuts, knowing mice were in the house.

A few particles indicate mice might simply be making a pit stop, but sometimes they set up housekeeping where you wish they wouldn't. I've lifted the hood of our car to check the oil, only to find a mouse nest on the engine. I once put my foot into my muckboot and found the boot toe full of something. Yanking my foot out, I turned my boot upside down and found that mice had stored a big handful of squash seeds in it!

Face-to-face encounters with those little pests have been rare, but one memorable day, I was cleaning a broken-up straw bale out of the garden shed and suddenly felt a lump around my toes. I looked down, and *Eeeeek*! A mouse had jumped into my boot!

Faster than you can yell *Gross!* I tore the boot off and dumped out the mouse. But it took days to get rid of that lumpy sensation on my foot.

Clipping thimbleberry at our fenceline one day, near a small tree, I saw something odd in my peripheral vision and did a double-take: there was a *mouse* perched on a branch. Upon closer inspection, I saw the critter was dead. Still, a mouse in a tree was so excessively weird I had to find John. "You're not going to believe what I just saw," I said, and told him about the rodent. "It wouldn't have climbed a tree to escape a predator, would it? Or do you think an owl got it, and just left it in the tree instead of eating it?"

John laughed so hard he nearly fell over. "Naw, it's just a dead one I must have thrown a little too high." I felt pretty silly, but at that point I didn't put anything past our resident rodents.

Soon after, our car developed a rattle every time you turned on the fan. The air conditioner wasn't a soothing hum anymore—instead, you'd hear an unsettling, knocking noise. When it was time for the vehicle's next oil change, I gave John a goodbye kiss as he prepared to head for the dealers. "Don't forget to have them look at the air conditioner."

"Will do," he promised. "Let's just hope it doesn't cost an arm and a leg."

When he returned home at the end of the afternoon, I met him in the driveway. "Did they find the problem?"

He smiled ruefully. "You're not going to believe this—mice had chewed through the air filter and built a nest inside the filtering system. The tech pulled out like, *buckets* of stuff."

Visualizing the technician pulling out leaf bits, seed fluff, and paper fragments, I said, "It's not like our car sits undriven for days or weeks at a time."

"It's pretty unbelievable," John commented, "but the tech said these nests inside your engine aren't uncommon."

I thought again of the spongy ground in our orchards. "You know, I swear our mouse and vole problem has gotten much worse since we lost the girls," I said slowly.

John reached into the car for the sack of groceries he'd brought home. "That could be another good reason for keeping hens."

PART IV

There and Back Again

'Twill be in the valley of love and delight.

—From "Simple Gifts"

61 ✆ Call of the Wild

Our Boomer Homesteaders' eggs were getting harder to find. For months, the village mom-and-pop grocery had reliably stocked an ample supply of their cartons—which regularly sold out. Given the popularity of the Boomers' eggs, John visited the store every week to score a couple dozen. But after coming home empty-handed for nearly a month, he said, "I wonder what's going on with our egg folks—it's too early for hens to take a break from laying."

Even more puzzling, each time I rode my bike past the Boomers' pasture, I'd see fewer birds. Maybe they're inside that cool mobile coop, I thought. Or the owners moved the flock behind their big hoop house. At any rate, with our local supply curtailed, and John and I being completely spoiled on pastured eggs, the only option was to buy them at the food co-op.

My next shopping trip, I found a carton from an organic egg operation less than twenty miles away. The farm had a vaguely familiar name. It took me a moment to recognize it—years ago, the owner had referred me to Shannon, who had sold us our six hens! Feeling like I wanted to do my part for such a worthy farmer, I reached into the dairy case, then spied the price…and cringed.

$7.50 a dozen!

Tempted to put the carton back, I thought, *Wait—these eggs are local, the owner did us a favor…they're worth it.* John and I wouldn't be getting any hens for the foreseeable future. So I would support our county's farmers—even if it blew my grocery budget.

John and I actually had a very good reason for *not* getting chickens.

All my years in the Foothills, I'd found plenty of cougar droppings on the road, but I'd seen a cougar only twice: the one in our yard that had killed our hens, and months later, a second big cat on the other side of our back fence. Shortly after that sighting, John and I learned our neighbor's Sharpei Ernie (a sturdy, medium-sized dog) had been badly mauled by a cougar. Ernie survived the attack, but every time I saw him after that, I could tell he'd lost some of his doggy joie de vivre.

Knowing these big cats really were closer and more active than I'd suspected, I visited our state's Department of Fish and Wildlife website. I discovered a male cougar will roam a home range of about 50 to 150 square miles, and a female about half that. Apparently they'll take about six months to cycle through a given hunting ground—and they definitely know how to stay out of view.

When it came to bobcats, especially after my cougar wake-up call with the chickens, I'd learned to recognize these medium-sized felines at a glance. John and I would find a bobcat skulking near the fence line every now and then, but we had the extraordinary experience of seeing one at close range. One August day when I was watering our biggest blueberry patch and John was working on the carport, a young bobcat entered our yard, and sat in the middle of the driveway.

I went very still, then John and I carefully walked closer. Yet the cat didn't seem at all spooked. The area was in the midst of a long dry spell—maybe the bobcat was thirsty and had smelled the water.

I put out a bowl of water as close to the animal as I dared, then retreated to a fair distance away, hoping it would take a drink. The cat lingered in the yard, but never did go near the bowl. I only hope it found water somewhere.

When it comes to bear sightings, I've never seen one on our ten acres. But this year, I'd spied more bear scat in the area than any other. Again, it was always in the middle of the road! I guess they like to take their breaks while keeping an eye out for danger. Although who's going to threaten a bear, I ask you?

As far as identifying bear scat: not to be too graphic, folks, but bear poo is easy to recognize. It will contain what appears to be undigested material, its appearance changing with the animals' diet.

At certain times of the year, bear droppings look like a small pile of asphalt. In the summertime, the scat has what appears to be fruit pits mixed in, likely from native bitter cherry or Indian plum fruit. The dead giveaway is that the amount of poo is generally much larger than what a dog or cougar might leave around.

Even if black bears stay on the down low on our property, I've spotted them nearby, usually when I'm riding my bike near our place. One day, I was heading out on my bike on the main road near our lane when an adult bear (huge!) followed by (count 'em) *three* cubs lumbered across the pavement. I quickly did a U-y, and backed up to watch them. The foursome disappeared into the woods on the other side of the road, but I could still hear a loud crackle through the brush. I kept watching, and within moments, the bear quartet appeared again, on a high ridge far above the road—heading up a near-vertical rock face. I couldn't believe how fast they could travel almost straight uphill.

Another time, I was riding about four miles from home when I noticed something odd: an overgrown apple tree at the side of the road was trembling violently, like an angry giant was shaking it. I heard a loud crack, then a limb broke and a young bear dropped out of the tree. Seemingly unhurt, it scurried into the brush.

My most recent sighting was also the funniest. I was again on my bike, and a short distance away, next to the road, I saw what looked to be a man. Dressed in dark brown, he was hugging a telephone pole! Or, I wondered, was it a guy taking a "comfort break"? But in full view of traffic?

As I got closer, I saw the pole-hugger was actually a young bear. He had both arms around the pole, and was moving up and down against it, apparently to scratch his tummy. As a car approached, he quit scratching. The driver stopped so the critter could cross the road, and he sauntered into the trees.

One afternoon, a state Fish and Wildlife officer visiting our lane pulled into our driveway to introduce himself. Rob was interested in our wildlife sightings, and spoke about the states various protective measures. My biggest takeaway was his cheerful advice about encountering wild creatures: "Just remember they're far more scared of you than you are of them."

I totally believed that—about bears at least: if you mind your own business, they will mind theirs. But cougars?

Not long after, John and I tooled down to the mom-'n-pop grocery, and discovered that the Boomers' eggs had once again been cleaned out. At the checkout, I said to the clerk, "What happened to your local eggs? We haven't seen any for a long time."

"They went out of the egg business," the clerk told us. "I heard animals got the hens."

It seemed unbelievable, yet in the space of a few short months, the Boomers' fifty or so hens had apparently been killed. After leaving the shop, John and I didn't talk much on the way home. Maybe he was thinking the same thing I was: Now *that* death toll was a good case for not keeping chickens.

62 🐦 Rock-a-Bye Baby

Another Foothills winter set in. Our eighth grandchild was due any day now—and Astoria had never seemed so far away.

Our area had already had an unusually cold start to the winter—a series of Northeasters kept many days below freezing. At Berryridge Farm, John and I could cocoon indoors and ride out any harsh weather, but in Astoria, my daughter Meghann's family had too much going on to take things easy. She and our son-in-law Matt were in the middle of moving to a bigger place, just as Matt was recovering from his second back surgery within a year. And Meghann's two boys and little Flora would need childcare while she was in the hospital. With Matt laid up, if ever John was needed to come with me to help out, it was this trip. We both had our bags packed.

All Meghann's babies had come early—so as the January days passed, my anxiety grew. Every time the phone rang, I felt a jolt of nerves, bracing for Carrie saying, "The baby's coming!" Although I was keeping a concerned eye on the forecast, I wasn't quite as worried about the new baby as I'd been with my daughter's previous pregnancy two years ago. Despite Meghann's constant Braxton-Hicks contractions while she was pregnant with Flora, the birth had been trouble-free. This time around, all we needed was for the weather to cooperate so John and I could get to Astoria safely.

So much for the best-laid plans.

Meghann had visited her midwife five times in the last two weeks, with one false alarm after another. Here at Berryridge Farm, the last day of January brought a grim forecast. A major regional storm was due to hit in a couple of days, with snow and frigid temperatures forecast all over the Western part of the state. My daughter Carrie, who's in constant texting contact with her younger sister, called mid-morning with an update. "Meghann's getting more labor pains, but they keep stopping. I'll call when they get more serious."

"I'll stay by the phone," I promised. After hanging up I checked the weather again on my tablet. "Look at this," and I showed John the screen as he was heating up his second cup of coffee. "They're saying snow for sure. If we don't leave for Astoria soon, we may not be able to get there until next week!"

"It looks that way," said John, his brow furrowed. "What do you want to do?"

I've never been good—actually, I'm pretty bad—about dealing with the unexpected. Or making snap decisions, especially when I'm stressed. But with Meghann's false labor pains turning into real ones, I knew there was only one thing to do. "We'd better go tomorrow, whether she's in labor or not."

February first, I awakened early to get ready for our trip. Another Northeaster was whistling around the house. I'd just heated the kettle for a cup of tea when the power went out.

John came into the kitchen, looking grim. "No power? The wind isn't even blowing that hard."

"Not yet," I said, practically hyperventilating. Even if our visit to Oregon was only for a few days, how could we abandon Berryridge Farm in the middle of a Northeaster? These winter storms practically guaranteed a power outage, often protracted ones. If John wasn't around to fire up the generator and keep our well pump operating, we'd risk our pipes freezing—or worse.

I blinked back tears. I wanted, *needed* John to come to Astoria with me—it was a long drive, and dicey weather would only make the trip more difficult. More importantly, Meghann and Matt could use every helping hand we could muster. But our place needed John too. "I hate to say it," and my voice cracked with strain. "But you'd better stay here. I'll go on my own."

On the freeway, a few snow flurries hinted at the coming storm. I arrived in Astoria by dinnertime, meeting up with Carrie at the motel she'd booked. "Before we even hugged, she said, "Still no baby."

When I called John to tell him I'd arrived safely, he said, "Guess what—the power came back on two hours ago."

"You are *kidding* me!" I said, chagrined. I'd played it safe and look what happened. "You could have come with me."

When John didn't answer right away, I was thinking, *you can still jump in the Ranger, come down by yourself.* Yet I knew in my heart that wasn't feasible. If the forecast was accurate, and we got a significant snowfall, John's light pickup wasn't safe to drive. "Well, maybe not," I amended. "Have we gotten any snow?"

"Not yet," said John, then added the obvious. "Well, what's done is done."

As Carrie and I showed up at Meghann and Matt's new place, among the greetings and hugs I could sense my son-in-law's disappointment at John's absence. "We had a power outage this morning," I said lamely. "We thought he'd better stay and make sure everything's okay." Then I had to admit, "But you'll never believe it—the power came back on this afternoon."

Saying it, I avoided looking at the two of them, lest I see any eye-rolling. But Meghann and Matt had to be thinking John and I were alarmists, making a big deal out of typical winter weather. Or worse, a couple of old fuddy-duddies who got their knickers in a twist over a little wind. Trying not to dwell on my rash decision to come by myself, I was impressed that our daughter and son-in-law, despite her advanced pregnancy and his post-surgery physical restrictions, had somehow managed to move all the main furniture and the basics of living from their former apartment.

Flora, just turned two, had wispy brown hair that curled at the ends, and tilted hazel eyes that made her look like she was smiling all the time. She was a smiley little person anyway, though she was still pretty shy with Carrie and me. However, as a *big* fan of the movie "Frozen," she could be distracted from any toddler apprehension as soon as you popped in the DVD.

That night, as I blew Flora a goodnight kiss, I wondered how much an entertaining kiddie film could keep her from missing her mommy and daddy. Because once her parents left for the hospital, it would me and her auntie looking after her, whether she liked it or not.

February second. Meghann's labor started in earnest the next morning. After kissing Flora goodbye, off she and Matt went to the birthing center, promising to call in a couple of hours. By noon, the new mommy was in heavy labor, and Matt's mom left work so she could watch Flora. Carrie and I headed immediately to the hospital, to be at Meghann's side.

Her previous deliveries had been, as Meghann would say, pretty easy-peasy, lemon-squeezy: several hours of serious contractions, a half-hour or so of pushing, and voila! A baby! This fourth time, however, wasn't going like the others. Lots of pain with very slow progress. The midwife, whom I'd met before, didn't seem worried, cracking her usual off-color jokes. Yet the fetal monitors Meghann was hooked up to showed the birthing process wasn't quite smooth sailing. The baby's heartbeat indicated our little guy was being affected by the long hours of labor.

With the obstetrical nurse checking the printouts every few minutes, Matt quietly reassured his wife. As he'd done when Flora was born, Matt was good at keeping his cool through uncertainty. By early afternoon, exhausted, and nauseous from the meds, Meghann finally got the midwife's go ahead to push. Shaking with nerves, I touched Meghann's hand. "Getting close now, Sweetheart." I took my place on one side of her, as Carrie stood on the other. Matt stayed at the head of the hospital bed to whisper encouragement.

Meghann smiled tiredly, then took a deep breath as the next contraction rolled over her.

As she continued to push, a second nurse joined the midwife, looking concerned. The baby's heartbeat was getting more erratic. Before long, an obstetrician came in, and the atmosphere in the room instantly changed.

The tension was palpable.

Meghann was still pushing, but the baby was losing ground, his heartbeat growing slower and slower. As a second doctor stepped in, I could feel my entire body quake with anxiety, and Carrie's eyes were turning red. I was bracing myself for one of the obstetricians to say, "caesarian" but the medical pros were talking about something else. A procedure I'd never heard of before.

In distressed childbirth, an apparatus can be affixed to the baby's head, using vacuum pressure to help pull the child out. It definitely was *not* an easy-peasy solution; in fact, it could lead to complications. Our little man was at a real risk.

By now, my heart pounding, I was praying with all my might. Carrie looked distraught. But Meghann, apparently spurred by the urgency of the situation, had a sudden, immense surge of strength. A few more mighty pushes, and little Lennox entered the world. Healthy and perfect.

The aftermath of a successful birth is probably the same for everyone all over the world, at once intimate and universal— laughing through your tears and hugging everyone within reach. And you can't stop your heartfelt thanks to the tender and compassionate medical staff who'd helped make the miracle happen. Ten years before, with John's medical scare one frigid winter night, I'd stood in our living room with the half-dozen first responders who'd brought him safely through a crisis, and felt an outpouring of love for these folks I'd never met before. Now on this wintry afternoon, in the birthing room with my daughter and new grandson safe, I felt the same affection for Meghann's midwife and nurses—and completely and utterly limp with relief.

I didn't get to indulge that weakness for long.

63 ☞ Sleepless in Astoria

Brimming with happiness, I phoned John that evening to tell him we had a new grandson, and related the baby's close call. I belatedly remembered to ask him how everything was at home.

"Well," he said ruefully, "it finally started snowing."

"How much?" I asked, still on my grandmotherly high, and not really worried. "And did the power stay on?"

"We've gotten a few inches," said John. "And yep, the power's good."

"*That's* a relief," I said fervently. Judging from past experience, any outage longer than a few hours was pretty bleak, especially after sunset, and *especially* when you're alone. If the electricity went out at Berryridge Farm again, hopefully it would be a short outage like the previous day—nothing to worry about. I asked him, "Are you set for groceries?"

"Got that covered," John said. "I got down to the village today for milk, in case I get snowed in."

John's Ranger could be safely driven with a light snowfall. Anything more than that, he'd be snowbound. Feeling confident John would be comfy, I ended the call on a high note—not knowing how prophetic his "snowed in" comment would be.

Carrie had recently gotten a big promotion at work.

The demands of her new position meant she could stay in Astoria for only another half-day. Yet in those few hours after Lennox was born, she got another kind of promotion. From little Flora.

With Matt at the hospital with Meghann and his new son, Carrie and I were keeping the home fires burning. Flora, a bit traumatized with this first-ever separation from her mommy, refused to go to sleep. Yet she seemed to be more comfortable with her aunt Carrie, and after several hours of fussing, my little granddaughter finally drifted to sleep in her aunt's arms.

They say siblings share far more DNA than parents and their children. And while Carrie and Meghann don't particularly resemble each other, I wondered if Flora had sensed something familiar in Carrie's tone of voice, or her maternal tenderness. Maybe Flora decided that if she couldn't have her mommy, her aunt was the best-ever substitute.

Besides "Frozen" (and her two big brothers), Flora's most favorite thing in the world is mud puddles. Not to admire, but to jump into. Astoria being one of the rainiest towns in the Continental U.S., Flora has mud puddles galore to enjoy. The next morning, when it was time to visit Meghann at the hospital, Flora's sneakers were still soaked from the last time she'd stomped through the neighborhood. Carrie didn't hesitate. Off went the three of us to the big chain store.

We trolled through the kiddie shoe section, overwhelmed by choices. Buy Flora another pair of sneakers? Despite being a puddle-jumper, she was a girly-girl too—how about patent leather Mary Janes? Then Carrie spied a stack of rain boots. There, front and center, was a pair of little aqua Wellingtons, decorated with Anna and Elsa, the two "Frozen" princesses. Flora's face lit up, and once we found her size, the deal was done.

From that moment on, Flora has called Carrie "Auntie Boots."

As the one family member on hand not tied to a nine-to-five job, I gladly stayed in Astoria to help out. The days—and nights—

passed in a happy blur, entertaining Flora (trying to get her "Frozen" boots off at bedtime), cooking and doing dishes, and staying awake into the wee hours rocking little Lennox so his mommy could grab a few winks in between breastfeeding. Since Meghann couldn't drive yet, I'd be up early to schlep my two grandsons to school, then do the afternoon pickup—quite a chunk of the day, since their school was a half-hour's drive away.

Once the boys were home, I'd run over to Meghann and Matt's former apartment. I was helping Matt move the remainder of their stuff, trying to do as much as I could so he wouldn't strain his back any more than he already had so soon after surgery. Once the place was empty, I worked on the post-move cleaning several evenings in a row. Immersed into the routine and responsibilities of my daughter and her family, after a week I was living on fumes.

As the days passed, I was too overwhelmed to keep in close touch with John.

64 🐾 Old Man Winter

Another Battle with Nature

I awakened to the crack of gunshots.

Looking blearily at the smoke alarm on our bedroom ceiling, I saw the dim green power light was off. *Not again!* The war was still on...

One week ago, the day Sue drove to Astoria, and the power came back by early afternoon, I figured the minor Northeast winds whistling through the Foothills wouldn't make much impact. Oh, how wrong could I be. Friday, two days after she'd left, it *really* started to snow. Then the "minor" Northeaster picked up speed, and within hours, the jet engine roar of the wind was unrelenting.

That night, the power went off in the wee hours, and the snow kept on coming. The next day, snow continued to fall, along with the temperature—my mom's little bluebird thermometer showed less than 20 degrees. Still without electricity after breakfast, I bundled up in my warmest outdoor gear—wind chills were probably in the single-digits—and headed out to the shop to start up the newer generator.

We'd bought this one over a year ago, to have a power source for the house. With only short outages the winter before, I'd never before needed to run this new machine. Today, though, was the day. I turned on the appropriate switches and pulled on the starter cord three or four times. Nothing. Then I adjusted and readjusted all the switches and dials, then repeated the drill, yanking over and over on the cord. Still nothing. I tried another half a dozen attempts with no success. Finally, I gave up—I was sure one more pull and I'd dislocate my shoulder.

Frustrated, I berated myself. Why didn't I get this darn thing tuned up in the fall? Going all those months without use, this new generator was deader than the proverbial doornail. I still had the first generator parked at the pumphouse, to power the well, but with hope springing eternal (that the power would come on any minute now!) I decided to hold off on starting it.

To keep busy, I shoveled pathways to the shop and the woodsheds, and again thinking positive, I cleared a track to the Ranger. Not that shoveling the driveway would do any good. Sue had taken our all-wheel drive Toyota to Astoria, and my lightweight truck would be useless in this kind of snow, even with chains.

That evening, I built up the fire and hunkered down in front of the woodstove, thawing some frozen soup on the stove's top. Sitting alone in the dark, I listened to the wind howl around the house. It was a long night. And still, it snowed.

There's something about a powerful Northeaster that wears on your spirit, especially when the storm knocks out the electricity. It's not only the roar of the wind, or the freezing cold. The hours drag by, because you know with a major system like this, it's going to be a while until the utility crews can restore power. Making your way around the house with only a tiny flashlight, you have no way to cook, listen to music or watch a movie, and every time you turn on the faucet you picture the water in the pumphouse tank dwindling down to a trickle. With the Internet kaput as well, you can only hope the charge on your e-reader holds out so you'll have something to do. You don't sleep well either, between the wind howling and worrying about how long the power outage will last. And when you're alone, all of these inconveniences seem like real hardships.

The next day, as I headed outside again, I guessed that so far, we'd gotten over two feet of snow. With more of the white stuff piling up, I shoveled the paths I'd cleared the day before. After starting up the pumphouse generator so the well pump could refill the water tank, I decided to venture down our lane to check out the road conditions.

It was quite the workout, wading through all the snow. The last two months, our rancher neighbor Michael, who lives next to the main road, had been great about plowing our private lane with his big farm tractor. But obviously, he hadn't been out. Our nearest neighbor, Toni, had a smaller tractor—yet when I reached her driveway, I could see she hadn't been out plowing either. As far as getting to the main road, I, along with the three other families on the lane, were completely snowbound.

Heading straight into the teeth of the wind, I encountered our new neighbors, Al and Gretchen, on snowshoes, bundled up in wool and Gore-Tex. "We're meeting Toni down at Michael's place," said Gretchen. "Yesterday, she parked her car next to the road, so she was able to make it to the village to get gas for her tractor."

"That was smart," I said. Toni, unlike me, Al and Gretchen, had a job she had to show up for.

"She said Michael blew a tire out on his big rig," added Al. "So he wasn't able to plow."

Well, that sure explained why there had been no sign of him. Not knowing when, or even if, Michael would have his tractor in operation, the three of us hiked down our mile-long lane. As I huffed and puffed, I got a new respect for snowshoes—Al and Gretchen were able to negotiate the tall drifts fairly easily, while I just had to flounder through.

Looking on the bright side, there's something about challenges that makes you more creative: when we arrived at the main road and found Toni waiting, I discovered she'd packed her son's snowboard in her car. She and Al tied her filled gas cans to the snowboard, then, as I brought up the rear, Toni and the two snowshoe-ers took turns dragging the snowboard the long mile back up the lane. Once Toni gassed up her tractor, she plowed out each of our driveways, plus cleared about two-thirds of the lane. When she reached the tallest drifts—the snow blowing off Michael's pasture had piled up about four or five feet—she turned her tractor around. There was still a long stretch that was impassable by car, but with this much of the lane open, Toni could hike the snowed-in portion on foot to reach her vehicle. One of us, then, could be in contact with the outside world.

Later that evening, the power came on. Hallelujah! I flushed the toilets, and since the temperature back in our bedroom was pretty bone-chilling by now, turned on the heat too. After plugging in my e-reader and tablet to recharge, I popped a DVD into the player. Warmth and light and TV—it felt like the height of luxury.

Another ten or so inches of snow fell that night, but in the morning, Michael showed up with his big farm tractor. He'd been able to get the tire repaired, and within a couple of hours, he had the lane cleared. Sue and I have always agreed we have the best neighbors—and they'd really come through for our little community.

I was finally able to reach Sue and related the events of one of the most severe storms we'd ever seen in the Foothills. I sensed she could hardly take in the kind of snowfall we'd had. Once she'd told me about her own filled-to-the-brim days at Meghann's, she added, "I still can't leave for awhile."

"Of course you can't," I agreed. "I'm just glad the family's doing well." After we said our goodbyes, I built the fire back up and envisioned smooth sailing for the rest of the winter.

It was early the next morning when I heard those gunshots.

It took my sleepy brain a second or two to realize the sound wasn't firearms—confirmed when I crawled out of bed and opened the curtains. I looked out into a world encased in ice. Alders and birches bent over, the tops and limbs snapping left and right. I couldn't help thinking there was a kind of evil beauty to the sight—our area looked like the WWI war-torn landscapes I'd seen in movies.

With no power, I fixed a cold breakfast. They say a watched pot never boils, but let me tell you, it takes *forever* to heat up a cup of leftover coffee on the top of the woodstove. After drinking a big mug of coffee, "starter fluid" as my dad always called it, I bundled up again and went outside.

I punched my way through the crust of ice in our driveway to find our lane was blocked again. This time it wasn't snow. Fallen trees and broken branches of every size littered the road. You couldn't get a tractor through this mess for love or money.

Peering through all the debris, I could see Al, Gretchen and Toni already at work, pulling wood material out of the crusty snow and shoving it to the side of the lane. I joined in, and by the end of the afternoon, we'd cleared about a third of a mile, and made plans to start up again in the morning.

I returned to the cold, dark house. It had been easy to keep my spirits up, working alongside our neighbors, but now that I was alone, I could feel myself getting really demoralized. Sure, no one really *needed* hot coffee, and if our bedroom got too cold I could sleep in the living room next to the woodstove. But if the power wasn't restored within the next day or two, did I have enough generator fuel to keep the water flowing? And with the second generator out of operation, what if I couldn't haul the pumphouse generator back to the shop, to hook to the Gentran so I could run power to our buildings? We could potentially face losing all the crops we'd put up in the freezer, plus everything in the house fridge besides.

With our area looking like a battlefield, what I was missing was my foxhole buddy. I didn't know when Sue would be able to leave Astoria—and being solo out here in the Boonies, without someone to share your troubles, it gets downright hard to stay upbeat. Even more, to keep putting one foot in front of the other. Especially when you feel you've taken one step forward, but two steps back.

65 ❧ There's No Place Like Home

After twelve days in Astoria, it was time to go.

I'd called John the day before and heard all about the ice storm. "The power came back on yesterday," John told me, "and we got the lane cleared enough to drive on."

"How about all that snow?" I asked, apprehensive about driving with three feet of snow on the ground.

"It's finally melting," John said.

I was quiet for a moment. "It's pretty strange, isn't it?" I said finally. "The way things worked out."

"Oh yeah," John said. He knew exactly what I meant. If we had disregarded that first power outage the day I left for Astoria, and he *had* come with me, who knows what could have happened to our place. Left to its own devices, Berryridge Farm could have turned into a real mess. We likely would have returned to busted pipes, and a ruined water system needing hundreds of dollars' worth of repairs. "Anyway," he added, "the roads should be safe by now."

Missing my husband, I reluctantly got off the phone. Now that our area's series of storms seemed to be over, and Meghann was able to drive again, I had no more excuses for staying in Astoria. The next day, after a tearful farewell to my daughter and her family, and one last look at Flora's beloved little face, I was on my way north.

After the five hours on the freeway, I headed into the snowy Foothills, hardly able to believe my eyes. The storm's destruction was immense—a tangle of broken trees filled both shoulders of the two-lane state highway. Everywhere I looked, I saw trees bent over double, or the tops sheared off. Some trees had busted right in half.

The private lane up to our place was barely passable in spots, piles of alders and cottonwoods sticking into the middle of the roadway. As I nosed into our drive, I sensed John had been through a far more challenging time than I'd ever suspected.

My smiling husband met me at the door. Hugging him close, I felt like Dorothy in the Wizard of Oz. "It's so good to be home!" I said over and over.

"It's so good to have you home," John answered every time. And in the next few days, I hugged him every chance I got, eternally grateful he hadn't made a fuss about my being gone so long, especially after what he'd been through.

As I unpacked, it hit me, then, that my husband and I had lived a winter-time parallel. Four years ago, John had had to leave Berryridge Farm to look after his son and I was the one who needed to stay home and keep our place going. This time, John was the one left to cope with far worse weather all by himself—and he'd done it gladly, without complaint. (Unlike yours truly.)

Yet after the worst winter weather we'd ever had, stuck at our place without help or support, John was seemingly just as grateful for our simple lives as he'd always been, just as eager to keep going together, here in the Foothills.

66 ☞ The Decision

John and I make most of our plans on the fly.

Our years in the Foothills have taught us to expect the unexpected—which means always being ready to improvise. Settling back into our Berryridge Farm routine, however, John and I realized that winging it was no way to get through the winter. We had a heart-to-heart about how unprepared we had been for this season's havoc, and felt a new resolve to avoid being caught with our proverbial pants down.

"These severe storms really came as a shock," said John. "I mean, in *February*."

In the past, by the third or fourth week of January, John and I always breathed a big sigh of relief—by then, the worst of the Foothills' cold and snow was pretty much over. So this year's huge snow dump and extreme cold, plus the ice storm, had *really* taken us off guard. I asked him, "We were okay as far as our food stores, though, don't you think?"

"We could do better," John said. Following his mom's example, he's very big on keeping a super-stocked pantry: lots of dried beans and grains that don't have a "Use by" date, and a large back-up jar of peanut butter. If not two jars. "But let me tell you," he added, "I'm definitely going to get both generators tuned up."

He also vowed to start up both machines every month to keep them operational, plus keep both gas cans filled up.

With March around the corner, I set aside my Irish novel to prepare a community college workshop focused on homestead food-growing. Thinking of John's long, snowbound days while I was away, I decided that building up a reliable cache of winter food would be Berryridge Farm's new zeitgeist. As I reviewed our gardening practices over the years—along with what I'd learned from farm visits, the workshops John and I had attended, and the hundreds of articles I'd read—a fresh wave of self-reliant fervor grew in me. After John and I gazed at his storm photos, showing two weeks of the Foothills' most extreme winter weather ever, my husband and I came to the same conclusion almost simultaneously.

We really *should* get chickens this spring.

Our snowshoeing neighbors, Al and Gretchen, had been keeping ten or so aging hens for their son's family. Running into the couple on the lane a few weeks after my return, I marveled a bit at their transformation. In place of the business-casual attire they'd worn at our first meeting, Al and Gretchen were dressed in backyard farming gear, in dusty Carhartts and fleece, each with a well-worn straw hat. I listened in awe, as John and our intrepid neighbors shared snowstorm war stories.

Despite the severe winter, Al and Gretchen smilingly related their plans: they were going to raise not only more chickens, but go for a half-dozen turkey poults, and in the future, even keep bees— jumping with both feet into the homesteading life.

As John and I walked home, I said to him, "Those two are amazing, aren't they? They make me feel lazy."

"That's for sure," John agreed. "I don't know where they get the energy to take on everything they're doing."

"Yeah," I said ruefully. "They're not quite the young Boomers we were when we moved here."

Fired up by Al and Gretchen's zest for homesteading, after I taught my April workshop, I had chickens on the front burner. But where I could source pullets was still up in the air. On my next visit to the food co-op, I reached into the dairy case for our favorite brand of farm eggs, produced by the Worthy Farmer—and hesitated. The price had gone up to *$7.99*.

Well. Sometimes you just have to draw the line—and that day, I considered it drawn. Even though, in the spirit of full disclosure, I admit I *did* buy the one-penny-shy-of-eight-dollar eggs. Still, I was so *done* with hemming and hawing about chickens. So *over* wondering if bringing hens to a cougar hunting ground was prudent. Never mind that our chicken run had once again deteriorated into a weed-choked jungle, and that we'd never had the heart to tackle (or gotten around to) repairing the fencing gaps.

And especially no dwelling on the Big Question: with eight grandchildren, and currently polishing my Irish farm novel for publication, did I really have the time to take on the responsibility of a flock?

When I got home, I pulled up the Worthy Egg Farmer's website. Having passed her operation many times on trips to town, I could tell that over the years, she'd expanded her farm with many more hundreds of chickens. Now I learned that besides her egg retailing, she was producing meat birds, and even sold homegrown, homemade chicken broth. With all those laying hens, I figured she'd have some to spare.

On the down-low (John was out doing errands), I fired off an email, asking her if she had pullets to sell, and pressed Send. Days passed without a reply, then weeks. Okay—it seemed obvious: she wasn't in the business of selling her future money-making birds. Plus she was too busy with her hundreds of chickens to let me know that. I felt silly for even asking her, but decided to keep trying.

Next, I called my favorite farmer's co-op store and asked if they were selling chickens. The clerk sounded surprised. "Sorry, we're all out of chicks."

"Oh," I said. "Well, thanks for your time." She'd said "chicks," so I surmised you couldn't go retail for pullets. If John and I wanted a flock this spring, it looked like we would have to take on baby birds. Which would entail a whole set of new equipment, plus an even bigger worry about predators.

Don't get discouraged, I told myself, and called my second-favorite farm supply shop. They were out of chicks too. Then I phoned the third and last store on my list. When I asked about chickens for sale, the clerk actually laughed. "*Chickens?* We sold out over a month ago."

"Thanks anyway," I said, crestfallen. Obviously, there was no point in trying the farm stores in the neighboring county. Spring chicks were gone.

On to Craigslist. I figured reaching out to the local community could be our chance to get pullets, and we wouldn't have to worry about trying to raise chicks! I was a Craigslist newbie, but without too much teeth-gnashing I found some hens for sale in the area, and even a few pullets. Yet each posting had one common element: warnings about bird flu.

Oh dear. I wasn't up for worrying about testing our theoretical new flock—and I certainly didn't want to risk bringing the deadly illness into the neighborhood, potentially affecting Al and Gretchen's birds. The other Craigslist drawback was that each viable offering was for *one* bird. Really disheartened by now, I closed the site.

After telling John what I'd discovered, I wondered if I'd given up too easily. But considering this unforeseen complication—trying to create a compatible flock of hens by combining birds from multiple sources—he and I came to the same, sad conclusion. We had no chance of getting hens, not until next spring. A whole year away.

67 ☞ First, The Bad News

I was still getting sticker shock every time I bought the Worthy Farmer's $7.99 eggs, but I had more to cope with than high prices. June was upon us—along with the crazy weeks of strawberry season. When I wasn't picking berries, I was rearranging the netting I'd set up to keep the chipmunks out. Chip (or Chips) seemed far more ingenious and aggressive than last year, breaching my complicated netting array as if by magic to steal our berries. After securing yet more stones around the edge of the nets to weigh them down, I'd be at the kitchen sink another hour or two every day to process the fruit for freezing.

John was building a shelter for his wood chipper. He wanted a bigger space for splitting and chopping firewood too, especially now that he had all kinds of busted-up trees from last February to process. Meanwhile, our next berry crop was in trouble.

Before the strawberries are done bearing, it's time to net the blueberries. Just like with the strawberries, keeping the robins out is easy compared to ol' Chip—each year, he and his homeboys have grown more unrelenting about stealing blueberries. Fortunately, this year our blueberry crop looked abundant—the shrubs had clearly rebounded from the two caterpillar plagues. And despite the hard pruning I'd given the bushes in spring to encourage more upright growth, the plants were laden.

I'd head into our two patches to look admiringly at all the healthy fruit set, clusters bursting with swelling white berries, taking on a bluish tinge—the first sign of ripening. Smiling to myself, I pictured the bowls of fresh berries we'd eat, the gallons of berries I could put up for freezing.

As the days went by, I discovered a mystery: shrubs that previously had been drooping with berries looked...emptier. I'd find berry stems with no berries on them, as if the robins had been gobbling them. But robins are smarter than that—they don't eat the white, sour fruit, they wait until the berries are blue and sweet, and *then* start attacking them.

After a week or so, I was getting really anxious: most of our blueberry bushes now held only a middling amount of berries. The fruit seemed to be disappearing before my very eyes. Poking around the shrubs, it was then I saw my problem: shriveled grayish-white bits on the ground, wrinkled little orbs that used to be blueberries.

I'd seen these tiny gray berries before—with spray-free blueberries, you'll find a number of them on every bush. In the past, I figured the berries dying was nature's way of preventing the shrubs from working too hard. But this year, I'd never seen so many, many dead berries. And large numbers of berries still on the bush were half-wrinkled and turning a sickly purple. You'd barely touch them and they'd fall off the stem. Something was definitely wrong.

I'd heard of mummyberry disease—and in my typical Pollyanna way, I told myself it was a problem only for *commercial* growers. (After all these years, I was still kidding myself.) After all, I'd faithfully mulched my berries to prevent the disease, along with meticulous pruning and watering. Yet this summer was shaping up to be a real scorcher—were the berries reacting to the heat?

When the numbers of shriveled bits were too alarming to ignore, I forced myself to face facts—the problem couldn't simply be hot weather. Prepared for some bad news, I Googled mummyberry disease. Reading the online articles, I sort of sagged in my chair: sure enough, our bushes had it. Mummyberry is yet another fungus—and one that attacks swiftly. Once afflicted, the berries drop to the ground within a day or two, looking "mummified."

It gets worse. If you don't pick up all your little mummies, *each one* develops into this mushroom-like thingy in the fall. Then in early spring, it releases like, *millions* of spores, thus setting you up for a worse fungal attack next year. Well, if picking up all the dead berries was what it took, that's what I'd do. Every day, I crawled under the nets and collected every last one of those little suckers. Fortunately, as blueberry season progressed, the die-off was decreasing. Still, for future crops, I vowed to mulch those mummies to kingdom come.

John and I had always thought we'd seen everything the Foothills weather gods had thrown at us: windstorms and blizzards and tree-splitting ice storms, along with drought and extreme heat. But yet another August heat wave brought a new twist: smoke.

A summer northeaster wind blew thick smoke into the region— and soon, it seemed like the whole Pacific Northwest was ablaze. Wildfires and forest fires on the eastern side of the state, over the border in Canada, and to the south. Around the Foothills, the air was choked with smoke; meteorologists said the air quality was between "marginal and poor."

Days passed, then weeks, as the thickening haze hung in the still air, and the hills surrounding Berryridge Farm were nearly obscured. Our county's iconic mountain had completely disappeared from view. At night, the moon was a bizarre blood-orange color. The whole landscape felt threatening, almost dystopian.

As a fresh air freak, I felt claustrophobic, forced to keep the house windows closed 24/7. Worse was staying indoors all afternoon. If you were outside, the heated smoke made your throat raw, and created a bitter taste in your mouth. The undone garden chores were piling up: weeds going unpulled, mulch going unmulched, bushwhacking going unwhacked. And every time the weather experts predicted that marine air was on the way, a cooling breeze that would dissipate the haze, the forecast would be proved wrong: the hot, heavy air mass that had trapped our entire region in smoke continued to linger.

It was mid-September before a steady flow of marine air cleared the last of the wildfire smoke.

Apple harvest time. Once the blueberries were done bearing, I always looked forward to the next round of Berryridge fruit, especially the Akane apples; this tree had beautiful rosy fruit, great flavor and crunch, and no whining, sniveling or apple scab! One afternoon, John and I collected a couple of boxes and ventured to our orchard to start picking. I could already taste our homemade applesauce and apple crisp.

For the first time in the eight years of bearing, however, the fruit was covered with little dots, with sort of dimples all over the skin. Well, growing without spray, John and I are accustomed to less than pretty apples, so we figured no problemo. Primed for my first taste of the season, I washed an apple and cut it in half to share with John. I could feel the apple's crunchiness as I wielded my knife, but as the apple fell into two halves, I wanted to cry.

The middle was full of trails of reddish-brown *stuff*.

Thanks to a recent article I'd read, I knew exactly what I was looking at. Those of you who have read *Little Farm in the Foothills* know what I mean when I write *stuff* (in italics)—that I've got a *really* big problem. In this case, this particular "stuff" was apple maggot larvae damage.

For some reason, I thought apple maggot flies wouldn't find Berryridge Farm (yep, doing my cockeyed optimism thing *again*). But clearly, here they were: the dratted creatures had laid their eggs on our baby fruits, and the eggs hatched into larvae. Those tiny worms had burrowed into our apples to feed, leaving the insides brown, mushy, and basically inedible. Our entire crop was ruined.

We ended up giving the apples to my horse-owning sister, whose critters don't mind half-rotten snacks. More discouraging was that even a cursory exam of our other apple trees showed tell-tale dimples on most of the fruit. If you're not too fastidious, you could use the fruit for cooking, but even with John's encouragement, I couldn't quite muster the intestinal fortitude to bake with such disgusting apples.

There were our future apple crops to worry about too. Even with this apple maggot infestation, John and I still wouldn't be spraying.

I heard commercial organic growers were encasing their entire *orchards* in fine mesh netting, but I couldn't envision us having the man-and-womanpower—much less the budget—for that kind of effort.

I'd also read you could prevent apple maggot damage by securing a plastic bag around each apple, but that seemed like extremely high maintenance. Same goes for inspecting each and every one of your baby apples for the larvae. You could then squish the tiny worms by hand, but that chore would feel like our caterpillar battles all over again. I also looked into homemade sticky traps, an option that felt more doable.

Despite all this summer's setbacks, with mummyberry attacking our blueberries, the smoke-filled weeks and our spoiled apple crop, I simply couldn't worry about next year. And we'd just gotten some good news—about the future of Berryridge Farm!—that put all these problems into perspective.

68 🌾 Ready, Set...Snafu

One late summer day, I ran into our neighbor Al, still clearing tree limbs on his property from the winter's destruction. Al now sported suspenders and a full beard, looking every inch the homesteader. As we chatted about our current projects, he mentioned their turkey poults had settled in nicely. "Say, we've ordered a bunch of chicks that'll arrive in a couple of weeks," he added. "Would y'all like us to set aside four or five of them for you?"

My heart leaped. "You mean it? We would absolutely *love* to buy a few of your chickens."

"It would be no problem," Al assured me. "We'll raise 'em for a couple of months, then they should be ready to move to your place around mid-October."

Elated, I thanked Al profusely, then hurried home. The twists of fate John and I have experienced always seemed to bring more problems. So for the Universe to move in such mysterious ways to our *benefit*—well, it felt like a miracle.

I found John working on his new shed. "You'll never guess what happened!" I told him my big news: that we wouldn't have to wait for the chickens we'd been hoping for.

"Wow," he said smiling. "I never thought we'd have hens this year."

"We've got so much to do first," I said, though John knew as well as I did how much work the chicken compound needed. Clearing the weed jungle. Redesigning the roost inside the coop. Cutting down the maple coppices that were threatening the integrity of the wire roof. And most of all, adding the critical fencing improvements to create a cougar-proof pen.

It's funny, that despite Al's offer to sell us some young birds, I was afraid to hope too much.

It seemed too good to be true—that John and I could obtain a new flock of hens with so little trouble, like manna from heaven. I know this superstition was the reason I put off whipping our hen compound into shape. Then, three weeks after Al and Gretchen's generous proposal, I saw not one, but two cougars on our lane only a hundred yards from our house…a sight that made me wonder if we really *had* made the right decision about keeping hens.

Yet one afternoon in early fall, when our poultry-raising neighbors invited John and me to stop by and check out their flock, I knew that 1) it looked like we really *were* going to get chickens, and 2) time was getting awfully short. During a break in the rain, we moseyed over to Al and Gretchen's place. As they gave us a tour of their poultry operation, I was nearly speechless with admiration. I briefly checked out the fishnet-covered shelter for their half-dozen turkeys, but I pretty much only had eyes for the chickens.

Ten or so older hens in a variety of breeds scratched around a separate pen, along with another couple-dozen, multi-colored young birds—a few of which would be ours before long. Al and Gretchen had two well-built coops that looked straight out of a homesteader magazine. One of the coops was a brand-new, airy, A-frame structure built off the ground, with a protected space beneath where lots of the "little girls," as Gretchen called them, liked to take shelter. A large fenced run with a few stacked straw bales gave both flocks lots of room to roam and climb. Their compound looked like hen nirvana.

"I thought I should give you fair warning," said Gretchen, "that these little girls probably won't be laying until spring."

"That's okay," I assured her. "We've waited this long for eggs, what's a few more months?"

When Al proposed that we pick up our five chickens in a couple of weeks, John and I were like, "Yes!" Yet after thanking Al and Gretchen and heading home, I felt more than a little inadequate. Our chicken set-up seemed ragged and careworn, not new or pretty or clean like theirs. And the weed-choked spots only made the whole place look worse. Still, when it came to selling us some pullets, Al and Gretchen were clearly all in. John and I had no more excuses.

The next day, John drove to the farmer's co-op and purchased two sacks of the same organic feed we'd bought for our first flock. Lucky for our budget, over the years, the cost of the boutique layer mix had gone down; now, instead of twenty-five pounds for $28, you got forty pounds for thirty bucks.

When he got home, he started collecting tree limbs to chip, so we'd have nice clean bedding for the hens. Meanwhile, I braced myself, and entered the safety zone to yank and clip the six-foot high vegetation to the ground—yet the weeds weren't the daunting part. Nor were the fifteen-foot limbs growing from the old maple stump in the compound. It was my fear that I'd find years-old chicken remains.

Since we could hardly introduce the little birds into a graveyard, though, I cleared every inch of the run. When the ground was free of weeds, I peered into every nook and cranny of the coppiced maple stump, where I'd found pieces of our girls so many years ago.

My next deep breath was one of relief. I didn't find any bones.

Despite our progress, there seemed to be a conspiracy afoot.

To keep John and me from getting chickens, that is. As mid-October arrived, my days were packed with a fuller-than-usual calendar of fall classes and author events—activities I'd lined up back in the spring, long before Al and Gretchen's chicken offer. Driving home from teaching a library program, I realized we'd made all these chicken plans without accounting for our upcoming trip to California. Of course, we couldn't leave our young chickens alone. I immediately phoned Al and Gretchen to ask if we could pick up the birds after our return.

Our easygoing neighbor didn't hesitate. "That's no problem," said Al. "Y'all just let us know when you're ready."

A couple of weeks later, on the plane trip home from LA, John felt sick. By the next day he was down with a respiratory bug—*down* being the operative word. He was knocked out for nearly a week, so I had to call Al and Gretchen and let them know we needed more time.

Then I caught John's illness, and had to phone our neighbors yet *again*. It was getting downright embarrassing, having to set another new date for picking up the birds. After making the call, I collapsed back on the couch and closed my eyes, fretting about all the work we had to do. And after putting off Al and Gretchen no less than three times, I couldn't help but wonder: would they think John and I weren't up to the task of looking after the young chickens they'd lovingly raised? Were we no better than a couple of flakey, hen-keeping wannabes?

69 ✺ Too Good to be True is Sometimes…True

A week before our poultry pick-up date, in early November, a Northeaster blew in, bringing five inches of snow. We'd never had a snowstorm like this so early in the season—and now John and I had to put our chicken tasks on hold until the snow melted.

With this wintry weather, I had a whole new complication to lose sleep over—the move would be difficult enough for the young birds. How could we bring them into their new home in sub-freezing temperatures? It was too late to back out, though; like Al and Gretchen, we were all in. As soon as the snow started melting, John started cougar-proofing the chicken safety zone. When he'd finished tacking poultry fencing in the roofline gaps, he fired up the wood chipper and began pushing the tree limbs he'd collected into it. Soon, he'd filled his new shelter full of wood chips, ready to be put to good use.

In the meantime, I released my fourth novel, *The Galway Girls*, a book that related a fictional version of some of the true-life events John and I had experienced at Berryridge Farm. Sitting at my desk one November afternoon, I had to marvel at the synchronicity: my heroine Kerry's story, which included lots of chicken adventures, was coming out when John and I were only days away from our long-awaited new flock of hens.

Once I'd recovered from my bug, John and I headed to our chicken compound together. He hand-sawed the maple coppice— the resulting stump would be our birds' jungle-gym—and with all the tree branches out of the way, made the last few tweaks to the fencing. An hour before we were due at Al and Gretchen's to fetch the birds, I brought in bucket after bucket of fresh wood chips for the coop floor and to spread around their safety zone. I sprinkled a thick layer of chips in the nest boxes too—the girls would have comfy-cozy nests for when they finally *did* start laying. At last, we were ready!

On a chilly November afternoon, John and I headed next door with a couple of boxes. Al and Gretchen were waiting, and had already separated out the young birds for us: three black Sexlinks, one Buff Orpington, and a reddish chicken that looked exactly like the hens we'd had the first time around. As Gretchen reminded us again that they wouldn't lay for many months, I eyeballed our five "little girls." They weren't exactly scrawny, but they'd have a lot of growing to do before they reached the girth of the older layers.

John, being sort of a "hen-whisperer," captured the birds with Al's help and put three in one box, and two in another. After John packed the boxes into the Ranger, I ventured to our neighbors, "So, what do we owe you?" We hadn't discussed the price of their chickens.

Al mentioned a far lower amount than I expected, so John and I persuaded him and Gretchen to accept several dollars more for each bird. Then after more effusive thank yous, John drove back to Berryridge Farm, chickens in tow.

I returned on foot, and met John, with the boxes, back in our chicken run. "I didn't let the girls out," he said. "I knew you'd want to be here."

"You know me so well," I said, smiling. As he carefully released the birds, I remembered the wild squawking our first hens had made when we unboxed them. These younger chickens didn't seem quite as freaked out, but were nonetheless too skittish to let John and me get too close.

We stepped away to let the little girls explore their new space. After some hesitation, they crept to the feeder and began to peck. Still smiling, I looked over at John. As our eyes met, I could see he was feeling the same way I was—that welcoming our new flock was an auspicious moment…and he felt the quiet joy that I did.

After more than four years since our first flock was killed, John and I had chickens again.

Epilogue 🐦 Full Circle

It hasn't taken long for John and me to settle into our former chicken-tending routine.

The little birds were very nervous and jumpy the first few days at our place, and mostly stayed in the coop, even during the daylight hours. But they've slowly grown more comfortable in their new home, and now they come running whenever John and I go outside. It helps that the girls know we're bringing food, but still. We like to think they just can't *wait* to see us.

These young ones aren't actual hens—not yet. Since they probably won't be laying eggs for a long while, I suppose we can't even call them pullets. Still, it's funny—it feels like these girls have always been here. Of course we've given each one a name: Buffy is the blond one, and the one I started calling "Red" turned into Red Rosie. One of the black chickens has a vivid ring of copper-colored feathers around her neck, and John decided she would be Penny. The two other black chickens are almost impossible to tell apart, and we were stumped for a while. Then, about a week after they arrived, John and I were watching the girls peck at the scratch I'd just tossed out. All of a sudden I thought of the three "girls" on our favorite show, "The Big Bang Theory."

"Since we've already got a Penny," I said to John, "what do you think of Bernadette and Amy?"

He got the joke immediately. "Amy Farrah-*Fowler*?" (The full name of the Big Bang character.) We had a good laugh, then it was back to our chores, firewood-splitting for John, and coop-cleaning for me.

Berryridge Farm is showing its age.

The woods look battered, the souvenir of last winter's ice storm. Several deer fence posts are listing sideways, the wood rotting, and three of our gates are sagging too. All the woodsheds need painting. The hazelnut trees are about five years overdue for a good pruning, and the woods and brush threaten to move into the yard. I still haven't figured out how John and I can hope for food self-reliance when the destructive pests and funguses we've been battling may ruin many of our future crops.

Still, John and I persevere, though we feel a bit battered by time ourselves. As the months and years fly by, our chores take longer, and keeping up our firewood supply gets harder. At the same time, the splitting maul feels like it's getting heavier, and suiting up to work outside takes more gumption when it's wet and cold. Yet my husband and I can't imagine ever leaving our place—Berryridge Farm is part of our blood and bones, like the people we love. Whatever comes, we plan to soldier on, and roll with whatever the future and Mother Nature has in store for us.

John recently came across an insight about living with a more spiritual mindset: if you think of praying as *talking* to the Universe, meditating can be *listening* to it. So that's what we'll keep trying to do. Listening to the Universe.

The holiday season brings another snowstorm. With the garden beds covered and the soil frozen, I have more time to think...and dream. Gazing at the snowy landscape, it comes to me that John and I found the slow life, all right...yet we learned long ago, our first year here, that our life isn't slow at all. Here in the peace and silence of the Foothills, it often feels like you're tied into a curious time-warp—the days will pass in a blink, the months will zoom by and you don't know how it happened. Leaving your little spot of heaven can be a pleasure, like visiting family and friends, or a necessity, like doing the shopping and seeing the dentist. So you go to town, you face civilization—yet secretly you know that it's not your real life. Because your Self, your soul, is connected to the land, to the rhythms of the natural world.

Despite the rush of time, what has truly slowed is your attention. As Christmas draws near, the landscape still encased in white, you notice little things—a mouse scurrying over the snow to disappear into a boot print, and the *clickitty-pop* of a raven's call. In the dark of midnight, looking at the woods, you can see the glint of moonbeams reflecting off drops of ice, so every tree seems to be sparkling with fairy lights.

Despite the cold and ice, in the daytime there's no time to snuggle in front of the fire; the hens need looking after. While it might be more rewarding to take care of chickens that are actually producing eggs, tending to these little girls is the most satisfying job on our place.

It's two days before Christmas. "Hey, Girls," I sing out and enter the run, shaking a quart container of layer feed. "Got some goodies for you!" Instantly I'm surrounded by the birds, making their funny clucks, like soft little horn sounds. I bring in a fresh supply of water—the girls seem to drink more if I hang out next to their waterer for a few minutes—then watch them peck at their food.

Before I leave, on impulse, I open the man door of the coop and peer inside, to make sure everything looks okay. I notice an odd sight—a hollowed-out spot on the floor, in the darkest corner of the coop. A Christmas present is waiting for us.

There, nestled in woodchips, lays a perfect little brown egg.

Excerpt from

Little Farm

IN THE FOOTHILLS

A Boomer Couple's Search for the Slow Life

Here's Chapter 1 of Susan and John's first memoir, *Little Farm in the Foothills*. Like *Little Farm Homegrown,* Book 1 in the Little Farm in the Foothills series is a warmhearted, true-life story for gardeners, nature-lovers, and dreamers of all ages!

1 🕊 Seeking Walden

It's said that if you want to figure out your life's passion, look at what you loved as a child. When I was growing up, I loved Barbies. You might think, there's a girl who'll go far, what with Astronaut Barbie and Internist Barbie and Professional Figure Skater Barbie. Actually, I predate all those ambitious, take-the-world-by-the-horns Barbies. In *my* time, back in the sixties, all Barbie did was sit around and look hot and wait for Ken to ask her out.

But I also loved to read, especially fairy tales like Sleeping Beauty, and stories about gutsy, courageous girls like Jo March and Laura Ingalls. And when I wasn't reading or hanging out with Barbie, Midge, and Skipper, I was playing in the woods behind our house. Maybe I was living out fantasies inspired by Sleeping Beauty's forest hideaway, or Laura's "Little House" series, but I found my bliss climbing trees, building forts and riding my bike around Woodland Hills, a new development perched on the rural edge of St. Cloud, Minnesota.

My husband, John, was an outdoorsy kid too, with a childhood a lot like mine. (Minus the Barbies.) Your mother sent you outside to play after breakfast, and except for lunch, you were supposed to stay there until it got dark or dinnertime, whichever came first. But then, you didn't really want to be indoors anyway. Certainly not John—from what I can tell, he *lived* "The Dangerous Book for Boys." He'd roam nearby woods and fields with his little gang of friends, playing Robin Hood or cowboys and Indians, coming home so dirty his mom would have to hose him down.

Later, as a young husband and father, John got his fresh air nurturing a small vegetable plot for his family. But it could be the outdoor activities so many of us love as adults, like camping, hiking, and gardening—and I hear vacations on working farms are getting popular!—are a way to free our inner tree-climbing, mud-lovin' child. To return to a simpler time, when most people lived on farms—or at least *knew* a farmer. A time when you spent far more of your life outside than in.

Whatever it is, I never stopped loving the outdoors, and John never lost his longing for wide open spaces...a love and longing we indulged with our mutual passion for gardening. But there came a time when we both yearned for a deeper connection with the land...for a more peaceful life, one more attuned to nature's pace. Okay, that sounds pretty highfalutin'—all we *thought* we wanted was more room for a kitchen garden, and a little quiet in which to enjoy it. Regardless of our goal, our journey to that life began the day we reached our tipping point with urban noise and traffic and crowds...when John and I bucked our play-it-safe, risk-averse natures and decided to leave the city. *Little Farm in the Foothills* is the tale of our fifty-something leap of faith, to seek out a slower, simpler, and more serene lifestyle on a rural acreage. And embrace a whole new way of living.

Who'd have guessed how complicated "simplicity" could get. Or that serenity and reinventing your life was no match made in heaven.

Before I hit my Boomer years, I'd never seriously considered living in the country.

Despite my woods-playing, I hadn't spent much time in the true boondocks. In elementary school, I'd been a Campfire Girl, but my group never went camping or sat around a campfire—much less lit one. I'd gone tent camping exactly once in my life, a post-high school girlfriend getaway memorable only for the fact that for the entire three days, we'd frozen our eighteen-year-old tushies off. In June!

Anyhow, I'm all for city comforts. Call me picky (I'm the first to admit I'm annoyingly germ-conscious), but I'd always been sort of revolted by the idea of an on-site septic system. There's all that "stuff" in a tank right next to your house, for Pete's sake. And I liked city water. The only well water I'd tasted was loaded with sulfurous compounds, and the rotten-egg smell wafting up from your glass would set off a gag reflex. I didn't want water from just *anywhere*—it could be unhygienic, okay? I have a B.S. in environmental studies. I *know* about contaminated groundwater. I wanted my drinking water from nice clean municipal water treatment plants.

But water was only a side issue. In my youth, I'd had the kind of country experience that would turn most people off permanently…

Little Farm in the Foothills is available at your favorite online retailer; you can also request an ebook or print copy at your local library, or order a print book at your neighborhood bookstore!

Dear Reader,

Thanks so much for your interest in Little Farm Homegrown. I'm always grateful for questions and comments from readers about my books, as well as insights about food-growing, homesteading, or backyard farming life! If you enjoyed this book, I would deeply appreciate your sharing it with your friends and family—and if you are so inclined, posting your thoughts about Little Farm Homegrown in an online review. In any event, I'm very grateful for your support, and would love to hear from you!

You'll find me online at my websites www.susancolleenbrowne.com and www.littlefarminthefoothills.blogspot.com.

Kind regards and happy gardening!

Susan Colleen Browne

Acknowledgments

Many thanks to the first readers of *Little Farm Homegrown*, Lish Jamtaas, Lori Nelson-Clonts, and Becky Burns, for their critical eyes, insightful suggestions and abiding friendship. I'm very grateful for the wise and big-hearted women of Northwest Authors4Authors, who have cheered me on as I wrote this book.

Big kudos to Courtney Lopes for another one of her beautiful cover designs, and to Amy Atwell at Author E.M.S. for her formatting expertise. And a big Foothills thank you to Al and Gretchen, poultry pros, wonderful neighbors, and backyard farmers extraordinaire.

John and I are thankful for The Willis Clan—we would never have gone to Ireland if it hadn't been for their Fan Tour! We will always treasure the memories of meeting this inspiring group of young people, and the lovely days in the West of Ireland.

Boundless hugs go to our wonderful family—especially our children and grandchildren, for all the love, friendship and joy they bring into our lives. To John goes my deepest appreciation for his ideas and artistic eye, and especially his support and encouragement—and not only during our collaboration on *Little Farm Homegrown*. I feel eternally blessed to have him as my true-blue partner all our years together.

About the Author

Susan Colleen Browne is a graduate of Huxley College of the Environment, Western Washington University. She weaves her love of Ireland and her passion for country living into her Village of Ballydara series, novels and stories of love, friendship and family set in the Irish countryside.

Susan is also the author of an award-winning memoir, *Little Farm in the Foothills,* the first book of the Little Farm in the Foothills series, as well as the Morgan Carey fantasy-adventure series for tweens. A community college instructor, Susan runs a little homestead with her husband John in the Pacific Northwest, USA.

When Susan isn't wrangling chickens or tending vegetable beds, she's working on her next Village of Ballydara book!

A retired police sergeant, John F. Browne graduated from Western Washington University with a bachelor's degree in Fine Arts. John is Berryridge Farm's head photographer, firewood slinger, and sodbuster; you can discover more of his photos online at www.escapetothefoothills.blogspot.com.

You can sign up for Susan's special offers and updates at
www.susancolleenbrowne.com.

You'll also find recipes, book excerpts and
tales from Berryridge Farm at
www.littlefarminthefoothills.blogspot.com.

Books by Susan Colleen Browne

The Village of Ballydara Series

It Only Takes Once
Book 1 (print and ebook)

Mother Love
Book 2 (print and ebook)

The Hopeful Romantic
Book 3 (print and ebook)

The Galway Girls
Book 4 (ebook, print on the way)

The Secret Well
short story ebook

A Christmas Visitor
short story ebook and the sequel to *The Secret Well*

The Morgan Carey Series for Tweens
set in the Pacific Northwest

Morgan Carey and The Curse of the Corpse Bride
Book 1, a lighthearted Halloween story (print and ebook)

Morgan Carey and The Mystery of the Christmas Fairies
Book 2, a gentle fantasy (print and ebook)

The Secret Astoria Scavenger Hunt
Book 3, a haunted house adventure (print and ebook)

Memoirs of Country Life

Little Farm in the Foothills: A Boomer Couple's Search for the Slow Life
(print and ebook)

Little Farm Homegrown: A Memoir of Food-Growing, Midlife, and Self-Reliance on a Small Homestead
(print and ebook)

Food Gardening and Backyard Farming Resources and References

Carpenter, Novella. Farm City: The Education of an Urban Farmer. Penguin Books, 2010.

Deppe, Carol. The Resilient Gardener: Food production and Self-Reliance in Uncertain Times. White River Junction, Vt.: Chelsea Green, 2010.

Kimball, Kirsten. The Dirty Life: A Memoir of Farming, Food and Love. New York: Scribner, 2011.

Kingsolver, Barbara, et al. Animal, Vegetable, Miracle: A Year of Food Life. New York: HarperCollins, 2007.

Pollan, Michael. In Defense of Food: An Eater's Manifesto. New York: Penguin Books, 2008.

Solomon, Steve. Gardening When it Counts: Growing Food in Hard Times. Gabriola Island, B.C., Canada: New Society Publishers, 2006.

Mother Earth News Magazine, www.motherearthnews.com

Joel Salatin, owner of Polyface Farms in Virginia and the author of many books including You Can Farm and Folks, This Ain't Normal; Mr. Salatin also appears in the documentary, "Food, Inc." www.polyfacefarms.com

For frost dates and other general food gardening and farming resources, consult your state's university agriculture extension programs.

"Simple Gifts" by Joseph Brackett

(the complete song)

'Tis the gift to be simple, 'tis the gift to be free
'Tis the gift to come down where we ought to be,
And when we find ourselves in the place just right,
'Twill be in the valley of love and delight.
When true simplicity is gained,
To bow and to bend we shan't be ashamed,
To turn, turn will be our delight,
'Till by turning, turning we come 'round right.

www.ingramcontent.com/pod-product-compliance
Lightning Source LLC
Chambersburg PA
CBHW030240030426
42336CB00009B/179